FORMS OF ASTONISHMENT

Forms of Astonishment

Greek Myths of Metamorphosis

RICHARD BUXTON

OXFORD
UNIVERSITY PRESS

OXFORD
UNIVERSITY PRESS

Great Clarendon Street, Oxford OX2 6DP

Oxford University Press is a department of the University of Oxford.
It furthers the University's objective of excellence in research, scholarship,
and education by publishing worldwide in

Oxford New York

Auckland Cape Town Dar es Salaam Hong Kong Karachi
Kuala Lumpur Madrid Melbourne Mexico City Nairobi
New Delhi Shanghai Taipei Toronto

With offices in

Argentina Austria Brazil Chile Czech Republic France Greece
Guatemala Hungary Italy Japan Poland Portugal Singapore
South Korea Switzerland Thailand Turkey Ukraine Vietnam

Oxford is a registered trade mark of Oxford University Press
in the UK and in certain other countries

Published in the United States
by Oxford University Press Inc., New York

© Richard Buxton 2009

The moral rights of the author have been asserted
Database right Oxford University Press (maker)

First published 2009

British Library Cataloguing in Publication Data
Data available

Library of Congress Cataloging in Publication Data
Data available

Typeset by SPI Publisher Services, Pondicherry, India
Printed in Great Britain
on acid-free paper by the
MPG Books Group, Bodmin and King's Lynn

ISBN 978-0-19-924549-9

1 3 5 7 9 10 8 6 4 2

Preface

For much of my professional life as a university teacher I have occupied myself with Greek mythology. To spend my time in this way has been, and continues to be, a pleasure and a privilege. Of all the specialisms within the field of classical studies, this one offers perhaps the greatest possibilities for kindling the interest of the general public: innumerable are the discussions which I have had with non-Hellenists about the ancient Greeks and their stories, discussions which—to me, at least—have been richly rewarding. But for the Hellenist, too, Greek myths exert an unusual fascination. In particular, they offer a way of addressing the perennially intriguing question: How far were the Greeks like ourselves? No stories raise this question with greater insistence than those which recount metamorphoses. I have been trying to come to terms with such stories for the better part of a decade; the result of these attempts is the present book.

Preliminary versions of various chapters have been presented to audiences in Basel, Bristol, Cambridge, Edinburgh, Leiden, Madrid, Moscow, Oxford, and Thessaloniki. In each of these places I received generous hospitality and valuable criticism. But of all the audiences the most exceptional was that in Leiden. My lecture was set in the context of a series of 'masterclasses' about metamorphosis which I had been invited to lead, the other papers being given by a group of outstandingly gifted Dutch research students. The mastery displayed at this event was emphatically theirs not mine.

In view of the ever-increasing demands upon the time of university teachers in the UK, obtaining periods of leave has become virtually a necessary condition for producing substantial research. This book would hardly have achieved completion without the generosity of the Leverhulme Trust, which elected me to a two-year research fellowship in 2002–4. More recently I spent a month in the wonderful library of the Fondation Hardt in Vandœuvres, Geneva, thanks to the organizing committee of that unique institution. Finally, I enjoyed a further spell of research leave funded by the Arts and Humanities

Research Council, whose grant, matched by that of the University of Bristol, enabled me to finish the book.

Numerous friends and colleagues have helped me along the way; far more than I can remember. But I single out a few, whom I sincerely thank for their kindness in offering me ideas, encouragement, or practical assistance: Lisa Agate, Mercedes Aguirre, Mihai Barbulescu, John Boardman, Jan Bremmer, Gillian Clark, Stephen Clark, Irene de Jong, Herbert González Zymla, Ken Lapatin, Geoffrey Lloyd, Roel Sterckx, and Marina Warner. In addition, since 2003, I have been lucky enough to be associated with the Fondation pour le Lexicon Iconographicum Mythologiae Classicae, at first in an editorial capacity, and since 2006 as President. It is impossible to exaggerate the respect which I hold for the scholars who collectively work for this Foundation, or the amount which I have learned through my contact with them. They have played a significant part in shaping this book, though neither they nor anyone else (apart from the author) should be held accountable for its defects.

In 2007 my mother and father both died. I dedicated my first book to them a quarter of a century ago. I now dedicate the present work to their memory, with renewed and heartfelt gratitude.

R.G.A.B.

Bristol
October 2008

Acknowledgements

Some preliminary thoughts on metamorphosis were sketched out in my article 'Metamorphose en religie bij de oude Grieken', *Raster* 95 (2001) 94–109 (published by De Bezige Bij, Amsterdam). I touched briefly on Homeric metamorphoses in my chapter 'Similes and Other Likenesses', in R. Fowler (ed.), *The Cambridge Companion to Homer* (Cambridge University Press, 2004) 139–55, at 142–3. Part of the material used in Ch. 6 of the present book also figures in my contribution to Jan Bremmer and Andrew Erskine (eds.), *Gods of Ancient Greece* (Edinburgh University Press, forthcoming). I extend my gratitude to those responsible for these publications for allowing me to make use of this material in the present work.

Contents

List of Illustrations

Translations and Transliterations

In order to make the argument of this book available to as wide an audience as possible, I have included translations of all quotations from ancient Greek. When I have borrowed or adapted existing published translations, I have acknowledged the fact. Where no such acknowledgement appears, the translation is my own; in such cases I have aimed (for I know my limitations) to privilege accuracy over anything resembling literary merit. When I cite the work of scholars writing in languages other than English, the translation is again my own.

Quotations of one or a few words of Greek within the main text are usually transliterated. In these cases, I distinguish short *e* and *o* from long *ē* and *ō*, but, to avoid visual confusion, I do not also indicate the position of the word accent.

So far as Greek proper names are concerned, there is, as is well known, no obviously 'right' policy. Usually I prefer a Greek-looking to a Latinate form (Aktaion not Actaeon), except in the case of household names such as Socrates, Oedipus, and Jocasta.

Abbreviations

Authors and titles of ancient works are normally abbreviated according to the practice of the *Greek–English Lexicon* of H. G. Liddell and R. Scott, 9th edition, revised by H. Stuart Jones, with Supplement (Oxford, 1968), and the *Oxford Latin Dictionary*, ed. P. G. W. Glare (Oxford, 1982). When I occasionally depart from this system it is to achieve greater clarity for the reader.

AJPh	*American Journal of Philology*
ANRW	*Aufstieg und Niedergang der römischen Welt* (Berlin, 1972–)
CQ	*Classical Quarterly*
DK	H. Diels and W. Kranz (eds.), *Die Fragmente der Vorsokratiker*, 6th edn. (Berlin, 1951–2)
FGrH	F. Jacoby (ed.), *Fragmente der griechischen Historiker* (Berlin, 1923–)
FHG	C. Müller (ed.), *Fragmenta Historicorum Graecorum* (Paris, 1841–70)
FI	P. M. C. Forbes Irving, *Metamorphosis in Greek Myths* (Oxford, 1990)
Fowler	R. L. Fowler (ed.), *Early Greek Mythography*, i: *Text and Introduction* (Oxford, 2000)
HSCP	*Harvard Studies in Classical Philology*
JDAI	*Jahrbuch des deutschen archäologischen Instituts*
JHS	*Journal of Hellenic Studies*
KRS	G. S. Kirk, J. E. Raven, and M. Schofield (eds.), *The Presocratic Philosophers: A Critical History with a Selection of Texts*, 2nd edn. (Cambridge, 1983)
LIMC	*Lexicon Iconographicum Mythologiae Classicae* (Zürich, 1981–)
PCG	R. Kassel and C. Austin (eds.), *Poetae Comici Graeci* (Berlin, 1983–)
PEG	A. Bernabé (ed.), *Poetarum Epicorum Graecorum Testimonia et Fragmenta, Pars I* (Leipzig, 1987)

PMG	D. L. Page (ed.), *Poetae Melici Graeci* (Oxford, 1962)
RE	*Paulys Real-Encyclopädie der classischen Altertumswissenschaft* (Stuttgart, 1894–1972)
REG	*Revue des études grecques*
RhM	*Rheinisches Museum für Philologie*
TAPA	*Transactions and Proceedings of the American Philological Association*
ThesCRA	*Thesaurus Cultus et Rituum Antiquorum* (Los Angeles, 2004–)
WSt	*Wiener Studien*
Würzb. Jbb.	*Würzburger Jahrbücher für die Altertumswissenschaft*

Introduction

In the year 1846, in a collection with the deceptively anodyne title *Mosses from an Old Manse,* Nathaniel Hawthorne published a short story entitled 'Drowne's Wooden Image'.[1] Drowne is a Boston wood-carver, who has fine technical skills but lacks flair. 'One sunshiny morning' he receives an unusual commission. He is to produce a figurehead for a ship, the work to be carried out according to the mysterious instructions (which the story never makes explicit) of a certain Captain Hunnewell, a seafarer recently returned from the Azores.

The carving which gradually emerges beneath Drowne's hands is that of a spellbindingly attractive woman of foreign aspect and dress:

The face was still imperfect; but gradually, by a magic touch, intelligence and sensibility brightened through the features, with all the effect of light gleaming forth from within the solid oak. The face became alive. It was a beautiful, though not precisely regular, and somewhat haughty aspect, but with a certain piquancy about the eyes and mouth, which, of all expressions, would have seemed the most impossible to throw over a wooden countenance.

When the work is complete, crowds flock from far and wide, eager to view the wondrous image, whose quality far exceeds anything which Drowne has ever produced before.

Then a remarkable event occurs. One fine morning, Captain Hunnewell is seen emerging from his house in the company of a woman who in every particular resembles Drowne's wooden image.

---

[1] Hawthorne (1846/1974), at 306–20 in vol. x of the 1974 edition. The story can also be found in Miles (1999) 398–408.

The couple walk through the streets of the town, to the astonishment of bystanders.

On the whole, there was something so airy and yet so real in the figure, and withal so perfectly did it represent Drowne's image, that people knew not whether to suppose the magic wood etherealized into a spirit, or warmed and softened into an actual woman.

'One thing is certain,' muttered a Puritan of the old stamp. 'Drowne has sold himself to the devil; and doubtless this gay Captain Hunnewell is a party to the bargain.'

'And I,' said a young man who overheard him, 'would almost consent to be the third victim, for the liberty of saluting those lovely lips.'

'And so would I,' said Copley, the painter, 'for the privilege of taking her picture.'

The last speaker is the celebrated artist John Copley, who has been observing the progress of Drowne's carving with awed fascination. When the Captain and his companion at length leave the public gaze and enter Drowne's workshop, Copley cannot resist the temptation to follow them. Inside he finds no trace of either the Captain or the lovely woman who had walked at his side. No one is within except Drowne, who is in the act of repairing the carved image; for the fan which the wooden figure holds has somehow become broken. Then, beyond a door which opens on to the waterfront, Copley hears the voice of Captain Hunnewell address-ing a lady; the two are evidently about to leave in a boat. The stroke of oars is heard. Neither the Captain nor his companion is ever seen again.

Drowne's work returns to its former mechanical quality; it is as if the events surrounding Captain Hunnewell's commission had never occurred. Yet there remains the question of how to explain those events. In ending his story, the narrator reports a rumour circulating in Boston, to the effect that a young Portuguese woman had fled from her home in the Azores and put herself under the protection of Captain Hunnewell. 'This fair stranger must', concludes the narrator, 'have been the original of Drowne's Wooden Image.' All seems accounted for, all rationally explic-able—except for one detail, which I have so far omitted to mention. Moments before Copley discovered Drowne mending the fan held by the wooden image, the flesh-and-blood woman walking with the Captain had been observed, as she was about to enter the workshop, 'to flutter her fan with such vehement rapidity that the elaborate delicacy of its workmanship gave way, and it remained broken in her hand'.

Hawthorne's story, wonderful and full of wonder, explores the boundary between the everyday and the uncanny, a boundary which the author consistently plays with and elides. In the process he explicitly highlights certain ambiguities central to the episode. Is there something divine at work here, or something devilish? Does Drowne's carving illustrate the power of human genius, or the possibility of an eerie overlap between the animate and the inanimate? If there *is* such an overlap, does it involve the coming alive of a block of wood, or the passing of a living human being into the form of a statue, or both? These ambiguities remain unresolved. What energizes the tale is a case—simultaneously real and imaginary— of metamorphosis: the breaking in of the astonishing upon the ordinary.

Astonishment is a reaction which metamorphosis has often been held to elicit, and the collocation of astonishment and metamorphosis will occupy us a good deal in this book. But what is metamorphosis? Or rather, what phenomena has the term been used to designate?

THE REACH OF METAMORPHOSIS

No one who viewed the splendid exhibition on 'Metamorphing' at the London Science Museum in 2002–3 could have remained in any doubt about the extravagant diversity of phenomena which can be brought under this heading.[2] There were painted or sculpted representations of a harpy, a werewolf, and a merman; a fine 1703 edition of Ovid's *Metamorphoses*; imaginary hybrids of human and animal (Miss Atkinson, 'The Pig-faced Lady', **Fig. 1**), and animal and vege-

---

[2] 'Metamorphing: Transformation in Science, Art and Mythology', curated by Marina Warner and Sarah Bakewell, 4 Oct. 2002–16 Feb. 2003.

Figure 1. *Miss Atkinson, the Pig-faced Lady.* Wood engraving, 19th century.

table (the Scythian Lamb, said to grow on a stalk, **Fig. 2**). Given that one of the co-curators of the exhibition had worked for many years at the Wellcome Library for the history of medicine, it was only appropriate that the display should have emphasized human anatomy and physiology, by including various kinds of instruments by which the form of the body can be altered (razors, tweezers, circumcision clamps). Since the body can be altered in other ways than through surgical intervention, there were also exhibits of masks from many cultures, not to mention corsets and a judge's wig. And change is nothing if not a matter of perception: so there was an opium pipe and laudanum and Prozac, as well as drawings and paintings executed while the artists were under the influence of these and other substances. And how could evolutionary transformation be left out? So other exhibits illustrated change through natural selection and genetic modification. As the booklet which accompanied the exhibition put it: 'Metamorphosis is all around us. It lies at the heart of almost every natural phenomenon we know' (**Fig. 3**).

Figure 2. *The Scythian Lamb*, from Claude Duret, *Histoire admirable des plantes*, 1605. This prodigious plant/animal (alias 'the Vegetable Lamb of Tartary') was much discussed and sought after in the 16th–18th centuries.

Figure 3. Daniel Lee, *Origin*, 1999–2003. A sequence of twelve digitally enhanced still photographs depicting an imaginary evolutionary sequence.

Even a cursory review of the history of representations of metamorphosis confirms this impression of prodigal diversity.[3] Some significant moments from this history will make the point.

1. Two texts surviving from the ancient Roman world develop the theme of transformation in contrasting but equally dazzling ways.

The work with which almost all scholars writing about metamorphosis take the subject *really* to begin is Ovid's *Metamorphoses*. This is perhaps understandable, given the mesmeric quality of Ovid's writing. In driving morality and psychology over every kind of transformational precipice, the Roman poet manages, by a supreme paradox, to make such changes seem both routine, in virtue of their sheer quantity, and consistently astonishing, in virtue of their prodigious variety.

A distinguishing characteristic of the Ovidian accounts of marvellous transformation is the fact that we mostly witness them as gradual processes rather than instantaneous shifts of state.[4] Choosing virtually at random we may cite the case of Kekrops's daughter Aglauros. Poisoned with envy at the thought that her sister has attracted the love of Mercury, she progressively leaves her humanity behind:

> Then, as Aglauros tried to rise, she found her limbs so sluggish and heavy that they could not be moved from a sitting position. She struggled to stand upright, but her knee joints had become rigid, a coldness pervaded her body to her very fingernails, and the blood drained from her pallid veins...She did not try to speak nor, had she tried, could her voice have found a way. Already stone held her neck in its grip, her lips had hardened, and she sat, a lifeless statue. The stone was not even white, for her dark thoughts had lent it their own hue.[5]

In addition to the poet's homing in on the gradualness of the transformation, other Ovidian traits are also recognizable: the expression of the human being's previous moral character within the new form, for example, and the stress on the *voice* as an index of what has changed or persisted.

---

[3] For some valuable pointers, see Brunel (1974); Skulsky (1981); Barkan (1986); Harzer (2000); Warner (2002).

[4] Cf. Frontisi-Ducroux (2003) 86.

[5] Ov. *Met.* 2.819–32; trans. Innes (1955).

The most remarkable aspect of Ovid's brilliance is the way he manages to turn a single mythological motif into a peg on which to hang the whole mythological tradition, from the transformation of universal chaos into order at the Creation (Book 1) to the climactic metamorphosis of the Roman state, as the civil strife unleashed by Caesar's assassination is healed by the triumph of Augustan order (Book 15). Thanks in considerable part to this virtuosity, the work was to exercise a phenomenal hold over the imagination of medieval and Renaissance Europe.[6]

Less influential than Ovid's metamorphic epic, but hardly less pyrotechnically daring, is Apuleius' irrepressible novel, again known as *Metamorphoses* (or *The Golden Ass*).[7] The centrality of metamorphosis within the work is claimed already in its first sentence: '... I want you to feel wonder at the transformations of men's shapes and destinies into alien forms, and their reversion by a chain of interconnection to their own', ('... *figuras fortunasque hominum in alias imagines conversas et in se rursum mutuo nexu refectas, ut mireris...*').[8] The plot turns upon the transformation of a young man called Lucius into an ass, and his eventual restoration to human shape thanks to the goddess Isis. Lucius' first-person narrative offers the reader the most extensive account to survive from antiquity of what it might *feel* like to be transformed into non-human shape (3.24):

... the hair on my body was becoming coarse bristles, and my tender skin was hardening into hide. There were no longer five fingers at the extremities of my hands, for each was compressed into one hoof. From the base of my spine protruded an enormous tail. My face became misshapen, my mouth widened, my nostrils flared open, my lips became pendulous, and my ears huge and bristly. The sole consolation I could see in this wretched transformation (*reformationis*) was the swelling of my penis—though now I could not embrace Photis.

---

[6] Among a torrent of recent publications about Ovid one may mention Latacz (1979); Graf (1988); Solodow (1988); Feeney (1991) 188–249; Schmidt (1991); Segal (1998); Feldherr (2002). Anderson (1963) is valuable for its initial setting out of the vocabulary of metamorphosis in Ovid, under the headings of e.g. 'form', 'change', 'continuity', and 'surprise', this last being a key motif in Greek texts also.

[7] 'Less influential'; but see Carver (2007) on the reception of Apuleius.

[8] Apul. *Met.* 1.1; here and subsequently I borrow from the translation by Walsh (1994).

The change had been only partly self-chosen, in that Lucius wished to turn into a bird but was misled by his girlfriend, the maid Photis, into using the wrong magical ointment. His eventual re-transformation to human form was, by contrast, entirely willed, since for eight books he had been trying to find and eat the prescribed antidote (roses). The process of re-humanization was astonishing, both for the bystanders ('the crowd stood amazed', *'populi mirantur'*) (11.13), and for the once-more anthropomorphic Lucius ('As for me, total astonishment rendered me speechless', *'at ego stupore nimio defixus tacitus haerebam'*) (11.14).[9]

This central narrative thread is interwoven with countless other motifs, many of which also involve amazing change. The Thessalian witch encountered by the character named Socrates changed three men with whom she quarrelled into, respectively, a beaver, a frog, and a ram (1.9). Other Thessalian witches could turn themselves into any shape they chose (2.22). Thessaly, indeed, is a place where appearances constantly shift before one's eyes (2.1):

I did not [reports Lucius] believe that anything which I gazed on in the city was merely what it was, but that every single object had been transformed into a different shape (*in aliam effigiem translata*) by some muttered and deadly incantation. I thought that the stones which caused me to trip were petrified persons, that the birds which I could hear were feathered humans, that the trees enclosing the city limits were people who had likewise sprouted foliage, that the waters of the fountains were issuing from human bodies...

Even the myth for which Apuleius' novel is best known—the tale of Cupid and Psyche—exploits the theme of metamorphosis, and in a psychologically suggestive way: to the unstable imagination of Psyche, the lover whom she has never seen oscillates between a divinely anthropomorphic and a hideously bestial shape.[10] In general, scarcely any character in Apuleius' novel turns out to be what she or he initially seems. Only at the very end of the work is some

---

[9] Cf. Lucius' own astonishment at seeing Photis' sorceress-mistress Pamphile change into an owl: 'I too was spellbound...I was rooted to the ground with astonishment at this event' (*'stupore defixus... exterminatus animi, attonitus'*) (3.22).

[10] Book 5, e.g. 5.21.

hint of order restored, as the god Osiris appears to Lucius *without* the mediation of metamorphosis (11.30):

He had not transformed himself into any other human shape (*non alienam quampiam personam reformatus*), but deigned to address me in person with his own august words.

2. Fundamental to most tales of metamorphosis are two antitheses: that between continuity and change, and that between body and mind/spirit/soul. These antitheses are of course fraught with complexity, which metamorphosis tales delight in exploring. Such explorations are a feature of numerous texts from medieval Christendom.[11]

Writing in the late twelfth century about his travels in Ulster, Gerald of Wales tells the story of a priest who met a werewolf.[12] When this wolf-husband asks the priest to administer the sacrament to his dying wolf-wife, the nature of a werewolf's identity—animal or human?—becomes of pressing theological importance. (In the event, the matter remains unresolved: when a local synod cannot decide, the priest is sent to Rome; with what result, we are not told.) To make sense of what kind of creature a werewolf might be, Gerald is prompted to review various aspects of extraordinary change, including Christ's incarnation, biblical miracles involving change of substance, and—arguably the most difficult issue of all—the alleged transubstantiation, during the Eucharist, of bread and wine into the body and blood of Christ.[13] On the last-mentioned point, Gerald admits defeat: while maintaining an orthodox stance (according to which the appearance persists whereas the substance changes—an inversion of 'Ovidian' change),[14] he adds, reasonably enough, that

---

[11] For some fine reflections on these matters in the context of the twelfth and thirteenth centuries, see Bynum (1998). More generally on metamorphosis in the Middle Ages: Barkan (1986) 94–136.

[12] For the first recension, see O'Meara (1949) 143–5, translated in O'Meara (1982) 69–72; for the second recension, see Dimock (1867) 101–7. Bynum (2001) 15–18 and 106–9 has a subtle analysis of the episode; cf. also Veenstra (2002) 148–50.

[13] For the complexity of the issue of transubstantiation, see Jorissen (1965); Lietzmann (1979); Feeley-Harnik (1981); more bibliography at Harzer (2000) 54 n. 23. What made transubstantiation so extraordinary was that it was a kind of metamorphosis; see Bynum (2001) 105.

[14] Warner (2002) 39.

'comprehending it is far beyond human understanding, and very deep and arduous'.[15] As for the phenomenon of the werewolf, comprehending it was no simple task:[16] if God created the species, whereas the Devil was unable to create, how could one explain the widely acknowledged perception of the reality of 'shape-shifters'? Augustine's answer had been that the Devil and demons had the power to change how things appeared to humans, though not to change their essence; later theologians added their own condemnations of the possibility of real metamorphosis.[17] In the twelfth and thirteenth centuries such views, informed by the reception of Aristotelian texts and by discussion about the theory and practice of alchemy, fed into the debate about the kinds of changes in matter which could be wrought by angels, by demons, and by God.[18] As for Gerald, his overall attempt to cope with the notion of the werewolf is a mixture of a fascinated acceptance of the possibility of an overlap between species, and a feeling that such miraculous boundary-crossing can in fact only be effected by God.[19]

As a second medieval example we may consider Dante's *Inferno*. Here the negative image of metamorphosis, so often associated with the Judaeo-Christian tradition, achieves its graphic apogee. In the words of Marina Warner, '[metamorphosis] distinguishes good from evil, the blessed from the heathen and the damned: in the Christian heaven, nothing changes, whereas in hell, everything combines and recombines in terrible amalgams, compounds, breeding hybrids, monsters—and mutants.'[20] While metamorphosis is by no means

[15] '*Quoniam supra humanam longe intelligentiam alta nimis et ardua est ejus complexio*'; text in Dimock (1867) 107.

[16] On werewolves, see Summers (1933), a still extraordinary work; to locate Summers within the tradition of modern witchcraft practitioners and believers, see Hutton (1999) 254–5. For an up-to-date account of werewolves, especially from late antiquity to the early modern period, see Veenstra (2002); for the classical period, see Buxton (1987). Clark (1997) 191–2 comments on lycanthropy beliefs in the early modern period.

[17] August. *C.D.* 18.18, with Barkan (1986) 98–101; Kratz (1976); Salisbury (1994) 159–66. What Augustine denies is the reality of the metamorphosis of humans into animals; he does not deny the possibility of *all* metamorphoses, e.g. those of rods into serpents in Exodus 7; see Bynum (2001) 242 n. 104.

[18] See Veenstra (2002) 146–8.

[19] Cf. Bynum (2001) 27–8; Mills (2003) 32–5.

[20] Warner (2002) 36.

the only figure through which Dante expresses the soul's physical torments, it is metamorphosis which, it has been argued, underlies the process by which sin is 'physicalized' when the fate of a sinner finds its corporeal counterpart.[21] At all events, those cases of explicit metamorphosis which we do meet are compelling and horrific.[22]

In Canto XIII Dante and Virgil are in a barren wood populated by those who took their own lives by violence. The scene is frightening, yet full of pity:

I heard from every side wailings poured forth and saw none that made them, so that, all bewildered, I stopped. I think he thought I thought that all these voices among the trunks came from people who were hiding from us, so the Master said: 'If thou break off any little branch from one of these trees, all thy present thoughts will prove mistaken.'

Then I put out my hand a little and plucked a twig from a great thorn, and its trunk cried: 'Why dost thou tear me?' And when it had turned dark with blood it began again: 'Why manglest thou me? Hast thou no spirit of pity? We were men and now are turned to stocks; thy hand might well have been more pitiful had we been the souls of serpents.'[23]

The speaker is Piero delle Vigne, former Chancellor to Emperor Frederick. However august his position in life, in death he shares the fate of other suicides. Even after the Last Judgement, the separation of body and soul will not be rectified: the bodies of the suicides will hang, each upon his own thornbush, for all eternity (103–8).

Grim though this episode is, its horror pales beside that of another, from much deeper in Hell. In the Dantesque imagination, thieving combines human intelligence with the traditional maliciousness of the serpent, in an act which dissolves the social order. Embodying such transgression is a series of hideous images of eternal dissolution and recombination. First (Canto XXIV) there is the brazen cut-throat Vanni Fucci, transfixed through the neck by a serpent, burned to ash, and then immediately reconstituted in human form. The following canto outdoes even this gruesome vision, in a manner which has left commentators unable to decipher with certainty the

---

[21] Barkan (1986) 140–2.
[22] For discussion of these cases, see Warner (2002) 37, drawing on Bynum (2001) 182–7.
[23] *Inferno* XIII.22–39; trans. Sinclair (1939).

complexity of that which the poetry evokes—because what is imagined defies complete interpretation. On one plausible reading of
the text, what we are shown is a group of thieves whose bodies merge
with those of serpents and lizards, which were themselves formerly
human.

While I kept my eyes on them, lo, a serpent with six feet darts up in front of
one and fastens on him all over; with the middle feet it clasped the paunch
and with those in front seized the arms, then set its fangs in the one cheek and
the other; the hind feet it spread on the thighs and thrust its tail between them
and stretched it up over the loins behind. Never was ivy so rooted to a tree as
the horrid beast intertwined the other's members with its own; then, as if they
had been of hot wax, they stuck together and mixed their colours and neither
the one nor the other appeared now what it was before . . . Now the two heads
had become one, when the two shapes appeared to us blended in one face in
which the two were lost . . . Each former feature was blotted out; the perverted
shape seemed both and neither, and such, with slow pace, it moved away.[24]

Thereafter, with an explicit claim to be *superseding* Ovidian metamorphosis, the infernal narrative goes on to describe, in terms which
challenge the capacity of language to express thought, how two
individuals, respectively in human and serpent shape, mutually
exchange their substance.[25] The whole canto is hard to parallel for
its enforcement of the equivalence between moral iniquity and material destabilization.[26]

   3. The post-medieval world offers a plethora of successors to
Ovid, Apuleius, Gerald, and Dante. Concerning the theme of metamorphosis in the Renaissance, the palm for scholarly analysis belongs
to Leonard Barkan, who gives a brilliant account of representations
of transformation in the art and literature of that period. However,
when referring to what precedes and follows his chosen period,
Barkan is understandably less authoritative. Writing of *Las Hilan-
deras*, Velázquez's multilayered depiction of the myth of Arachne and
Minerva, Barkan observes that this painting 'may illuminate the end
of the metamorphic tradition as well as Ovid's account illuminates

---

[24] XXV.49–78; trans. Sinclair (1939).
[25] XXV.94–151; the reference to Ovid is at 97. On the whole passage, see Ginsberg
(1991).
[26] See Barkan (1986) 153–8, with more bibliography at 323 n. 37.

the beginning'.[27] The implication that Ovid's transformational poem stands at the *beginning* of such a tradition requires no further comment at this stage (beyond the observation that it is a central purpose of the present book to call such a view into question). I concentrate, therefore, on the post-Renaissance connotations of Barkan's remark.

Although Barkan uses the word 'illuminates' rather than, say, 'constitutes', he seems to suggest that the mid-seventeenth century witnessed in some sense the running-of-its-course of 'the metamorphic tradition'. However, as the distinguished Germanist and literary analyst Theodore Ziolkowski has shown, from Ezra Pound and T. S. Eliot, through Franz Kafka's *Die Verwandlung* and David Garnett's *Lady into Fox*, to the more recent work of C. H. Sisson, Salman Rushdie, and Christoph Ransmayr, the literary exploitation of metamorphosis continued with undiminished vigour;[28] and one may add two late-1990s best-sellers, namely Ted Hughes's masterly poetic reworking of Ovid, and Marie Darrieussecq's novel about a woman-turned-sow.[29] Nor is this far-from-extinct tradition restricted to the world of texts. While in the field of more recent art it may be hard to parallel the Renaissance proliferation of Aktaions, Daphnes, and Ledas, the dream world of Salvador Dalí—to take a single example—inhabits a landscape where the visual fabrication of one mode of existence from another is the norm rather than the exception (**Fig. 4**).[30]

4. All this is without stepping outside the confines of the imaginative tradition which inherited and reinvested the legacy of Greece and Rome. As soon as we look beyond those confines, an even greater richness and diversity of belief and representation comes into view. In ancient Egypt (with a few exceptions, such as the almost invariably anthropomorphic Ptah and Osiris) divinities had the capacity to manifest themselves in a variety of non-human forms.[31] Hindu religion abounds in deities who self-transform into an appearance which is entirely or partially zoomorphic.[32] In relation to traditional

---

[27] Barkan (1986) 5.
[28] Ziolkowski (2005). Note also the essays in Barta (2000) for the theme of metamorphosis in Russian modernist writing.
[29] Hughes (1997); Darrieussecq (1996).
[30] See Raquejo (2004).   [31] See below, 180–1.   [32] See below, 178–80.

Figure 4. Salvador Dalí, *The Three Sphinxes of Bikini*. Oil on canvas, 1947. Multiple metamorphosis: the nuclear cloud forms a human head, which changes into a tree, then back to a head . . . © Salvador Dalí, Gala-Salvador Dalí Foundation, DACS, London 2009.

beliefs about the creation of the landscape, metamorphosis has been described as 'the great spiritual theme common throughout Aboriginal Australia' **(Fig. 5)**.[33] Mesoamerica, with its powerful shamans endowed with the ability to transform themselves into jaguars, is another prime location for metamorphosis beliefs.[34] The list could be extended almost indefinitely.[35] One particularly fascinating case is, however, worth looking at more closely.

In no civilization is the presence of metamorphosis beliefs more strikingly pervasive than in China. In his splendid study of the role of

[33] Caruana (1993) 176.
[34] See Hugh-Jones (1979) 124–5; Krasniewicz (2000) 41–58; Lewis-Williams and Pearce (2005) 93.
[35] For other comparative material, see Brunel (1974).

Figure 5. Jimmy Midjaumidjau, *Nadulmi in his Kangaroo Manifestation.* Painting on bark, 1950. Nadulmi is an ancestral being who figures in Australian Aboriginal art. Out of his internal organs—laid bare in this 'x-ray' representation—Nadulmi created aspects of the landscape of western Arnhem Land.

animals as presented in the writings of the Warring States and early imperial China, Roel Sterckx locates such beliefs in the context of '[t]he absence of a strict separation between a realm of the divine and an immanent world of natural creatures'.[36] In such a situation, a permanent state of interchangeability between human and animal becomes a principle underlying the order of the world.[37] A passage from the Daoist work the *Lieh-tzŭ* shows how the principle works out in practice:

Sheep's liver changes into the goblin sheep underground. The blood of horses and men becoming the will-o'the-wisp; kites becoming sparrow-hawks, sparrow-hawks becoming cuckoos, cuckoos in due course again becoming kites; swallows becoming oysters, moles becoming quails, rotten melons becoming fish, old leeks becoming sedge, old cwes becoming monkeys, fish roe becoming insects—these are all examples of things altering.[38]

Although the paradigm of the Chinese metamorphic animal is the dragon, that creature's power is replicated throughout the animal

---

[36] Sterckx (2002) 166.   [37] Cf. D. G. White (1991) 20.
[38] Graham (1991) 21; cf. Sterckx (2002) 169.

world, not least in the transformational skill of the silkworm.[39] On the basis of the assumed pervasiveness of metamorphosis, the possibility of such changes was frequently regarded as fundamental and natural rather than anomalous and surprising[40]—a significant contrast with one aspect of Greek metamorphosis beliefs to which we shall repeatedly return, namely the *astonishment* which transformations usually provoke. Yet the Greece/China contrast should not be made to bear *too* much weight in this respect: in China changes of form in the natural world *could* be felt to be portentous, in virtue of being anomalous. Metamorphoses of chickens, for example (as in the case of a hen reported as turning into a rooster), were variously alleged to portend the rise of a rival contender for power, or to come about when women usurp government.[41]

5. In the life sciences, concepts of metamorphosis raise all manner of fascinating problems. Drawing the definitional circle of the term 'metamorphosis' rather narrowly, we may take it to designate a particular kind of biological development involving an abrupt and conspicuous change of form. Although this phenomenon is found among very many types of living creature, especially marine animals, the best-known examples are doubtless those of the frog and certain insects. So far as frogs are concerned, the crucial stage is that which results in the growth by tadpoles of hind and then fore limbs, while their gills and tails are correspondingly lost. In the case of insects such as flies, moths, and butterflies, metamorphosis takes place during the pupal phase intermediate between the larval and adult stages.

On a broader definition, however, biological metamorphosis may be regarded as involving 'the whole question of the origin and development of species',[42] given that (1) evolutionary theory is con-

---

[39] Dragons: see e.g. *Guanzi jiaoshi* 39 ('Shui di'), 14.351; cf. Sterckx (2002) 179–80. Silkworms: Sterckx (2002) 184.

[40] Sterckx (2002) 169.

[41] *Hou Hanshu,* 'zhi', 13.3273–4, 60B.1999, 60B.2000 n. 2; see Sterckx (2002) 196. For further aspects of the China/Greece contrast, see G. E. R. Lloyd (1996) 104–25, and (1997), especially on Aristotelian views of the fixity of species as contrasted with the greater Chinese openness to the concept of metamorphosis, consonant with the greater stress in many Chinese texts, especially the *Huainanzi*, on the fluidity of boundaries between natural kinds.

[42] Massey (1976) 3; cf. Ziolkowski (2005) 78.

cerned precisely with the gradual mutation of one form of living thing into another, and (2) such mutations might be regarded as instances of 'metamorphosis'. A still wider range of phenomena could be considered in the context of the *history* of science: it might, for example, be appropriate to include under the same metamorphic umbrella the astonishing changes posited by alchemy.[43]

6. Finally we must highlight a development, advancing now at an exponential rate, involving a complex of increasingly interfused media ranging from cinema and television to computer graphics.

From its inception cinema could justifiably claim a significant generic role in the history of metamorphosis. What else did cinema depend on, after all, but the perceptual shift whereby the brain transformed a series of still images into the illusion of movement? But cinema's association with transformation was also more specific. The animated cartoon, with its creation of an infinite plasticity of image, earned the respect of so thoughtful a practitioner-critic as Sergei Eisenstein, who likened its 'plasmatic' power to that implied by the myth of the shape-shifting sea-god Proteus. Thanks to the quality of 'plasmaticness',

a being of definite form, a being which has attained a definite appearance and which behaves like the primal protoplasm, not yet possessing a 'stable' form, but capable of assuming any form and which, skipping along the rungs of the evolutionary ladder, attaches itself to any and all forms of animal existence . . . [44]

Elsewhere Eisenstein singles out Walt Disney's use of

the *protean element*, for the myth of Proteus (behind whom there seems to be some especially versatile actor)—or more precisely, the appeal of this myth—is based, of course, upon the omnipotence of plasma, which contains in 'liquid' form all possibilities of future species and forms.[45]

Classic instances of the plasmatic quality of animation are the productions of the Fleischer Studios, such as *Betty Boop's Snow White*

---

[43] Cf. also the processes identified by Goethe in his *Metamorphose der Pflanzen*, on which see Harzer (2000) 31–2; Ziolkowski (2005) 28; von Mücke (2006).

[44] Eisenstein (1988) 21.

[45] Eisenstein (1988) 64; see Solomon (2000) 16–17. For the topic of metamorphosis in the cinema of Eisenstein, see Nisbet (2000).

(1933).[46] A landmark of a different sort, involving not animation but the painstaking manipulation of the human form, was Lon Chaney Jr.'s performance in *The Wolf Man* (1941), in which many hours of the gradual application of prosthetic facial features, hair, claws, and fangs created, through the use of stop-go filming, a still impressive illusion of astonishing change.[47] Subsequent movies on the werewolf theme have refined the technique (**Fig. 6**).

From the late 1980s computerized techniques of 'warping' and 'morphing' made possible the representation of metamorphosis with hitherto undreamed-of detail and vividness.[48] Notable examples are *The Fly* (1986), *Willow* (1988), *Terminator 2: Judgment Day* (1991), and *Death Becomes Her* (1992), followed by a tidal wave of successors which shows no sign of abating. Towards such imagery, a double attitude seems in place. On the one hand, there is the sense of wonder and astonishment, as morphing creates images which defeat expectations and break all manner of natural laws.[49] On the other hand, such is the present ubiquity of this type of transformational image that it is pertinent to ask whether visual metamorphosis is not in the process of being repositioned—shifting, that is, from the astonishing to the expected. Whether this contemporary banalization of transformation will in turn generate an anti-(meta)morphic reaction, it is too early to say.

GREEK METAMORPHOSES

The foregoing is the briefest sketch of what might be and what has been held to fall under the heading of metamorphosis. It would be impossible to cover all this ground within the pages of a single study, and I have no intention of trying to do so. Instead I propose to focus on selected aspects of metamorphosis to be found in just one culture,

---

[46] See Klein (2000) 26–9. The tradition continues with the sublime *Wallace and Gromit: The Curse of the Were-Rabbit* (2005).

[47] See Sobchack in Sobchack (2000) 133.

[48] See Gomes et al. (1999).

[49] Cf. Krasniewicz (2000) 46, in relation to *Terminator 2: Judgment Day*.

Figure 6. Man becomes wolf: stills from *Legend of the Werewolf*, 1975, with David Rintoul.

where we can identify the roots of some of the developments which I have just been outlining. This culture is that of ancient Greece.

Even within the Greek context only, the notion of metamorphosis might be considered to bear radically diverse meanings. It could, for instance, be taken to refer, by extension, to *any* kind of change, whether corporeal or non-corporeal. Or it might be taken to denote any one of a number of non-corporeal types of transformation, for example the psychological alteration experienced by an individual participant in one of the Mystery cults.[50] However, in the present study I shall restrict myself to analysing narratives about certain sorts of drastic, corporeal transformation, narratives mostly drawn from the area usually called 'mythological'.

Although metamorphosis, in this limited sense, is one of the most arresting motifs in Greek traditional stories about gods and heroes, it has only rarely been tackled head-on. Otto Kern's remark, that there existed in his day (1930) no full treatment of Greek and Roman metamorphosis, is no less true today.[51] The dissertation by W. Bubbe is broad in scope, but brief and unanalytical.[52] Moreover, a strong Ovidian emphasis is usually evident both in those who confine themselves to the classical world and in those with a later focus.[53] Irving Massey does devote two-and-a-half pages to the *Odyssey*, but fails to convey the central position occupied by metamorphosis in the poem.[54] Even the sophisticated book by Friedmann Harzer places great weight on Ovid but little on his predecessors.[55] One exception, now largely forgotten in respect of this aspect of his work, is Jacob Burckhardt, who set an account of Greek metamorphosis beliefs at the head of his long section on the *Religion und Kultus* of ancient Greece.[56] For Burckhardt, the context of these beliefs is a pervasive assumption according to which the whole of nature—not just

[50] Cf. Harzer (2000) 29.
[51] Kern (1930) 203.
[52] Bubbe (1913).
[53] Classical: Lafaye (1904); Castiglioni (1906); Jannaccone (1953). Later: Barkan (1986); Warner (2002). Zgoll (2004) is an exception, for he offers a painstaking discussion of metamorphosis in Augustan poetry to the exclusion of Ovid.
[54] Massey (1976) 20–2.
[55] Harzer (2000).
[56] Burckhardt (1898–1902) ii. 5–18, with *Nachtrag* at 438–43. One modern scholar who does not forget Burckhardt is Harzer ((2000) 7–8).

humans and animals, but plants, stones, and water—is alive. Burck-hardt's discussion contains characteristically intelligent discrimin-ations about what it is or is not useful to regard as metamorphosis. But, at just eighteen pages, his analysis is inevitably limited in scope. With P. M. C. Forbes Irving's study we come at last to a book-length work which does focus on Greece.[57] This account is valuable for reference and as a point of departure, and it contains many helpful observations. However, its author devotes little time to ana-lysing metamorphosis tales within their diverse and detailed narra-tive contexts, nor does he tackle several major interpretative problems which his material ought to raise. Nevertheless, I would not wish my not-infrequent criticisms of this work to overshadow its utility. It has been constantly at my elbow.

Less comprehensive, but more thought-provoking, is a recent work by Françoise Frontisi-Ducroux, which asks important ques-tions and usually answers them persuasively.[58] Although its special strength is the analysis of visual images, the book is suggestive in other areas too; among these are valuable pages devoted to the vocabulary used to evoke the experience of the victims of transform-ation and of the deities who bring it about.[59] Still, like Forbes Irving's book, this treatment too leaves unexplored many details of meta-morphosis narratives in their diverse contexts.

My aim will be to build on earlier accounts, and to take forward our understanding by means of several particular emphases. My first emphasis is on how metamorphosis was explored in different narra-tive contexts; this will be the burden of Part I. I begin with Homeric epic, principally the *Odyssey* (Chapter 1), and then turn to the tragic and comic drama of Classical Athens (Chapter 2). As well as being evoked in literature, mythological transformations were depicted in visual art. Given the special kinds of challenge faced by artists wishing to represent or allude to metamorphosis, it is not surprising that the strategies they developed differ from those adopted by verbal narrators. Such matters will be addressed in Chapter 3. It has often been remarked that a notable expansion of the imaginative explor-ation of metamorphosis took place during the Hellenistic period; in

---

[57] Forbes Irving (1990), hereafter abbreviated as FI.
[58] Frontisi-Ducroux (2003).   [59] Frontisi-Ducroux (2003) 183–5.

Chapter 4 I consider how transformations are narrated in that period. I devote most attention to two Hellenistic poems: the epic *Argonautika* of Apollonios of Rhodes, and Moschos' smaller-scale *Europa*. As a conclusion to Part I, I examine in Chapter 5 metamorphosis narratives in several post-Hellenistic texts, especially the luxuriant forty-eight-book *Dionysiaka* by Nonnos.

After reviewing the evidence from specific narrative contexts, I turn in Part II to a cross-contextual examination of representative aspects of the logic of transformation. The examples I select are self-transformations of the gods (Chapter 6), and metamorphoses of mortals into landscape (Chapter 7) and into plants and trees (Chapter 8). In my penultimate chapter (Chapter 9) I ask how we should locate 'the metamorphic tradition' in relation to other kinds of speculation about the categorization of humanity vis-à-vis animals/plants/gods. In particular I attempt to place metamorphosis stories against the background of views expressed by certain Greek philosophers and other exponents of wisdom who, from various motives, wished to challenge or deny metamorphosis. Finally (Chapter 10) I return to an issue raised at various points earlier in the book, namely the question of how far a contextualizing approach to interpretation should affect the way we interpret 'strange' beliefs such as that in metamorphosis.

Although, in the course of these explorations, I shall cite visual images on numerous occasions, the predominant emphasis will be textual. It is therefore important to stress that my analysis will not be directed towards just one single word, or group of related words, which the Greeks might have used to denote 'metamorphosis'.[60] Occurrences of the noun μεταμόρφωσις (*metamorphōsis*) are rare and (from the perspective of a literary tradition going back to the eighth century BC) 'late'. The first time the word appears in our extant texts is in a passage by the first-century AD geographer Strabo, who seems to be using it in the fully-fledged sense of 'astonishing transformation in a sacred context'. He employs the plural form *metamorphōseis* to denote one item in the catalogue of (for Strabo) marvellous but incredible events which Homer narrates in the *Odyssey*: 'Okeanos,

[60] For the discussion of vocabulary I am much indebted to Frontisi-Ducroux (2003) 183–5.

Hades, cattle of Helios, entertainments by goddesses, metamorphoses, the hugeness of the Cyclopes and the Laistrygonians' (1.2.11).[61] Yet—the point bears repetition—the presence of the word *metamorphōsis* can never be used as a litmus test for the presence of the idea.

We shall, then, have to do not with one word group, but with several. There are compounds involving the prefix μετα- (*meta-*), implying 'change', e.g. μεταβολή (*metabolē*) with the cognate verb μεταβάλλω (*metaballō*), as well as other words with a similar connotation, notably ἀλλάττω (*allattō*), 'I change' (transitive), ἀμείβω (*ameibō*), 'I exchange', and ἀλλοιόω (*alloioō*), 'I alter'. There are nouns meaning 'form', especially μορφή (*morphē*), but also εἶδος (*eidos*), which denotes the 'appearance' of something or someone, and is related to the verb εἴδομαι (*eidomai*), 'I look like'. A cluster of other terms similarly implies some sort of 'resemblance' or 'likeness', or 'as-ness', for instance the participle ἐοικώς (*eoikōs*) and the adjectives ἐναλίγκιος (*enalinkios*) and ἴκελος (*ikelos*).[62]

Then again, many cases of metamorphosis involve not just a change of appearance but a process or a moment of 'becoming'. The most indicative word in these cases is usually γίγνομαι (*gignomai*), 'I become'. A passage in which someone or something is said to *look* different, while (it may be implied) 'really' remaining the same underneath, *may* need to be distinguished from one in which a person or object is said, perhaps more radically, to 'become' something or someone else. However, there is more to a text than the words in it and, as we shall see in due course, the 'seem'/'become' distinction needs to be handled with the greatest care.[63]

Turning from the perspective of one who undergoes metamorphosis to that of one—normally a god—who causes it to happen to someone or something else, we must mention the verbs ποιέω (*poieō*), 'I make', and τίθημι (*tithēmi*), 'I put (into a certain condition)'—the simplicity of the action conveyed by the verb corresponds to the effortlessness with which a god can effect a change.[64] Finally, in

---

[61] In his monumental commentary Radt (2002–) passes over the word in silence.
[62] For this cluster, see below on Homer, 34.
[63] See below, 169–70.
[64] Frontisi-Ducroux (2003) 185.

a book which includes the notion of 'astonishment' in its title, we can hardly omit a word group which is used to express not the process of change, but its effect: θάμβος (*thambos*), 'consternation', and θαμβέω (*thambeō*), 'I am astounded'.

From vocabulary I turn to more general questions, relating to interpretation. In the course of this book, various such issues will be raised. One concerns how we locate metamorphosis stories in relation to the perceptions of everyday life. Did Greeks take the possibility of metamorphosis 'seriously'? If they did take it seriously, did they do so all the time, or only some of the time, or only in some contexts? For the modern observer, thinking about transformation is an excellent way of getting to grips with the distinctiveness of Greek mentality, since some kinds of belief in metamorphosis can indeed seem to have about them a powerful air of the strange, and, as the historian Robert Darnton has observed, 'anthropologists have found that the best points of entry in an attempt to penetrate an alien culture can be those where it seems to be most opaque'.[65]

Metamorphosis stories posit overlaps between classes of beings/ objects which are normally regarded as separate. Moreover, meta- morphoses take place at moments of potential danger, for example when the human comes into contact with the divine in a context where nothing—sacrifice, temple, prayer, for instance—intervenes in order to mitigate the explosion of power represented by the presence of a god, or when a human individual is jolted out of one form into another.[66] Such moments of abnormal crossover clearly have the potential to shock those present as witnesses. And indeed our Greek evidence is full of references to and depictions of bystanders being struck with 'astonishment'—*thambos*—when they observe the process or consequences of transformation. One of our aims will be to register and discuss the presence of *thambos*, or its absence: for, just occasionally, the most notable feature of a metamorphosis is the fact that it arouses *no* consternation.

Another cluster of interpretative issues concerns religion. What do metamorphosis stories tell us about the forms in which the Greeks

---

[65] Darnton (1984) 78. Compare also the work of Clifford Geertz, especially (1973), in which an 'oblique' entry, via an analysis of the Balinese cockfight, introduces us to central questions relating to Balinese society.

[66] See Frontisi-Ducroux (2003) 17.

imagined their gods? How do such stories impinge upon the contrast between anthropomorphism and theriomorphism, a distinction which has been so influential in shaping scholarly and popular views of Greek religion? Does the fact that Greek divinities could be thought of as changing shape constitute a diminution of their power, or an enhancement of it? Is a propensity for metamorphosis an essential part of divinity, or merely marginal? These questions will be addressed as appropriate, but particularly in Chapter 6.

The present book does not offer a continuous or exhaustive account of perceptions of metamorphosis in ancient Greece. It sets itself, rather, the more modest goal of dwelling on certain moments in the history of Greek storytelling, and on some interpretative issues generated by consideration of that history. Even an enterprise of such relatively limited scope, however, provokes fundamental questions about the world of the ancient Greeks, and about our own understanding of that world. Not the least intriguing of such questions concerns our own capacity to be astonished. Can we still be shocked by a group of tales which have become so familiar to us? Caroline Walker Bynum concludes her analysis of the concept of wonder in the medieval period with these words: 'Not only as scholars, then, but also as teachers, we must astonish and be astonished.'[67] This is sound advice in relation to any intellectual endeavour, but it applies with particular force to the subject addressed in the pages that follow.

[67] Bynum (2001) 74–5.

Part I

Narratives and their Contexts

Part I

Narratives and their Contexts

1

The *Odyssey*

As we examine the significance of corporeal transformations within the Odyssey, *our point of departure will be what is, apparently, nothing but a tiny detail. However, the scholarly debate over this detail repays scrutiny. It raises large questions not only about metamorphosis in Homer, but also about the nature of Greek religion, and about the assumptions of those who attempt to understand it.*

COMMENTARY AND THE EYE OF THE BEHOLDER

Telemachos has sailed to Pylos in search of news about his long-absent father; the young man is accompanied by Athene, who has adopted the form and voice of Odysseus' trusty companion Mentor. Having assured herself that Nestor, the stalwart old ruler of Pylos, has granted Telemachos a splendidly hospitable reception, Athene can, for the time being, leave the action to the mortals. Here is how the departure of the goddess is narrated (3.371–3):

> Ὣς ἄρα φωνήσασ᾽ ἀπέβη γλαυκῶπις Ἀθήνη,
> φήνῃ εἰδομένη· θάμβος δ᾽ ἕλε πάντας ἰδόντας,
> θαύμαζεν δ᾽ ὁ γεραιός, ὅπως ἴδεν ὀφθαλμοῖσι·

So saying, green-eyed Athene went away, likening herself to a vulture, and astonishment (*thambos*) took hold of all those who were looking, and the old man was amazed (*thaumazen*), as he saw it with his eyes.

'Likening herself to a vulture' is my translation of *phēnēi eidomenē* (φήνῃ εἰδομένη). *Phēnēi* is a noun in the dative case denoting a type of bird; *eidomenē* is a participle deriving from the verb *eidomai* and

meaning 'resembling' or 'looking like'. Richmond Lattimore is also of
the view that Athene went away 'in the likeness of a vulture'.[1] Another
translator, Walter Shewring, agrees that she left 'in the likeness of' a
bird (he calls it an osprey),[2] while the classicist and naturalist John
Pollard (who identifies the predator as the great lammergeier) talks
of the 'form' which the goddess adopted.[3] Similarly W. B. Stanford
comments: '[a]n actual metamorphosis, not a simile'.[4] This interpretation is by no means new: already in 1860 A. Kirchhoff referred
to Athene 'in the form of a bird', a view echoed by the great Swedish
authority on Greek religion Martin Nilsson: 'Athene appears... in
the form of a bird.'[5] Such a reading rests on a common Homeric
usage, found in the *Odyssey* and *Iliad* alike, according to which
certain parts of the verb *eidomai*, and specifically its participles
governing the dative case, are employed in contexts where corporeal
resemblance is incontrovertibly involved. A straightforward instance
is Athene's taking of the appearance of the Taphians' leader Mentes,
eidomenē... Mentēi (*Od.* 1.105), from which moment, until her
departure (1.319), she is treated by Telemachos simply *as* Mentes.
An example involving the adopting by a god of animal rather than
human form can be found in the *Iliad*, when the wind-god Boreas
couples with the mares of Erichthonios 'having likened himself to a
dark-maned stallion' (*Il.* 20.224), the word translated as 'having
likened himself' being *eisamenos*, an aorist participle from *eidomai*.
All this would seem to constitute respectable support for the view
that, in our starting passage too, Athene adopts the *form* of a bird.

There is, however, an alternative interpretation, according to which
Athene does not turn into a bird at all; rather, her departure is merely
compared to that of a bird. This was the view of, among others,
Christian Gottlob Heyne and Walter Otto, while Franz Dirlmeier, in
his detailed study of the problem, is emphatic: there is no bird trans-

[1] Lattimore (1965).
[2] Shewring (1980).
[3] Pollard (1977) 79–80, 155. Another classicist and naturalist, Geoffrey Arnott,
takes *phēnē* to cover what are now identified as two separate species, the lammergeier
and the black vulture (Arnott (2007) 188). A precise identification, even were one to
be possible, would be irrelevant to our concerns here.
[4] Stanford (1965) on 3.372.
[5] 'in... Vogelgestalt' (Kirchhoff (1860) 330–1); 'erscheint Athena... in Vogelgestalt' (Nilsson (1967) 349, with n. 4).

formation; rather, Athene/Mentor quits the scene *with the speed of* a bird.[6] Dirlmeier makes a virtuoso attempt to combat the advocates of transformation, for example in his discussion of the Boreas episode from the *Iliad* which we mentioned just now. He maintains that, because 'dark-maned' is elsewhere an epithet of Poseidon, what is happening is that Boreas is being likened, not to just any horse, but to Poseidon-as-horse, which means that Boreas is turning himself temporarily, not into an animal, but into another god; but this (Dirlmeier argues) is a totally different situation from the one in our *Odyssey* starting passage, since what would be at stake on the 'metamorphosis reading' of *that* passage would be the transformation of Athene, not into a bird-goddess, but just into an ordinary bird.[7] Unsurprisingly, many have remained unconvinced by these extraordinary contortions.[8] Dirlmeier fails to undermine the linguistic grounds for translating *eidomenē/eisamenos* as 'taking/having taken the form of'; and to suggest that what arouses Nestor's astonishment in our starting passage is the *eagle-swiftness* with which Athene departs the scene is to introduce an element ('as swift as . . .') which is absent from the text. So Stephanie West, in her note on the passage in the Oxford *Commentary on Homer's Odyssey*, seems to me perfectly justified in observing that *eidomenē* 'must mean that the goddess assumes the form of a bird'.[9]

Why would accomplished scholars have resisted this apparently obvious interpretation? Much more is at stake here than the understanding of a single Greek verb. The possibility that a Greek goddess could have been envisaged by Homer as transforming herself into a bird exposes a raw nerve for those critics who see such a possibility either as conflicting with their notion of what it is appropriate to expect to find in Homer, or with their notion of what it is to be a Greek divinity, or both.[10] Dr West identifies the relevant implicit agenda: 'To some scholars,' she writes, 'the notion that the Olympians

[6] Heyne (1802) i, n. on *Il.* 7.59; Otto (1929) 268; Dirlmeier (1967) 24. Note also the translation by Aurelio Privitera (1991): 'la glaucopide Atena andò via *come* un vulture' ('green-eyed Athene left *like* a vulture'); my emphasis.

[7] Dirlmeier (1967) 25–6.

[8] For criticisms see Bannert (1978) and Erbse (1980).

[9] Heubeck, West, and Hainsworth (1988) on 3.371–2.

[10] Bushnell ((1982) 9) goes so far as to speak of Dirlmeier's 'distaste for the idea of gods appearing in bird form'.

might thus manifest themselves in the guise of birds ... has seemed to imply unacceptably theriomorphic conceptions of divinity.'[11]

Indeed, an enormously influential way of reading the development of Greek religion has been to see it as embodying the triumph of anthropomorphism, a characteristic which, furthermore, is usually seen as distinguishing Greek religion from other ancient Near Eastern religions. In the words of Wilamowitz: 'The great superiority of the Hellenes over the Orientals and the Egyptians lies in the fact that they conceived their gods in a form which was beautiful, human, and unaffected by the disfigurements of old age; and it was Homer who first taught them this lesson.'[12] Greek religion, on this view, witnessed the superseding of non-anthropomorphism (for example, theriomorphism) by anthropomorphism, even though certain beliefs and practices redolent of non-anthropomorphism obstinately survived. Such a view of the general history of Greek religion (a view to which we shall return later)[13] naturally has consequences for the reading of the individual texts—and the individual passages, such as the one we began by considering—which form part of that history. In particular, an interpretation of Homeric epic which minimizes the extent to which the poems depict the gods in non-human form has the effect of placing Homer in the anthropomorphic religious vanguard as opposed to the (allegedly) outdated theriomorphic past.

Let us return once more to our starting passage, looking at it this time from a different angle:

> Ὣς ἄρα φωνήσασ᾽ ἀπέβη γλαυκῶπις Ἀθήνη,
> φήνῃ εἰδομένη· θάμβος δ᾽ ἕλε πάντας ἰδόντας,
> θαύμαζεν δ᾽ ὁ γεραιός, ὅπως ἴδεν ὀφθαλμοῖσι·

So saying, green-eyed Athene went away, likening herself to a vulture, and astonishment took hold of all those who were looking, and the old man was amazed, as he saw it with his eyes.

Here is another observation from the Oxford *Commentary*, an observation which at first sight appears uncontroversial. 'Mentor vanishes,

---

[11] Heubeck, West, and Hainsworth (1988) on 3.371–2.

[12] Wilamowitz-Moellendorff (1931–2) i. 144. Cf. also Nilsson (1952) 74: 'The Greek form of imagination is anthropomorphic'; 143–4: 'we have been educated by the Greeks to a consistent anthropomorphism, and this is something specifically Greek.'

[13] See below, 177–90.

and the spectators see instead a vulture flying off.'[14] Stephanie West is far from being the only scholar to speak of Athene 'vanishing': virtually every critic makes the same assumption. Herbert Bannert describes the scene like this: 'Everyone looks on as the stranger beside Nestor suddenly disappears, and high in the air there flies a sea eagle.'[15] The difficulty, however, is that the notion of 'vanishing' is nowhere to be found in the Greek. Now, when we are attempting to understand phenomena with an uncanny quality to them—and that is certainly Nestor's view of what has occurred, since his immediate inference (3.377–9) is that he has been in the presence of a goddess—it is more than usually important to attend to the exact words used in a text (or, as the case may be, to register the precise details of a visual image). To say that Athene-as-Mentor vanishes, and that a bird *then* flies off, is to bleach out some of the strangeness of what we actually have before us. In this metamorphosis there is no description, in the manner of an Ovid or a Bernini, of elongating and feather-covered fingers. All we know is that *somehow* Athene/Mentor took the form of a bird. If the interpreter punctuates this mysterious shape-shifting with a disappearance—a 'blank' covering the gap between Athene-as-Mentor and Athene-as-bird—the effect is to render an enigmatic and baffling occurrence just a shade more rationally acceptable than it would otherwise have been. This is not to say that *no* Greek texts narrating metamorphosis involve an intermediate stage of disappearance; many of them explicitly do, and we shall come across examples in due course. It is just that in the present passage there is no evidence of such a notion.

I have been suggesting that a critic's perception of whether a metamorphosis occurred, and of how it occurred if did occur, may be influenced by fundamental assumptions about the historical development of Greek religion, and about the representation and understanding of 'uncanny' behaviour. I want now to widen the perspective, in order to see whether these two observations remain valid when viewed in the light of certain other Homeric passages which, once more, involve birds.

---

[14] Heubeck, West, and Hainsworth (1988) on 3.371–2.

[15] Bannert (1978) 31. For distinctions, in a Greek context, between eagles, lammergeiers, and other large raptorial birds, see Pollard (1977) 76–82, and Arnott (2007) under the relevant entries; but see my comment at n. 3 above.

The *Iliad* and *Odyssey* contain several episodes in which the narrator represents gods in the form of—or perhaps as simply 'like'—
birds. At *Iliad* 7.58–61 Athene and Apollo, 'resembling birds (*ornisin
eoikotes*), vultures, settled in the high oak tree of their father, Zeus of
the aegis'. At *Iliad* 14.286–91 Sleep, before Zeus could spot him, sat in
a pine tree 'like a singing bird' (*ornithi ligurēi enalinkios*). At *Iliad*
15.236–8 Apollo comes down from Mount Ida 'like a hawk' (*irēki
eoikōs*). At *Odyssey* 5.51–4 Hermes speeds over the waves 'like a
seagull' (*larōi ornithi eoikōs*); 'in such a likeness (*tōi ikelos*) Hermes
rode over the many waves.' A little further on in the *Odyssey*, at
5.352–3, the sea-goddess Leukothea, having lent Odysseus her
harm-averting veil, 'in the likeness of a shearwater (*aithuiēi eikuia*)
slipped back into the heaving sea, and the dark wave closed above
her'. Finally, at *Odyssey* 22.239–40 Athene, in the midst of the battle
against the suitors, 'in the likeness of a swallow to look upon (*che-
lidoni eikelē antēn*), shot up aloft and perched on the roof-beam of
the smoky palace'. In the scholarship on these episodes we find the by
now familiar polarization: for some critics, these are accounts of
transformations; for others, they involve nothing more than similes.
Often the argument is linguistic: it revolves around asking whether
there might be significant distinctions between the usage of different
Greek words for 'likening', 'like', 'resembling', etc. But equally often
the argument rests, explicitly or more often implicitly, on assumptions about what it is plausible or appropriate to find depicted in
Homer. In relation to *Iliad* 7.58–61, Heyne considered it 'ridiculous
. . . if Athene and Apollo are turned into vultures or assume the
appearance of vultures'.[16] Leaf took the opposite view, in favour of
a 'metamorphosis reading' of the scene[17]—which is, according to
Dirlmeier, just what one would anticipate: 'That the English, with
their passion for folklore, should opt for the bird-transformation was
only to be expected';[18] for Dirlmeier, the Leafian approach entailed
ascribing to Homer a 'reversion to prehistoric theriomorphism'.[19]
However, Leaf's view was by no means confined to the English. Pierre
Chantraine was unambiguous in stating that 'Athene and Apollo

---

[16] Heyne (1802) v. 318, n. on *Il.* 7.59; cf. Dirlmeier (1967) 5.
[17] Leaf (1900) n. on *Il.* 7.59.
[18] Dirlmeier (1967) 9.   [19] Dirlmeier (1967) 35.

perch on an oak in the form of vultures', and interpreted several other Homeric passages along similar lines, hazarding the opinion that such passages *might* preserve the memory of ancient theriomorphic divinities.[20] Hartmut Erbse also followed Leaf's general line, but added his own twist to it, arguing that Homeric gods could adopt non-human forms as 'masks': although the gods' essence remained unaltered, their external appearance was indeed transformed.[21] Erbse was thus able to accommodate both the fact that the Homeric Olympians sometimes assume the form of animals, and the 'superiority' of anthropomorphism: he speaks of a *Tiergestalt* as a survival which Homer 'degrades' into the form of a mask.[22]

Just as the transformation-versus-simile debate, with its wider implications regarding theriomorphism/anthropomorphism, replicates itself in relation to a range of passages throughout Homeric epic, so too does the 'Does she vanish?' problem, along with *its* implied, wider question: just how 'astonishing' are the events portrayed in the Homeric narrative? An episode from Book 1 of the *Odyssey* offers a useful point of entry.

By 'likening herself' (*eidomenē*) to Mentes, guest-friend of Odysseus' household, Athene gains the confidence of Telemachos (1.105). Two hundred lines later, after urging the young man no longer to cling to childhood, she leaves Ithaca (319–23):

> Ἡ μὲν ἄρ' ὣς εἰποῦσ' ἀπέβη γλαυκῶπις Ἀθήνη,
> ὄρνις δ' ὣς ἀνοπαῖα διέπτατο· ...
>   ὁ δὲ φρεσὶν ᾗσι νοήσας
> θάμβησεν κατὰ θυμόν· ὀίσατο γὰρ θεὸν εἶναι.

So spoke the goddess green-eyed Athene, and she went away, *ornis d' hōs anopaia dieptato*...and he noticed in his mind, and he was astonished (*thambēsen*) in his heart, for he thought it was a divinity.

Controversy over the meaning of ὄρνις δ' ὣς ἀνοπαῖα διέπτατο (*ornis d' hōs anopaia dieptato*) is as at least as old as the ancient scholia. The disagreement even extends to accentuation and word division. The Alexandrian scholar Aristarchos thought the reading should be

---

[20] Chantraine (1954) 62–3.
[21] Erbse (1980).
[22] Erbse (1980) 273. On Homeric gods 'masking' themselves, cf. Reinhardt (1961) 280.

ἀνόπαια (*anopaia*), understood as the name of a kind of bird; his rival Krates was among those who took ἀν' ὀπαῖα (*an'opaia*) to mean 'through the smoke-vent in the roof'. What I want to draw attention to here, though, is not these differences over translation, nor indeed the metamorphosis-versus-simile dispute—which rages over this passage too—but rather a comment, once more in the Oxford *Commentary*, on the smoke-vent option:

On this interpretation it is difficult to avoid the inference that Athene is supposed to be transformed into a bird, not merely, as some have thought, compared to one. Though διέπτατο [*dieptato*; 'flew'] might be used of swift movement other than literal flying..., it is absurd to imagine Mentes suddenly levitating towards the roof and squeezing out through a chink in the tiles; we are surely meant to suppose that he suddenly vanished and Telemachos saw instead a bird flying overhead.[23]

The commentator is quite prepared to entertain the possibility that Athene might be represented as undergoing metamorphosis, but draws the line at taking a further step in the direction of, as she sees it, absurdity. The solution is to introduce a disappearance. Vanishing is appropriate, levitation definitely not. The scene is allowed to be astonishing, but not *too* astonishing.

A more general approach to the metamorphosis/vanishing conundrum is that of Françoise Frontisi-Ducroux:

For the Greeks, metamorphosis happens in the twinkling of an eye, that is to say at the moment when vision is blocked. Metamorphosis belongs to the sphere of the non-visible, since it occurs in response to a divine command. The gods are invisible to humans, since human sight is too weak...The immediacy of the aorist tense, regularly used in the case of metamorphosis, may signify that the gods' actions cannot be grasped, and that divine temporality eludes the perception of mortals.[24]

I agree with every word of this, especially because it retains uncanniness as a fundamental part of the bystander's experience of metamorphosis. But the next step taken by Frontisi-Ducroux seems to me less persuasive:

---

[23] S. West in Heubeck, West, and Hainsworth (1988) on 1.320.
[24] Frontisi-Ducroux (2003) 91.

In the two cases [sc. two instances of Athene-as bird in the *Odyssey*] no change is described: there is a verb to denote taking-wing, and a simile or an epithet expressing likeness to denote the new form already taken. These divine metamorphoses are above all disappearances.[25]

As I suggested a few moments ago, it is not that to talk of 'disappearance' is to introduce a motif which is *intrinsically* inappropriate to metamorphosis. It is just that to talk of disappearance *in these cases* is to compel the text to say something about which it is silent.

THE CENTRALITY OF TRANSFORMATION IN THE *ODYSSEY*

So far in this chapter I have sought to identify assumptions which seem to me to lie beneath what others have written. However, there is something uncomfortably facile (even though it was a standard intellectual gambit in the 1980s and 1990s) about positioning the interpretations of others without having the will, or perhaps the courage, to make interpretative statements oneself. But the act of interpretation is not *entirely* constituted by the interpreter's assumptions: it remains possible—indeed it is the *point* of interpretation— to marshal evidence in as self-aware and judicious a manner as possible, and then to bring that evidence to bear upon the text. In this spirit, as I widen the perspective for a second time, embracing now the role of transformations in the *Odyssey* as a whole, I propose to indicate how I myself see the place of this theme within the narrative.

The first point to emphasize is that self-transformation by the Olympian gods constitutes only a part of the picture. This brings us to the two divinities whom the poem identifies most closely with metamorphosis, and who live far removed from Olympos: Proteus and Circe.

Proteus is the evasive sea-god whom Menelaos encounters in Egypt. The narrative stresses both Proteus' isolation and his margin-

---

[25] Frontisi-Ducroux (2003) 90.

ality. Menelaos relates that he came upon the Old Man on the island
of Pharos, said to be a whole day's sail from the coast even for a vessel
enjoying a following breeze (4.355–7). (Since Pharos, later the historical location of the lighthouse of Alexandria, was actually situated
less than a mile from the Egyptian coast,[26] we might detect here a
refocusing of real-world knowledge in the interests of a desired
narrative emphasis precisely upon Proteus' remoteness.) As for marginality, this applies quite literally to Proteus, since it is onto the sea
shore that he emerges in order to count his seals (450). To overcome
him, Menelaos and three of his men must themselves undergo a
quasi-metamorphosis, hidden under the noisome sealskins which
the daughter of the Old Man spreads over them (440). Deceived by
the stratagem, Proteus mistakenly counts the four humans as seals, as
if this were an actual and not a pretended transformation (452).
When seized by the Greeks, he goes through a terrifying metamorphic repertoire (4.454–9):

With a shout we rushed upon him, locking him in our arms. But the Old
Man had not forgotten his tricky skill. First he became (*geneto*) a great
bearded lion, then a snake, then a panther, then a mighty boar; he became
(*gigneto*) running water, and a tall, leafy tree. But we held resolutely on to
him with enduring spirit.

But at last defeat compels him to revert to his original form. He has
no choice but to recognize his foe's identity and to predict for him
what the future holds in store.

The other non-Olympian divinity linked with metamorphosis is
Circe. Like Proteus she is isolated; like him, she dwells on an island:
Aiaia.[27] Any real-world geographical analogue for this island is beside
the point; what is relevant is that Aiaia is, in terms of Odysseus'
journeys, his last stopping place on the way to the Land of the
Dead—as far off the track beaten by the living as it is possible to be.

Circe's special powers enable her to alter the form of those who
come to visit her: so, for the first time in our discussion of the poem,

---

[26] S. West in Heubeck, West, and Hainsworth (1988) on 4.354–9.

[27] 10.135. Contrast the variant chosen by Apollonios of Rhodes and by Virgil, for
both of whom Circe's dwelling is on the Italian coast between Rome and Naples (Ap.
Rhod. *Arg.* 3.312, 4.850; Verg. *A.* 7.10–24); cf. Hunter (1989) on *Arg.* 3.311–13.

we encounter the transformation of human beings. The victims are some of Odysseus' companions (10.233–40):

She brought them inside and seated them on chairs and benches, and mixed for them a potion of cheese and barley and pale honey and Pramneian wine, but put into the mixture harmful drugs, to make them utterly forgetful of their own country. When she had given them this and they had drunk it all down, suddenly she struck them with her wand and drove them into her pig sties. They had the head and voice and bristles and body of pigs, but the mind within them stayed as it had been before.[28]

It is worth noting the *elaboration* of Circe's technique: making the victims sit, administering to them a concoction laced with drugs, striking them with a wand. Unlike the great Olympian deities, Circe cannot effect metamorphosis by an instantaneous and unmediated act of will. Rather she resembles the Helen of *Odyssey* Book 4 (219–33), whose power of inducing temporary forgetfulness of unpleasant memories is similarly mediated by a potion. Circe is also the antecedent of later semi-divine or human sorceresses such as Apollonios' Medea, Theokritos' Simaitha, and Apuleius' Pamphile, all of whom use complex techniques to effect metamorphosis or to carry out other ritual practices.[29]

The metamorphosis of Odysseus' men, together with its reversal after Odysseus has resisted Circe's potion thanks to the herb *mōly*, poses many problems for the interpreter.[30] Several scholars have read the episode in terms of a contrast between epic, on the one hand, and folktale, with its allegedly distinctive aura of magic and fantasy, on the other. It has commonly been maintained that (1) the story of Circe reveals traces of 'folktale elements'—wicked witches who transform their victims, magical antidotes to transformation, heroes who break the spell and undo the metamorphosis, and so on; but that (2)

[28] The view that Odysseus' companions are merely *like* pigs is expressed by the twelfth-century commentator Eustathios (on *Od.* 10.383), within the framework of his allegorical reading of the poem: to be 'like a pig' is to be 'swinish' in one's behaviour; cf. Skulsky (1981) 20–3.

[29] Note though that *sometimes* the Olympians too use mediation, as when Athene employs a *rhabdos*, 'wand' (e.g. *Od.* 16.172, 456). In the study of the pluralistic world of Greek myth, there is almost always room for an 'And yet...'; see 166 below.

[30] *Mōly*: 10.305. For the self-transformation of Hermes himself, in the passage immediately preceding this episode, see 42 and 168 n. 25 below.

such elements are minimized in the *Odyssey*. Alfred Heubeck's observations are representative:

Traits from... [folk-tale] are to be seen in Circe, but, as is characteristic of the epic treatment, the central elements of the folk-tale are restricted to a minimum. Pure magic is to be found only in the few lines which deal with the companions' actual metamorphosis and transformation back into human form. We are not told how, or indeed if, the magic plant Moly works on Circe. The action is set on as realistic a level as possible, and transferred from the alien realm of magic and irrational fantasy to the epic world... But the greatest advance on the traditional story is the depiction of Circe herself. She is a highly individual character, full of contradictions.[31]

It goes without saying that the complexity of Circe's character is indeed one of the countless, marvellous subtleties of the poem; but such complexity is perfectly compatible with the presence of 'magic' and 'fantasy'. What of Heubeck's other comments? First, the notion of folktale. Although Homeric scholars routinely invoke this term,[32] work on tale-telling has shown that 'folktale' is a concept invented at a particular time with a particular agenda—nationalist movements in late eighteenth- and early nineteenth-century Europe—and with doubtful relevance to classical antiquity.[33] Secondly, if we do allow the relevance of 'folktale' evidence, many of the examples which are said to reveal the state of the traditional story before Homer actually date from long after the composition of the Homeric poems; and it is

[31] Heubeck in Heubeck and Hoekstra (1989) on *Od.* 10.133–574 (p. 51).

[32] Page (1973)—in a work uncompromisingly entitled *Folktales in Homer's Odyssey*—surprisingly (but perhaps prudently) confines his *definition* of 'folktale' to a footnote (117 n. 2), which begins, moreover: 'I should prefer to shirk the task of defining precisely what I mean by "folktale"'! But the footnote does give some clues about what Page understands by the term. He speaks of '[a] broad and obvious line [which] may be drawn between a species of "folktale", as concerned with creatures of grotesque form and supernatural powers, living in an imaginary world, and a species of "saga", as concerned with persons believed to be historical and represented as behaving realistically in the actual world.' Page's remark ad loc. that in the *Odyssey* the distinction between folktale and saga is 'deliberately blurred' assumes, of course, that such a distinction is both prior to, and implicit in, the poem. A more recent critic illustrates just how persistent Page's approach is: in his excellent survey of Homeric scholarship, Richard Rutherford (1996) at one moment (3) expresses scepticism about imposing such terms as 'folktale' on Homer, yet later (66) echoes the usual view that 'comparison with parallel folk-tales suggests that Homer has somewhat reduced or underplayed the magical aspects'.

[33] See Burke (1978) ch. 1; Buxton (1994) 13 n. 19.

highly questionable whether the later evidence can be combined with the earlier to generate a 'universal folklore'.[34]

Thirdly, we need to examine just how far magic and fantasy are in fact played down in the Homeric narrative about Circe. For Heubeck, 'pure magic' is confined to the 'few lines' describing the companions' transformation.[35] Now it is by no means clear what we are to understand by 'pure magic', an expression which sounds naive in the light of the huge contemporary bibliography about what is at stake in defining 'magic'.[36] Even if we leave aside the definitional point, it is difficult to recognize in our Odyssean text a deliberate minimizing of the fantastic. At the centre of this issue is the depiction of metamorphosis, which, so far from being circumscribed within a few lines, in different ways pervades the entire Circe episode. The moment Odysseus' men enter Circe's domain (10.210) they come across mountain wolves and lions, which/who fawn on the new arrivals in the manner of tame house-dogs. Although the hearer/reader is theoretically free to interpret the behaviour of these creatures as the product of Circe's 'evil drugs' (213) *which merely turned wild animals to tame*—rather than causing, on this occasion, the more drastic change from human to animal—it must, first, be doubted whether such a domestication could be called 'evil', and, secondly, be relevant that Eurylochos instances Circe's transformational powers by warning that she can turn human beings into pigs, *wolves, and lions* (433). In short, the overall weight of the narrative supports the view that the wolves and lions first encountered by Odysseus' men are transformed humans.[37]

---

[34] Page (1973) 57.

[35] This echoes Page (1973) 57: 'The transformation into pigs is the one unrealistic element in the tale of Odysseus and Circe; it is therefore reduced to the smallest possible measure'; Page is followed by Skulsky (1981) 15.

[36] Cf. for instance R. Gordon in Flint et al. (1999) 159–275; bibliography in *ThesCRA* iii. 286–7 (compiled by R. L. Fowler and F. Graf); Bremmer (2008) 347–52.

[37] It has even been suggested that the stag killed by Odysseus is itself not just monstrously big (*pelōros*, 168) but monstrous *tout court*, on the grounds that it too is a transformed mortal. Certainly the lions and wolves enchanted by Circe are also described as *pelōra* (219). But nothing in the narrative suggests that Odysseus and his men are doing anything out of the ordinary in eating the stag; and, in a poem so overwhelmingly sensitive to the social/cultural/religious import of that which is eaten, such dietary matter-of-factness would be inconceivable if there were the slightest hint that the venison in question were formerly human. For the contrary but quite unconvincing view, see Roessel (1989).

In due course, the newly arrived humans are themselves transformed. When Odysseus starts up from the seashore to investigate,
the narrative highlights yet another transformation, though a less
radical one. Odysseus meets Hermes 'in the likeness of (*eoikōs*) a
young man' (278). When Hermes gives Odysseus *mōly*, and when
Odysseus uses the plant to block Circe's sorcery, this is surely another
example of the poem's non-avoidance of 'the fantastic'. It will be
recalled that Heubeck wishes to play down the strangeness of the
episode ('We are not told how, or indeed if, the magic plant Moly
works on Circe. The action is set on as realistic a level as possible').
But the remarkable effectiveness of *mōly* is beyond dispute, even if
the effect defies analysis in terms of magic or pharmacology. As
Hawthorne's tale of Drowne's wooden image reminds us, the sense
of the uncanny surrounding a transformation can perfectly well be
conveyed by a gap, or a silence.

Circe concedes that she is powerless to vanquish her adversary by
effecting his metamorphosis out of human form. However, though
she cannot abolish Odysseus' humanity, what she can do is enhance
it, by bathing, anointing, and re-clothing him (360–70). She performs a similar service for Odysseus' companions, not just re-
humanizing them (a rare event in Greek narratives about
metamorphoses of humans) but rejuvenating them, like a 'good'
Medea (388–96):

So I spoke, and Circe walked out through the palace, holding her wand in
her hand, and opened the doors of the pigsty, and drove them out, looking
like (*eoikotas*) nine-year-old porkers. They stood facing her, and she, making
her way among them, anointed each of them with another drug. The bristles,
which had grown upon them through the evil drug which Circe had placed
upon them before, now fell away from them, and they became (*egenonto*)
men again, younger than they had been, and taller and more handsome to
the eye.

Is this 'magic', or even 'pure magic'? It all depends what you mean
by... At all events, Circe's craft remains undiminished, even though
it was momentarily neutralized when she came up against (by proxy)
the power of one of the Olympians.

In view of the geographical remoteness of Proteus and Circe, could
we go on to suggest that metamorphosis, too, is a kind of isolated and

'fringe' element, to be contrasted with the poem's magic-free, anthropomorphic centre? To do so would be quite wrong. Such a move,
like other attempts to rescue the poem from fantasy and so render it
more 'real', is not only unsustainable but also unnecessary. For
transformation happens in Ithaca, no less than on the 'fringes'.
Odysseus can change himself, by telling stories, into many different
men—or, as in the encounter with the Cyclops, into No Man—and
he can do it beside his own hearth just as well as beside that of the
Cyclops. Furthermore Athene can change Odysseus not just metaphorically, but literally. This happens in Phaiakia, as during her
protégé's encounter with Nausikaa (6.229–31):

Athene, daughter of Zeus, made him seem taller to look upon, and thicker,
and on his head she made his curling locks hang down like hyacinth petals.

But later too, back on the good old solid earth of Ithaca, Odysseus is
once more altered, this time in the presence of Telemachos (16.172–83):

So spoke Athene, and she touched him with her golden wand. First she put a
fresh clean mantle and tunic over him, and made him taller and younger. His
dark colour came back to him, his jaw grew firm, and the beard on his chin
became (*egenonto*) black. Having done her work Athene went away once
more, but Odysseus went back into the hut. His dear son was astonished
(*thambēse*) and turned his eyes away, fearing this might be a god, and spoke
to him and addressed him in winged words: 'Suddenly you seem changed
(*alloios... phanēs*), Stranger, from what you were before; your garments are
different, and so is the colour of your skin. Surely you are some god, one of
those who hold the high heaven...'

Telemachos' amazement is a classic way in which characters in this
poem react to the perceived irruption of the sacred. But not *every*
case of metamorphosis has astonishment as its sequel. After revealing
his identity to his son, Odysseus must for the moment resume the
hunched shabbiness of the beggar (16.454–8):

But Athene stood by Odysseus, son of Laertes, and touched him with her
wand and made him (*poiēse*) once more an old man, and put dirty clothing
upon his skin, in case the swineherd might recognize him when he looked
upon him...

The transformation is effected in such a way as to block recognition,
avoiding the astonishment which would otherwise inevitably ensue.

As a final illustration of the presence of metamorphosis at the heart of Ithaca, I want to discuss a unique passage from Book 19, a passage which demonstrates just how disconcertingly fluid can be the poem's representation of the human. Odysseus, clad in rags, is huddling beside his own hearth, unrecognized by the wife with whom he is conversing. Having discovered in this enigmatic Stranger a friend in whom she can confide, Penelope asks him to interpret a dream which has come to her. She keeps, she tells the Stranger, twenty geese in the house, which she loves to watch. In her dream, a great eagle swooped down from the mountain, killed every one of these geese, and then soared away into the air; Penelope (still in her dream) cried out in sorrow at the slaughter. But then the eagle returned, and perched on the roof of the palace. Yet a change had come over the eagle (19.545–53):

> He now had a human voice, and checked my lamentation: 'Take heart, daughter of far-famed Ikarios. This is no dream, but a happy waking vision, destined to be accomplished. The geese are the suitors, and I, who was the eagle, am now your own husband, come home, and I shall bring shameless destruction on all the suitors.' So he spoke; and the honey-sweet sleep released me. I looked about and saw the geese in the palace, feeding on grains of wheat by the trough, as they always did.

The 'real' but still disguised Odysseus interprets this dream as portending death for the suitors. But Penelope is not so sure: after all, two sorts of dreams visit mortals, the true and the deceptive—and it is hard to distinguish between them.[38] No wonder Penelope cannot be confident of the Stranger's interpretation; for the dream she has recounted to him is extraordinarily intricate. To begin with, it is not simply a dream, but an omen-within-a-dream, which, moreover— the omen, that is, not the dream—delivers its own interpretation. This interpretation is given by the eagle, one of the very birds whose behaviour is the object of the interpretation. Furthermore, although the eagle still (we must infer) retains its avian form, it now has a human voice, with which it tells Penelope that it has abandoned its

---

[38] The truth status of dreams is hard to fathom even for one with far greater divine backing than Penelope enjoys. When Aineias leaves the Underworld, he does so through the Gate of Ivory—through which *false* dreams pass in order to reach mortals (Verg. *A.* 6.893–9).

role as bird-omen to become Odysseus-in-the-form-of-a-bird, and left behind its status as dream to become 'reality'. The transition from dream to waking, with the corresponding shift from Odysseus-as-bird/omen-and-as-omen-interpreter to Odysseus-as-disguised-Stranger, rounds off an episode for which it is impossible to find a parallel elsewhere in the poem. Nor is it surprising that we should find such a passage at such a juncture. Penelope is surrounded by the 'false' stories of the disguised Odysseus, who 'knew how to say many false things that were like true things' (19.203)—another dimension of his metamorphic skill. The drive of the story towards revelation and openness is increasingly insistent—only Odysseus' hand over Eurykleia's mouth imposes a temporary check upon it—but years of empty disappointment have shrivelled Penelope's capacity to believe, or to take a decision. And yet, whatever she believes, she does decide: to set up the contest with the bow. By a process about which the narrative never fully comes clean, the astonishing account of the dream/omen has acted as a catalyst upon her imagination. Quite apart from the shifting emotional drama which it implies for Penelope, this passage embodies a fascinating exploration of the relations between different modes of access to the sacred: omen, dream, and metamorphosis.[39] Let us reiterate the point: metamorphosis is to be found, among other places, at the very hearth and heart of Odysseus' home.

I began this chapter by arguing that whether a metamorphosis has taken place, and if so, how it has taken place (with or without an intervening disappearance), are questions the answers to which may be inflected by the interpreter's assumptions. I went on to offer some comments of my own about the place of metamorphosis in the *Odyssey*, highlighting the various corporeal changes which take place across the full geographical sweep of the poem, and not just on its fringes. Against this background, I shall now look again at some interpretative issues raised earlier in the chapter.

---

[39] It is worth noting the contrast with the far simpler omen at 15.160–81. As Telemachos and Peisistratos set out from Sparta, an eagle carries a goose in its talons. There is no framing dream, no metamorphosis of the eagle, no crying out by Penelope at the slaughter of the goose. But then, in Book 15, the emotional situation has not reached the complexity of Book 19.

The *Odyssey* presents us with a spectrum of kinds of transformation. At one end we have 'mere' similes, according to which a person or thing may be 'like' another, without being identified with it. At the other end we have Proteus, and the victims of Circe, and Athene-as-Mentes; about all of these the narrative leaves no room for doubt that a corporeal transformation is to be understood to have taken place. Between these extremes is a range of textual phenomena, some inclining towards the status of simile, some seeming to imply full bodily transformation, many, though, resisting such binary analysis: for it is sometimes *impossible to decide*, on the basis of the text, whether what is at stake is a transformation or a comparison.[40] I would exemplify that in-between category with the description of Hermes speeding over the water like—or in the form of—a seagull (*Od.* 5.51–4). Hermes is alone: there is no astonished internal spectator in this episode, as Nestor was astonished at Pylos, to prompt us into ascribing this or that appearance to the travelling god. What was 'actually seen' cannot be determined. Nor is there anything in the least surprising about such indeterminacy. Since one of the attributes of Greek divinity can be mystery, it is entirely appropriate that this should be reflected in narrative ambiguity or openness (just as a different kind of mystery is reflected in the ambiguous, open text of Hawthorne's tale of Drowne and his image). Could one, then, cut the knot of the avian simile/transformation debate by allowing 'openness' to *all* these problematic passages? That would be a major mistake: it would reduce the subtle differentiations of the Homeric narrative to a flat homogeneity.

Within the fictional world of the *Odyssey*, then, certain kinds of change-of-form are central, integral, pervasive. Many such changes involve shape-shifting by the gods, although there are changes also to human form (Circe's victims; the transformations of Odysseus). However, the changes in this poem are hardly ever of the type which sees the human permanently metamorphosed into the non-human. It may be significant that in Book 19, when Penelope invokes the tale of the nightingale lamenting the dead son whom she has slain (518–23), there is no explicit reference to what would become the

---

[40] Cf. Burckhardt (1898–1902) ii. 7; Fränkel (1921) 81; de Jong (1987) 134–5; Buxton (2004a) 143.

ubiquitous end-point of this tale for later myth-tellers, namely the transformation of the three protagonists (often named Tereus, Prokne, and Philomela) into birds.[41] In the *Odyssey,* metamorphosis does not embody an exit route for the human who has been driven beyond the limit. The only boundary which limits human action, and which gives it meaning, is death. The form of the hero is not *ultimately* malleable: neither Odysseus nor any of the other principal characters will leave their human shape behind. That outlet is for other types of narrative to exploit.

CODA

What of the *Iliad?* We touched on Iliadic examples of god-into-bird transformation earlier in this chapter; but a final, more general comment may be appropriate.

The thrust of an influential paper by Jasper Griffin was to isolate the uniqueness of Homer by bracketing the *Iliad* and *Odyssey* together and contrasting them with the Epic Cycle: 'the fantastic', so the argument went, played a much smaller role in the *Iliad* and *Odyssey* than it did in the Cycle.[42] Griffin does occasionally distinguish between the two Homeric epics ('It is at once evident that the Cycle contained a number of things to which the *Iliad,* and *to a lesser extent* the *Odyssey* also, was inhospitable'),[43] but the distinction needs greater clarity. As regards the issue which is our focus in this book, the *Odyssey* extends the possibilities of metamorphosis into areas which the *Iliad* does not. Although in both poems the Olympians habitually shift shape, in the *Iliad* there is no Circe; the goddess Thetis—who in other narrative variants is (as we shall see) prone to change her shape serially—stands in the *Iliad* as the poignant embodiment of anthropomorphic motherhood; nor do corporeal

[41] The 'state of the myth' at the time of the epic's composition is extremely uncertain; cf. Russo, Fernandez-Galiano, and Heubeck (1992) on 518–24; Martín Rodríguez (2002) 35–6. A typically crystal-clear account of the evidence is to be found in Gantz (1993) 239–41.

[42] Griffin (1977).

[43] Griffin (1977) 39; my emphasis.

changes overcome Iliadic heroes in the manner experienced by the polytropic Odysseus of the *Odyssey*. Of course, even in relation to the *Iliad* we must not deny altogether the presence of fantastic, divinely caused metamorphoses within the natural-mortal world. Zeus at Aulis (2.308–20) sends an omen whereby eight sparrow chicks and their mother are eaten by a snake, which Zeus then turns to stone; unsurprisingly, the bystanders are 'astonished' (*thaumazomen*, 320). Again, when Achilles tries to encourage Priam to relent from his grief in order to eat, he cites the precedent of Niobe: her children having been struck dead by Apollo and Artemis, she broods still, petrified, like the rest of her community, whom Zeus also turned to stone (24.602–17).[44] Yet these remain exceptions. It is fundamental to the *Iliad* that, for animals and humans alike, there is ultimately no way out of life but death. On *this* point—notwithstanding the greater role accorded in the *Odyssey* to *certain* types of metamorphosis—it is indeed legitimate to bracket together the two great Homeric epics.

---

[44] See Gantz (1993) 536–7, and 201–2 below.

2

Athenian Drama

With its masked actors and its location in the theatre of Dionysos, god of reversals, Attic drama may be said to have at its very core a set of 'metamorphic' features, at least in an applied sense of the term. More specifically, however, the plots of some plays turn upon a change of shape by one or more of the characters. By analysing how this motif is contrastingly handled in tragedy and comedy, we can illuminate fundamental differences between the genres. At the same time we can begin to confront a difficult question: how far was metamorphosis 'taken seriously'?

TRAGEDY: ASTONISHING CHANGE AND ITS LIMITS

Athenian tragedy dramatized extreme situations within which human lives were 'tested to destruction'.[1] Through myths retold in tragic drama, Athenian society examined moral, political, and religious issues in such a way that, however catastrophic the outcomes within the dramatic frame, the society which held that frame could continue to function.[2] Disruption of order, transgression of boundaries: these are the life-blood of tragedy; and one of the motifs which sometimes accompanies—indeed, literally embodies—disruption

---

[1] Cf. Buxton (2002a) 184, for a discussion of this phrase borrowed from engineering.

[2] Osborne (1993) 34 interestingly argues that 'the city's promotion of dramatic competition implies a confidence that the political effects of promoting certain issues can be controlled'.

and transgression, is metamorphosis.[3] We begin with a tragedy featuring a god who is often taken to show a peculiarly intimate connection with transformation: Dionysos.

Forms of Dionysos

Euripides' *Bacchants* is dominated by changes of appearance. As early as the fourth line of his prologue Dionysos establishes that he has 'taken the shape (*morphēn*) of a mortal in exchange for that of a god'; to remove any doubt—for the point will be crucial to the audience's appreciation of the plot—he drives the message home at the end of the speech: 'I have taken and keep the appearance (*eidos*) of a mortal, and I have altered my form (*morphēn... metebalon*) to that of a man' (53–4).[4] Although it is not always easy to specify exactly *how* the form of a god differs from that of a human, the distinction is nevertheless fundamental. It may even be a matter of life and death, as it was for Dionysos' mother, whose fate is vividly present on stage in the shape of the still-smouldering ruin of her home (6–9). Semele had wished for Zeus to appear in his true form, which, as she found to her catastrophic cost, entailed the thunderbolt and the lightning flash as well as magnificence.[5]

As the action unfolds, changes of form multiply. The fawnskin-clad chorus of Bacchants embody Dionysos' power symbolically to assimilate humans to animals, a point reinforced when Teiresias and Kadmos enter dressed likewise in fawnskins. The transformations which Dionysos himself undergoes are, however, more than a matter of clothing: such changes indicate just how kaleidoscopic this divin-

[3] For brief remarks on tragic metamorphoses, see FI 16–19.

[4] Dodds's defence of the text against charges of tautology is conclusive: he speaks of 'the necessity of making it quite clear to the audience that the speaker, whom they accept as a god, will be accepted as a man by the people on the stage' (Dodds (1960) on lines 53–4).

There is a parallel case in Aischylos' *Edonians*, where Dionysos appears as a stranger unrecognized by his adversary, the Thracian King Lykourgos (F 61 Radt; cf. Henrichs (1984) 86). Note also the situation in Sophokles' *Inachos*, in which a stranger is said to have created disruption in Argos by transforming Io into a heifer (F 269a, 36–45 Radt). The stranger is, of course, Zeus. Detailed commentary in Carden (1974) on *P.Oxy.* 2369; on *Inachos*, see also Seaford (1980).

[5] See below, 148–50; 158–9.

ity is.[6] For Teiresias, this divine power—newly arrived and simultaneously age-old—is a liquid, who/which can be poured out as a
libation in the form of wine (284). To Pentheus, what seems most
striking about the Stranger is his femininity (353; cf. 453–9), a
characteristic which, in Pentheus' eyes, both enables him to corrupt
the Theban women sexually and sets him apart from Pentheus' own
world of men's men.[7] With the entry of the Servant, yet another
perspective on the Stranger develops: he is a *thēr*, 'wild beast' (436),
the most persistent variety of imagery in the play.

In the first confrontation between Pentheus and Dionysos, the
unrecognized god tells the mortal the precise truth about his ability
to shift form, although to Pentheus' ears what he says is mere
nonsense (477–9):

Pen. You say you saw the god clearly. What appearance did he have?
Dion. Whatever appearance he chose. It was not I who decided that.
Pen. Again you diverted that skilfully, with words that are nonsense.

Soon Pentheus experiences at first hand this Dionysiac power over
form. When the palace has been struck by a divinely provoked
earthquake, the god causes a bull to appear where he himself had
been imprisoned (618), and creates in the courtyard a kind of apparition, which Pentheus vainly attacks, 'as if', comments Dionysos, 'he
were killing me' (629–31).[8] Each new Dionysiac miracle confirms the
power of the new divinity to effect metamorphosis, but the most
shocking substantiation follows the shattering monosyllabic cry
which stops Pentheus dead in his tracks: 'Ah!' (810). At this instant,
which marks an unfathomable combination of temptation with sub-
jugation, Dionysos overturns the mortal's mind. After that, changing
his appearance is literally a mere formality, as the Theban ruler agrees
to don the complete costume of a maenad (827–43).

---

[6] For the multiple perceptions of Dionysos in *Bacchants*, see Buxton (1989) and
(1991).

[7] Male/female in Dionysos and his worship: Lada-Richards (1999), esp. 23–6;
Buxton (2009).

[8] However, the Greek word evoking this apparition is textually uncertain: φάσμα
(*phasma*), 'apparition', is an emendation of the manuscript reading φῶς (*phōs*),
'light'; cf. Seaford (1996) on 630–1, arguing that we should retain *phōs*.

When Pentheus and Dionysos face each other on stage for the third and last time, the mortal's transformation is complete. Pentheus resembles 'in form' (*morphēn*) one of the daughters of Kadmos (917; cf. 925–7). His wits, too, are altered, incapable as he is of distinguishing the Stranger's human shape from that of a bull (920–2). This collapsing of the human into the bestial is celebrated in the frenzied song of the chorus after Pentheus' departure for Mount Kithairon (977–1023): Bacchants—those wearers of the skins of timid fawns—are the swift hounds of Madness (977); the mother of their human prey is herself inhuman, either a lioness or a Gorgon (988–90); the god of the Bacchants is summoned to appear as bull, many-headed serpent, or flame-breathing lion (1017–19). In the narrative of the Newsbringer (1043–1152), the assimilation of human and bestial reaches its climax. At first the maenads are likened to animals (fillies, 1056; doves, 1090). Then, as Pentheus desperately struggles to re-erect the barrier between humans and animals ('Mother, I am your son Pentheus!', 1118–19), the maenads ecstatically ignore it: the intruder is a 'climbing wild-beast' (1107–8) whose head, ripped from its body and impaled by Agaue on her Bacchic *thyrsus*, is like that of a mountain lion (1141–2).

The chorus' reaction to this terrifying narrative is to re-emphasize Pentheus' falling-short of his proper humanity: he is the 'offspring of a snake' (being descended from one of the teeth of the Theban Serpent) who dressed as a woman (1155–7). The state of mind of Agaue, Pentheus' mother and murderer, is quite different. Though she talks of having engaged in an animal hunt (1174, 1185), for her this hunt—especially the head she bears as a trophy—has nothing to do with her son. Only in dialogue with Kadmos does she recover her previous mind, so as to be in a position to reaffirm the separation between beast and human (1283–4):

Ka.   Surely this doesn't appear to you to be a lion's head?
Ag.   No! In my wretchedness I hold Pentheus' head in my hand.

Not only is metamorphosis a central feature of the play's power to unsettle and unnerve: without the premiss, established in the prologue, that Dionysos can transform himself undetectably into human shape, the drama falls apart. That premiss guides us into the heart of the play's meaning, in relation to the ultimate distinction between humanity and divinity.[9] Dionysos' form is throughout presented as mobile, fluid, unbounded: as the chorus expresses it in the coda (a formulaic Euripidean ending, but never more relevant than in this play): *pollai morphai tōn daimoniōn*, 'Many are the forms of divinity' (1388).[10] Pentheus, on the other hand, seeks, not to dissolve order, but to impose it; when he is induced to relax a boundary—that between male and female—the result is at first ridiculous and then horrific. For Pentheus, to become female is to be diminished. But when Dionysos assumes new forms—including that of a feminized mortal man—this constitutes not a diminution of his divinity, but an extra dimension to it.[11]

The horned woman

Whereas in *Bacchants* transformation is a leitmotif throughout the play, in *Prometheus Bound* its presence is felt in one scene only.[12] But in the context of the fully extant tragedies that scene is unique, since it brings the audience face to face with a victim of animal metamorphosis.

The plot centres on the agony of an immortal who has dared to cross the will of Zeus; but entanglement with the supreme god can be equally disastrous for a mortal. Halfway through the play Io, an Argive maiden, bursts in upon the remote and craggy wasteland where the Titan Prometheus has been fettered. The shock value of the scene lies in the motif of metamorphosis, for Io has been transformed into a cow, a fact represented on stage by her wearing of horns (674).[13] Her distress is intensified by the relentless stinging of a gadfly. The wordless screams of the guiltless maiden signal the surreal, less-than-human state into which she has been plunged, a state in which physical pain is compounded by psychological distress:

---

[9] Henrichs's brilliant paper (1984) insists on the importance of this distinction in *Bacchants*.

[10] The line recurs at Eur. *Alc.* 1159, *Andr.* 1284, and *Hel.* 1688.

[11] See Buxton (2009), for the notion of feminization in this play and in other tragedies.

[12] For discussion of modern—not ancient—doubts about Aischylean authorship, see the summary in Griffith (1983) 31–5.

[13] Compare Pollux 4.141, for a reference to a tragic mask of the horned Aktaion.

she imagines she is being persecuted by the ghost of her former guard Argos, a persecution which she experiences visually but also aurally, through the remembered, haunting pipe-music which she associates with his killing.[14]

Prompted by the curiosity of the chorus of Oceanids, Io relates her extraordinary history. Visions, she recalls, came every night into her bedroom, beguiling her with the prospect of yielding her virginity to the supreme god of Olympos. When she told her father Inachos of these dreams, he naturally sought guidance from the gods' oracles. At first their voice was ambiguous, but at last they spoke clearly: he must drive his daughter out of her home into wandering exile, or else Zeus' thunderbolt would destroy the entire family (645–68). Against his will, Inachos carried out the command. Immediately Io suffered a transformation to whose effect her body still bears witness (673–82):

> At once my form (*morphē*) and mind were distorted.
> Horned, as you see, stung by the gadfly's sharp goad,
> I rushed with crazed, convulsive step to Kerchnea's clear stream
> And Lerna's spring. The earthborn cowherd Argos,
> Boundless in wrath, followed my every step
> With relentless eyes. A sudden unexpected fate
> Took life from him. But I, whipped by the gadfly's god-sent lash,
> Am driven on from land to land . . .

In keeping with the obscurity which clouds Io's fate according to her own narrative—after all, she is a mere mortal, the victim of powers beyond her comprehension—she leaves the metamorphosis unattributed to a particular divinity. She blames Zeus for her sufferings (577–8), but the metamorphosis itself was something which just happened, out of the blue. Nor does Prometheus, for all his near-omniscience, clarify the point; although he talks of Hera's role in Io's anguished wanderings (703–4), this carries no necessary implication that Hera might have effected the transformation.[15] *Prometheus Bound* does not, then, follow the version of events given elsewhere, for example in Aischylos' *Suppliants*, according to which the deity responsible for the transformation is unequivocally Hera, as she

[14] Are they the pipes of the herdsman Argos himself, or those of Hermes, who lulled Argos to sleep? The text is enigmatic (574–5).

[15] The same is true of the chorus' general reference to Hera's cruelty to Io (899–900).

attempted to block Zeus' passion by transforming its object ('The Argive goddess made (*ethēken*) the woman into a cow', is the view of, at any rate, the Argive king; *Supp.* 299). Whereas Zeus' role in *Suppliants* is relatively positive, culminating in the gentle breath with which he brought to Io both respite and impregnation, in *Prometheus Bound* the emphasis falls predominantly on Zeus' malignly causative role.[16] Only after Io's journeyings beyond number will rest and sanity replace exhausting madness when, at the touch of Zeus, she conceives and brings forth a son; but all that lies in the future, couched as it is in the form of a prediction by Prometheus (848–9).[17]

Io's story is relevant in multiple ways to the themes of the play.[18] Her fate both parallels and contrasts with that of Prometheus. Like him, she is a victim of Zeus' violence: political/cosmic violence in Prometheus' case, sexual in hers. Like Prometheus, she glimpses the distant prospect of a release from agony (Prometheus will ultimately be released thanks to Herakles, who will be a descendant of Io— another link between the two). Yet Io is a wanderer, whereas Prometheus is immobile; and she is mortal, which at least prevents her from anticipating her future suffering, whereas he, Forethought personified, can foresee only too clearly the torment to come. All this has repeatedly been commented on by critics.[19] Two other matters, however, have attracted far less critical attention.

The first concerns astonishment. We saw repeatedly in discussing Homer, and we shall see repeatedly again, how metamorphosis is usually represented as the irruption of the sacred into the everyday world of mortals, an irruption which typically generates astonishment among those who witness it. In *Prometheus Bound* the on-stage audience—Prometheus and the Oceanids—consists entirely of div-

---

[16] Aesch. *Supp.* 574–81.

[17] For other Greek versions of the Io myth, see Gantz (1993) 198–202. The Ovidian account is different again, being unambiguous in its setting out of the motivations of the tit-for-tat domestic squabble between Jupiter and Juno. Jupiter covers the world with a dark cloud to facilitate his adulterous passion; Juno dispels the darkness; Jupiter turns Io into a cow to try to fool Juno; she asks him for the cow as a gift, and places it under Argos' surveillance; Jupiter sends Mercury to kill Argos, whom Juno immortalizes by setting his hundred eyes for ever in the peacock's tail (*Met.* 1.583–750).

[18] See Murray (1958) 46–55; Conacher (1980) 56–65.

[19] E.g. Taplin (1977) 265–7; Buxton (1982) 99–102; Griffith (1983) 12.

inities; thus Io's arrival is an inversion of the usual pattern: it is an astonishing irruption of mortality into the world of the gods. For, even for the gods, Io's fate is, literally and metaphorically, an outlandish one. The Oceanids shudder at the sight of what has happened to her (695), and describe her account of her transformation as 'strange words' such as they never heard before (688–9). So strange can the fact of metamorphosis be that it retains its capacity to astonish even in this company—after all, the Oceanids themselves are no strangers to strangeness, for they flew onto the scene either on winged chariots or, conceivably, mounted on the backs of sea creatures, provoking alarm even from Prometheus (127).[20]

The second issue is, from the point of view of our enquiry, more fundamental. It concerns what we are to make—or what a Greek audience would have made—of the appearance on stage of a human metamorphosed into a cow. It is extraordinarily difficult to answer such a question, not only because of the inevitable plurality of any audience response, but also because of the absence of anything resembling contemporary extra-dramatic testimony. But one inference can be made from the play itself: Io's metamorphosis is no less solid a part of the staged fiction than is the rest of the tale. Significantly, after Io's departure the chorus dwells on aspects of her fate which have nothing to do with her status as cow, and everything to do with the exemplariness of her fate for mortal women: fearfully considering Io's fate, the Oceanids wish never to be joined in marriage with a god (894–900). More generally, within the dramatic universe of *Prometheus Bound* there is nothing which ridicules or in any other way undermines the terrifying convincingness with which Io's disoriented madness is portrayed. Within the frame of the tragic genre, her metamorphosis is unquestionably 'taken seriously'.

Mythical logic and interpretative charity

In *Prometheus Bound* an already-completed metamorphosis provides a graphic correlative to the extraordinary mental state which a mortal character experiences in the dramatic present. But a different tragic

---

[20] On the possible modes of arrival of the Oceanids, see Griffith (1983) n. on 128–92.

pattern involves reference to a future metamorphosis, which places a kind of ultimate, immortalizing seal upon the staged action, immobilizing it and yet also, paradoxically, prolonging it indefinitely. One play in which this motif figured was Sophokles' *Tereus*, which depicted a vicious sexual transgression and its horrific and ultimately metamorphic consequences. Tereus, husband of Prokne, raped her sister Philomela, then cut out her tongue to prevent her revealing the truth. However, when Philomela wove her experiences onto fabric which she sent to her sister, Prokne took a ghastly revenge, killing her own son Itys and serving up the corpse as a meal to the boy's unwitting father. At this point, according to a summary of the play, the gods took pity on the two sisters by transforming them into birds; Tereus too was transformed.[21] Because *Tereus* is so fragmentary, we know few details about how the metamorphoses were treated.[22] Nevertheless, the mythical logic is plain: the characters' traumatic experiences found eventual, emblematic permanence in the shapes of the hoopoe (Tereus, dwelling in the lonely wilds), the nightingale (Prokne, pouring out her endless lament for her child), and the swallow (Philomela, obliged ceaselessly to twitter since, lacking a tongue, she could never sing again).[23]

Sometimes, though, we have to work much harder to recover a connection between a human fate and its theriomorphic prolongation. An example is the metamorphosis alluded to at the end of Euripides' *Hekabe*. In the course of the play the audience has witnessed the repeated humiliation of the eponymous Trojan queen at the hands of the victorious Greeks. But from one of those responsible for her grief and moral collapse she exacts a dreadful punishment. The Thracian king Polymestor has treacherously killed one of Hekabe's sons; now, with the aid of women companions, the Trojan queen kills Polymestor's children and blinds their father. In a grim

---

[21] Tzetzes on Hes. *WD* 566, quoted by Radt (1977) 435; cf. also the summary in *P.Oxy.* 3013, which *may* be the hypothesis to Sophokles' play; see Radt (1977) 435–6; Gantz (1993) 240–1.

[22] For speculations see Cazzaniga (1950–1) i. 45–64; Calder (1974); Kiso (1984) 51–86 with 139–47; Sutton (1984) 127–32; Hourmouziades (1986); Dobrov (1993); Dunbar (1995) on *Birds* 101; Fitzpatrick (2001); Martín Rodríguez (2002) 56–65.

[23] We may compare and contrast this with the version at Homer *Od.* 19.518–24; cf. 46–7 above.

illustration of the link, so often made by Greeks, between blindness
and prophecy, Polymestor predicts that Hekabe's sufferings are destined to come to an unusual end: during the voyage which is intended to transport her to a life of slavery in Greece, Hekabe will be
transformed into a bitch with fire-red eyes, will climb the ship's mast,
and will then plunge into the sea to her death; her tomb will be a
landmark for sailors on the coast of Thrace.[24]

What is the mythical logic here? Hekabe's metamorphosis is not an
alternative to death but—far more unusually, in relation to other
Greek metamorphosis narratives—its immediate precursor. But is it
a blessed release or a cruel punishment? There is no *deus ex machina*
to solve the riddle, and Judith Mossman has persuasively argued that
this is deliberate on Euripides' part, since 'he wanted an embittered,
confusing ending, with none of the certainty and order which a
theophany would have introduced'.[25] But in any case: why a bitch?
If we see ourselves in the role of charitable interpreters—interpreters
who do everything to understand an apparently strange belief by
locating it within its context[26]—we can point to aspects of the story
which may anticipate and so explain Hekabe's particular metamorphic destination. First, the degeneration into wild bitterness
which she undergoes during the play—Polymestor calls her and the
other women 'murderous bitches' (1173)—would seem to find an
appropriate counterpart in her transformation into a dog. (This view
is sometimes spelled out in later sources, even though Hekabe's
emotional state is more commonly identified as anguish rather
than bitterness.[27]) Then, since dogs are associated with the goddess
Hekate, and since specific reference is made to Hekabe's *tomb*, it may
be that the particular character of the metamorphosis implies something about the continued eerie numinousness of Hekabe after

---

[24] Blindness and prophecy: see Buxton (1980) 28–9.

[25] Mossman (1995) 201.

[26] See below, 59–61; cf. 248–52.

[27] On the extent to which Hekabe's conduct can be seen as bestial, see Mossman
(1995) 194–201. Bitterness: Cic. *Tusc.* 3.63. Anguish: Q.S. 14.347–51. In the latter
passage Quintus of Smyrna sets out a characteristic sequence of events: (1) Hekabe
transformed into a bitch; (2) bystanders astonished (*thambeon*); (3) a god turns
Hekabe to stone; (4) this is a great marvel (*mega thauma*) for generations to come.

death.[28] We might add that there would then be a parallel with the play's prologue, spoken by the ghost of Hekabe's dead son Polydoros, who is himself located at the edge of the Thracian shoreline. Thanks to a moderate dose of interpretative charity, therefore, we can at least partially 'make sense' of even so apparently recalcitrant a story as that of the transformation of Hekabe.

But even charity has its limits. In our discussion of *Bacchants*, one aspect of metamorphosis remained unconsidered: the future transformations predicted by Dionysos *ex machina* at the very end of the work. Addressing Kadmos, the founder of Thebes, the god prophesies as follows (1330–9):

> You shall change your form (*metabalōn*) and become (*genēsēi*) a serpent.
> Harmonia, whom you, a mortal, took as wife from her father Ares,
> Shall change her shape (*allaxei tupon*) into that of a snake,
> Turning into a beast. As the oracle of Zeus foretells,
> You, leading a barbarian host, shall with your wife
> Drive a wagon of yoked oxen. With your countless army
> You shall destroy many cities; but when they plunder
> Loxias' oracle, they shall find a wretched homecoming.
> But Ares shall preserve both you and Harmonia, and establish you
> To live in the Land of the Blessed.

In one respect this prophecy is satisfying in its logic: Kadmos, whose Theban career began with a confrontation with Ares' snake, will finally be transformed into the same type of creature—this time with Ares' blessing. But that is far from being the end of the matter so far as interpretation goes. E. R. Dodds, usually a convinced advocate of the value of anthropological parallels for the understanding of Greek culture, describes this prediction as 'bizarre', and is forced to opt for the kind of syncretistic explanation to which classicists often resort when faced with recalcitrant mythological data: 'The story bears traces of having been put together at a relatively late date out of heterogeneous older elements.'[29] Richard Seaford notes that the passage 'jars with the [Kadmos] we have seen so far; but predictions with no apparent connection with the events

---

[28] Dogs and Hekate: FI 208–9; Mossman (1995) 197–8.
[29] Dodds (1960) n. on 1330–9.

of the play are found elsewhere in Euripides' finales'.[30] More outspoken than either Dodds or Seaford is R. P. Winnington-Ingram, who calls the prophecy 'dry, pedantic, unreal', 'a rigmarole of odd mythology', whose 'quaint' details are 'incongruous in their association with the human, prosaic Kadmos'. According to Winnington-Ingram, this incongruity is precisely Euripides' point since, here and in other plays, his final scenes 'offer, upon divine authority, a solution which is either inadequate or irrelevant'.[31]

What *does* the charitable interpreter do with this prophecy? Taken individually, its principal elements are congruent with assumptions underlying many Greek myths. (1) That city-founders, such as Kadmos and Harmonia, should be identified with snakes—tutelary, (auto)chthonic creatures, according to Greek religious perceptions—is a notion which can easily be paralleled elsewhere, for example in the Athenian tales of their anguiform founder-ancestors Kekrops and Erechtheus.[32] (2) That Kadmos and Harmonia should be linked both with oxen and with a 'barbarian' (i.e. non-Greek) army echoes the link found elsewhere in Greek tradition between Kadmos and the Illyrian settlement of Bouthoe ('*Bou-*' means 'ox'), a settlement which he was said to have founded.[33] (3) That Kadmos should be destined to plunder the Delphic oracle, and to suffer dire consequences as a result, corresponds to an oracle in circulation during the Persian Wars, as recorded by Herodotos, and said by him to refer to an Illyrian invasion.[34] (4) That Kadmos and Harmonia should, after all their tribulations, be at length translated to the Land of the Blessed corresponds to the belief, as old as the *Odyssey*, that just such a happy fate lay in store for mortal males who had married goddesses. The 'rounding off' at the end of the tale is made even neater by the fact that, according to a tradition going back at

---

[30] Seaford (1996) n. on 1330–9. As an example of an 'unconnected' Euripidean finale Seaford cites *Andr.* 1257–62; there, what Thetis predicts is not the metamorphosis but the deification of her husband Peleus.

[31] Winnington-Ingram (1948) 145.

[32] See Bodson (1978) 77–86.

[33] *Etym. Magn. s.v.* Βουθόη; cf. Dodds (1960) ad loc.; Vian (1963) 124–33; Roux (1970–2) on *Ba.* 1330–9.

[34] Hdt. 9.42–3; cf. Dodds (1960) ad loc.

least to the fifth century, there was a place in Thebes—perhaps the acropolis itself—known as 'The Isles of the Blessed'.[35]

The problem for the charitable interpreter lies not in the separate details, but in their presentation as a continuous narrative. As Dodds trenchantly asks: 'Was Kadmos already a snake when he drove the ox-wagon...? and is he still one in Elysium?' Winnington-Ingram even suggested that part of Euripides' intention may have been 'a faint ridicule of the mythology itself'.[36] In that case there must have been, in the context of this speech in this play, something 'faintly ridiculous' about imagining a formerly human snake in the act of driving an ox-wagon. The thrust of this argument recalls the approach taken in the Oxford commentary on the *Odyssey* towards the vanishing/ levitating Athena:[37] the possibility of metamorphosis into a snake is regarded as allowable, but the idea of a snake driving an ox-cart is felt to be just too weird to be acceptable, or at least to be taken 'seriously'.[38]

Over the question of the Kadmos/Harmonia metamorphosis, I admit that I simply do not know whether or not the poet would have been felt to have tilted the tonal balance of the myth towards 'the ridiculous'.[39] Or, to phrase the matter less in terms of personal inadequacy: 'It is in the nature of interpretation that some things are

---

[35] Schol. Lyc. *Alex.* 1204; Armenidas *FGrH* 378 F 5; cf. Dodds (1960) ad loc.; Vian (1963) 123; Roux (1970–2) on *Ba.* 1338–9.

[36] Dodds (1960) ad loc.; Winnington-Ingram (1948) 145.

[37] See 35–6 above.

[38] Surviving images do not help us visualize those aspects of the transformation which commentators have found incongruous. Philostratos (*Im.* 1.18) does describe a painting in which, alongside the rending of Pentheus and the mourning of his family back in Thebes, there is a depiction of Harmonia and Kadmos in the process of transformation: 'Harmonia and Kadmos are there, but not as they were before; for already they are becoming (*ginontai*) snakes from the thighs down, and already scales are forming on them. Their feet are gone, their buttocks are gone, and the change of appearance (*hē metabolē tou eidous*) is creeping upward. They are amazed (*ekplēttontai*) and embrace each other as though holding on to what is left of the body, so that this at least may not escape them.' The presence of amazement, that standard human reaction to metamorphosis, is acknowledged; but there is no ox-wagon on the scene.

[39] Seidensticker (1982) 115–29 discusses comic elements in *Bacchants*, but does not deal with the snake metamorphoses. Intriguingly, even Ovid, that consummate exploiter of the potentially absurd, makes no reference to snakes driving ox-carts: his story concludes with the transformation of Kadmos and Harmonia into 'friendly snakes' (*Met.* 4.576–603).

impossible to interpret.'[40] There are, however, two more general points which I do feel confident in making. The first is so often taken for granted that it is hardly ever mentioned. In contrast to other kinds of mythological narrative, drama was distinguished by its playing out of even the most extraordinary plots and characters on a visibly human scale, for the obvious reason that, despite all variations of mask and costume, the actors doing the playing were of human stature. That is to say, ancient representational drama depended on the constant, implicit presence of a canon of anthropomorphic normality. Any major departure from such a canon, any excessive stretching of the bounds of the credible, might generate a tension, a potential incongruity, between medium and content; and incongruity is a necessary ingredient of comedy.

But what follows from this? I come to my second point. Just because the theatrical medium created a space within which incongruity *might* be represented, it does not follow that it *was* represented. Each representation has to be judged on its own terms. When a character—perhaps even Kadmos—in an unknown Euripidean play utters the contextless couplet:

> Alas, half of me is becoming (*gignetai*) a snake;
> My child, embrace what is left of your father![41]

we have no information with which to assess the tone. Anyone who wishes to see this as an example of a Euripidean importation of the accents of comedy into tragedy cannot be proved wrong.

As the examples of Kadmos/Harmonia, Tereus/Prokne/Philomela, and Niobe show, tragedy *could* make room for mortals permanently to abandon their human form, either as a consequence of extreme transgressions of the norms of human behaviour, or in a state of unbearable suffering. Yet in the tragic world such exits are few. For most tragic heroes and heroines—for Agamemnon, Clytemnestra, Phaidra, Aias, Antigone, Deianeira, Hippolytos, Jocasta, Eteokles, Polyneikes—the ultimate boundary of humanity is still, as it was in Homer, death.

Two passages will make the point. When the chorus of *Agamemnon* compares Kassandra's lamenting of her own imminent death to

⁴⁰ Obeyesekere (1992) 180.   ⁴¹ Eur. F 930 Radt, with discussion ad loc.

the song of the nightingale crying for the loss of her son Itys, Kassandra herself sees not similarity but difference. The gods, she recalls, gave the nightingale wings and a sweet, grief-free life; but for Kassandra there remains only butchery by the two-edged sword (*Ag.* 1140–9). Escape via metamorphosis is peripheral, a far-off echo of the possibility of release and relief; at the *centre* of the fortunes of the House of Atreus, by contrast, is a series of *in*escapable deaths.[42] The second passage is from the end of *Hippolytos*. When Artemis, speaking *ex machina*, reveals to Theseus the horror of his misguided cursing of his innocent son, she raises the possibility of two strategies for him: to hide his body beneath the earth, or to take on a winged existence 'beyond suffering' (*Hipp.* 1290–3). But in fact neither form of escape will be available to Theseus: he must live with what he has done, the paradigm of frail and anguished humanity.[43]

In general, then, tragedy affirms a strong sense of the *ultimate* boundedness, integrity, and centrality of the human form. But another dramatic genre, tragedy's complement, is boisterously cavalier about humanity's limits. For a vision of a world open to radical change of form, it is to comedy that we must turn, and specifically to the comedy of Aristophanes.

ARISTOPHANES AND THE NORMALITY OF TRANSFORMATION

Men into birds

The gap between ordinary life and the speculations and explorations of myth is one of the favourite engines which drives Aristophanic

---

[42] Cf. Eur. *Hel.* 375–80, where Helen contrasts with her own unending anguish the relief from pain which transformation into a bear afforded Kallisto.

[43] In the same way the blinded Polymestor wishes he might have wings to soar to the stars or to plunge to Hades (*Hec.* 1099–1106); but instead he must face, unwinged, the reality of his pain. In *Ion*, too, Kreousa wishes she might fly away from earth into the sky; for her servants, once their mistress's failed plot on Ion's life is discovered, taking wing is one of the escape options which they entertain (*Ion* 796–9, 1238–43). But of course neither she nor they could possibly see their wishes realized. Cf. also Eur. *Or.* 982–3 and 1375–9.

comedy. Not that Aristophanes maintains the gap. Far from it: he elides it, distorts it, collapses it. Nowhere is this demonstrated with greater virtuosity than in *Birds*, a work in which metamorphosis, and the incongruities which it generates, play a pivotal role.

As the play begins, its two principal human characters stand in what will have been, for the audience, a normal, everyday relationship to birds. Peisetairos and Euelpides, two elderly Athenians, have purchased a jackdaw and a crow in the Athenian market. Although people usually bought birds in order to eat them, bait them, or keep them as pets, these two gentlemen plan to use their purchases as guides.[44] Dissatisfied with life in Athens, Peisetairos and Euelpides are proposing to emigrate. To this end they propose to consult Tereus, in view of the broad experience, both geographical and psychological, which crossing the species divide has conferred on this man-turned-hoopoe. At first, communication between the Athenian duo and the bird world is notably unsuccessful: although birds were traditionally supposed to offer humans signs via augury, Peisetairos and Euelpides fail dismally to divine what, if anything, their two guides are trying to tell them. These two humans may metaphorically have flown from Athens, but they have done so with feet planted firmly on the ground (35).

Before long, though, they are taking their first, tentative steps towards birddom. Unnerved by the sudden appearance of Tereus' formerly human and now feathered servant—for the transposition of the motif of metamorphosis into comedy means that it becomes associated with that fundamental comedic theme, the master/slave relationship—they identify themselves as birds (64–8). Then, in conversation with Tereus himself, they propose a venture to be undertaken jointly with the real birds: the foundation of a city. This will be situated between gods and humans, for the human world is now 'below' the stage action, as the divine world is above it (175–8). So, just by walking, Peisetairos and Euelpides have arrived at the airy place where the birds dwell. This has happened with a wave

---

[44] Dunbar (1995) on 13; 70; 533–8; 704–7; 1297–9. One may perhaps disagree with Dunbar's view that the crow and the jackdaw were real birds (p. 130); funnier, surely, and certainly more practical, if the two intrepid Athenians had a pair of dummy birds on their wrists.

of Aristophanes' dramaturgic wand.[45] With another wave, something else happens. Whereas at the outset the crow and the jackdaw were bird-sized and the humans human-sized, henceforth birds will be represented by human actors (the 'real' birds 'fly off' at 86–91; presumably at this point the actors simply threw away the dummies).[46] No wonder the immediate reaction of Peisetairos and Euelpides on seeing the hoopoe's human-sized servant is to void their terrified bowels (66–8).

If any character illustrates the truth that Greek culture's representation of mythology was pluralistic, it is Tereus. In the majority of narratives about mortals who leave human form in extreme circumstances, the nature of their day-to-day existence after transformation is passed over in silence. Not so in *Birds*. But how will the post-metamorphosis Tereus behave towards his spouse? Forgotten is the vicious rapist who violated his wife's sister and then cut out her tongue: the Aristophanic Tereus lives a life of admirable political correctness and affectionate domestic tranquillity. As for his public persona, he is clearly a bird of considerable authority with his peers, yet he will only join the two humans in their scheme 'if the other birds agree' (197), for all the world like those paragons of democratic royalty, Pelasgos in Aischylos' *Suppliants*, and Theseus in Sophokles' *Oedipus at Colonus* and in Euripides' *Suppliants*. On the domestic front, hoopoe and nightingale (at least according to Tereus' presentation of things) live in marital harmony, quite literally (209–22):

> Come, nest-mate of mine, wake up from your sleep!
> Issue forth all the strains of the sacred chants
> In which you lament, with a mouth that's inspired,
> For the child of us both, oh piteous Itys!
> Let your voice thrill the air with its liquid notes,
> Through your vibrant throat! For your song is so pure
> As it echoes around, through the rich-leaved trees,
> Till it reaches the throne of Lord Zeus up above,
> Where Phoibos as well, golden-tressed god of song,

---

[45] Something similar happens in *Peace*, in which Trygaios 'travels from Athens to Olympus and back again: first by dung beetle, then on foot—and with no change of scenery...With comic lightness, with almost magical ease, the comic hero moves back and forth between houses, between town and country, and even, like the comic playwright himself, between different levels of reality' (Reckford (1987) 208).

[46] Cf. n. 44 above.

Hears your grief and responds on his ivory lyre,
As he summons the gods to take part in the dance.
Then is heard from above an immortal choir,
    All in unison clear,
As the gods cry in grief for your plight.[47]

Not a whisper about how Itys died; it is as though a fond couple had lost a beloved child through accident or illness. The reaction of Prokne/nightingale to all this is anyone's guess: she never speaks.[48] But she is not altogether silent, for an *aulos*-player represents her lovely voice (223). And her attractions are not lost on her husband, a strong interest in sex being one characteristic which the tragic and comic Tereuses have in common.[49]

As the plot unfolds, the mainstay of the comedy continues to be the incongruous juxtaposition of the humanness of the birds with the birdiness of the humans. The arrival of the chorus prompts Peisetairos and Euelpides to notice resemblances between particular birds and well-known, contemporary humans ('This bird is a "gobbler".' 'Is there any other gobbler (=glutton) but Kleonymos?' (288–9); etc.). At first the chorus resists the intrusion of the two Athenians: humans are humans, birds are birds, and the two groups should keep well apart. But Tereus, the species-crosser, stresses the link rather than the division: 'They're relatives, yes kinsmen of my wife' (368; Prokne was an Athenian). So the chorus-birds are induced to hear out Peisetairos' persuasion.

True to his name ('Peis-'='persuade(r)'), he wins them over, with a mixture of crudity, fable, and anecdote. Birds, he argues, had once ruled the universe, only to be ousted by the Olympians; but with the help of Euelpides and himself this ancient wrong can be righted. The new city in the sky will institute a blockade: there will be no free passage for descending gods on their way to lie with mortal women,

---

[47] Trans. Halliwell (1998). Halliwell's translation, and his extensive introduction to the volume in which it appears, are both excellent.

[48] How different from the lamenting wife of Tereus evoked by the tragic chorus of Aischylos' *Suppliants* (60–8): 'exiled from the haunts familiar to her, she sings the tale of her son's death; how he perished by her hand, the victim of a cruel mother's wrath.'

[49] Cf. 203: 'When I've aroused my nightingale (*aēdōn*).' The related word *aēdonis* was used by the Archaic poet Archilochos as a euphemism for female genitals (Hsch. *s.v. aēdonis*; Dunbar (1995) on *Birds* 207–8).

and no upward mobility for sacrificial savours rising from earth to Olympos. Only one obstacle stands in the way of a true partnership between the Athenian pair and the real birds: Peisetairos and Euelpides are still in human form. Tereus/hoopoe has the answer: 'There is a little root: if you eat it, the two of you will sprout wings' (654–5). Commentators have suggested a link with Circe's potions and Hermes' antidote to them, or have sought and found parallels in folktales.[50] The truth is that we have no idea whether the allusion refers to a commonly held belief.[51] If it does, it throws an interesting sidelight on Forbes Irving's assertion that '[w]e can assume, I think, that most ancient Greeks were not seriously worried that they would suddenly become animals'.[52] Worries, even serious ones, can manifest themselves in all kinds of half-hidden, barely expressed ways, like cobwebs in the sharp corners of 'rational' experience; and a cobweb is every bit as real and functional a part of the world as a sharp corner.

When Prokne/nightingale is summoned for the second time by Tereus/hoopoe, she appears on stage (667), to the intense delight of Peisetairos and Euelpides; the latter expresses the wish to 'get between her thighs' without more ado. In her commentary on the passage, Nan Dunbar rightly points out that we are in the dark about the relationship between language and staging here. When Prokne is described as 'delicate' and 'white' (668), we 'cannot tell whether these adjectives matched what Aristophanes' audience saw—a man wearing a bird-mask...but also flesh-coloured tights representing a naked female body...or were comically incongruous with what they saw—an all-over bird-costume, which Peisetairos proceeds to praise in terms suiting only a human Prokne. Either would be effective.'[53] In any case, Euelpides is aroused by what he sees, and clearly views the species barrier as no impediment to his urgent ambitions.

---

[50] Dunbar (1995) on 654–5, citing Page (1973) 67. On the problems about invoking folktales, see 39–41 above.

[51] The parallels cited by Bowie (1993) 159 n. 44, namely Paus. 9.22.7 and Athen. 296e–7a, concern Glaukos, a fisherman who ate a herb and thenceforth became a sea divinity—not explicitly a change of *shape*, but a dramatic enough alteration nevertheless.

[52] FI 60; see also 252 below.

[53] Dunbar (1995) on 667–8.

The chorus leader invites pleasure-seeking humans to come and join the birds (753–4), and amplifies this by explaining the advantages of having wings: if you want to leave the theatre to eat, defecate, or commit adultery, wings are just the thing—they serve, in other words, three of the great Aristophanic themes: food, excrement, and sex (785–97). Peisetairos and Euelpides themselves now take one more step along the road to metamorphosis by donning feathers (801–8), like common-or-garden variants of Daidalos and Ikaros. By this time the fantasy is soaring as high as Peisetairos' megalomania. After a series of cameos by characters keen to be involved in the act of foundation, Iris, messenger of the gods, flies in to lodge a protest, but takes off again in a hurry when Peisetairos threatens her with rape. A herald then enters with news that humans are queuing up to emigrate to the new city; Peisetairos gives orders to assemble some basketsful of wings to kit out the newcomers (1305–12). And in they come: the father-beater looking for an escape route, the dithyrambic poet longing to be a nightingale, the political informer keen to 'swoop' on his victims. The fantasy attains its climax when, after receiving shrewd advice from Prometheus (who is hiding from Zeus under a parasol), Peisetairos negotiates with a delegation from the gods until he gets the terms he wants: Zeus is to restore the sceptre of power to the birds, while Peisetairos is to have as his bride Basileia, the sexy girl—and, it is to be presumed, divinity—who keeps Zeus' thunderbolt.[54] With this riotous realization of the ultimate power-fantasy, in which Peisetairos leaves the scene in the guise of the new Zeus, the comedy concludes.

What makes metamorphosis ideally suited to the plot of *Birds* is that the play is about a new beginning, a city foundation; and any metamorphosis is itself a new beginning. But since this is Aristophanes, the relationship between these beginnings is inverted and distorted.[55] Foundation myths frequently symbolize the formation of a new population by using the image of physical transformation: Cypriots come from wasps, Myrmidons from ants, even the whole

[54] 1600–2; cf. 480, 554, 635; 1537–41.
[55] In what follows I am greatly indebted to the excellent comments of Bowie (1993) 159–60, 166–9, 172–5.

of humanity from stones after the Flood.[56] Analogously, Peisetairos and Euelpides acquire wings as their new foundation receives approval from the bird community. However, as Angus Bowie notes, whereas the usual foundation myth involves a non-human population changing into human form, *Birds* is a tale of two humans wanting to leave their humanity behind.[57] Another inversion, again highlighted by Bowie, is that, whereas a common pattern in metamorphosis myths shows suffering and crime reaching some kind of end-point through transformation (as in the Sophoklean version of the Tereus story), in *Birds* the new society into which Peisetairos and Euelpides propose to fly is to be marked by all kinds of transgressive behaviour: adultery and diverse types of violence will be sanctioned, while Peisetairos goes so far as to roast rebellious birds, thus taking on the cannibalistic role played by pre-transformation Tereus (1583–5).[58] Fantastic the new city may be, but it is hardly paradise.

What *Birds* does *not* do is depict the very notion of corporeal transformation as beyond belief: the dramatic vision is more inclusive, more richly hospitable than that. Within the world of *Birds*, metamorphosis is accepted as a perfectly comprehensible possibility, no more and no less plausible than the notion of a man buying a bird in the market, or an Athenian marrying the keeper of Zeus' thunderbolt. For the duration of this extravaganza, all those things are equally likely.

The adult fantasies of Aristophanes

As we look beyond *Birds* to the genre of which it formed a part, we find that fantastic transmogrifications are a central feature of Greek Old Comedy. The bird-dancers on an Attic black-figure vase may represent one such episode (**Fig. 7**). Another can be seen on the much-discussed vase formerly housed in the Getty Museum, and now repatriated to Italy (**Fig. 8**). Whatever the uncertainties about

---

[56] Wasps: Philostephanos *FHG* 30 F 10 = Alexandros Polyhistor *FGrH* 273 F 144. Ants: Hes. fr. 205 MW; cf. Vian (1963) 170. Stones: Hes. fr. 234 MW; Pi. *O.* 9.41–6; Apollod. *Bibl.* 1.7.2.

[57] Bowie (1993) 160.

[58] Auger (1979) 84; Bowie (1993) 168.

Figure 7. Dancers costumed as birds. Attic black-figure oinochoe, 510–490 BC.

Figure 8. Two cocks: a scene from a drama. South Italian red-figure krater, late 5th cent. BC.

the interpretation of this image, it vividly evokes the kind of meta-morphosis which could be, and regularly was, enacted on the comic stage.[59] In *Frogs* Dionysos dresses up as Herakles; in *Women at the Thesmophoria* Euripides' kinsman dons female garb in order to penetrate the women's festival, and is then obliged to play Helen to Euripides' Menelaos, and Andromeda to his Perseus; Praxagora and her female followers dress as men with beards in *Assemblywomen*; in *Acharnians* Dikaiopolis disguises himself as (Euripides') Telephos, who is in turn disguising himself as a beggar; in *Peace* Trygaios takes the role of Bellerophon as he rides his dung beetle (= Pegasos) up to Olympos; in *Wasps* Philokleon seeks to escape imprisonment by imitating the Odysseus of *Odyssey* Book 9, who evaded the Cyclops by hiding under a ram. The characters of comedy habitually and riotously pass themselves off as what they are not.

Complexity is piled on complexity. In *Wasps*, for instance, the roles of all the characters and all the chorus members are—of course—taken by human actors, yet amongst the stage figures are included two dogs (plaintiff and defendant in a lawsuit) and a cheese-grater (one of the witnesses). Within the fiction, these are not cases of metamorphosis, or even of disguise, but they certainly broaden the range of possibilities for the elision of the human/non-human boundary. What, though, of the chorus? These 'wasps' are not wasps as the chorus of *Birds* are birds; rather they are old men, fanatical jurors, with the *characteristics*—behavioural, but, on the fantastic Aristophanic stage, doubtless also physical—of that particular stinging insect. They represent one more position on the sliding scale of Aristophanic metamorphic virtuosity.

From one point of view these pretences and impersonations are no more than extensions of the fundamental illusion upon which de-pend all the major types of Greek masked theatre, whether tragedy, satyr play, or comedy: namely, the transformation of ordinary cit-izens into participants in a spectacular fiction. But of the three genres it is Old Comedy which exploits this transformation most richly. Old Comedy thrives on games with form, on the bodying-forth of meta-phors. In *Frogs*, lines of poetry are weighed on scales (1365–1410); in

---

[59] For discussion, see e.g. Green (1985); Taplin (1993) 101–4; Csapo (1993).

Peace War pounds cities in a mortar (228–31). Formal rigidity is up for grabs; it is there for the taking. That excellent student of comedy Kenneth Reckford makes the following remark in his exuberant book about the most exuberant of comedians:

Actors appear in the very transparent guise of dogs and cheese-graters, hoopoes and barbarian gods. Choruses of clouds, birds, or frogs sing and dance and join in the action. Part of comedy's delight is therefore, as Plato noticed, the vicarious liberation it provides from our ordinary roles in life that nature and society join to enforce, firmly distinguishing female from male, human from beast, animate from inanimate nature. For a brief time, the barriers are broken down.[60]

Indeed. But then Reckford, with his infectious love of fairy tales, and with his constant reference to them as analogues of Aristophanic fantasy, goes on to locate the extravagances of Old Comedy not only Outside but also Before:

We can be children once more. We can 'be' dogs, or frogs, or birds. We can relapse into an animistic frame of mind in which we are no longer isolated from the rest of nature, but enjoy communion with birds and beasts, and trees, and even gods.[61]

This is a step in the wrong direction. With each successive context in which we find Greek metamorphosis narratives occurring, it becomes progressively less convincing to marginalize them as the regressive fantasies of childhood.[62] More plausibly we should regard transformation as a central feature of Aristophanic comedy—central, in particular, to its representation of character and its exploitation of language.

On character, Michael Silk puts the matter well:

The switches, the transformations, the reversals embodied in Aristophanic characters are . . . something more than incidental odd moments in otherwise tidy or homogeneous wholes. They represent a pervasive and essential

---

[60] Reckford (1987) 99.

[61] Reckford (1987) 99. Cf. 178: 'One of comedy's gifts is to restore to us what we enjoyed in childhood.'

[62] See G. E. R. Lloyd (2007) 112, on the analogous danger of assimilating (1) beliefs in supernatural causation held by adults from non-Western societies to (2) apparently comparable beliefs held in Western societies by children.

fact of Aristophanic drama and, as such, may quite naturally constitute the most important part of a single character's presentation.[63]

Philokleon in *Wasps* 'begins his play as a sort of caricature of Athenian legalism and finishes it as a sort of personification of the self-expressive life-force'.[64] Other examples of such development are Demos in *Knights*, Trygaios in *Peace*, and Aischylos in *Frogs*. Especially notable is *Women at the Thesmophoria*, in which transformation transcends character to become a pervasive dramatic theme, with cross-dressing and other types of role-play proliferating.[65]

But Aristophanic metamorphic virtuosity is a matter of language as well as character. Instances of the sophisticated turning of one word/idea into another can be found on virtually every page of a text of the plays. A striking example can be found at the beginning of *Wasps*, when the slaves Xanthias and Sosias recount a pair of dreams involving transformations. Xanthias' vision was of an eagle swooping down into the agora to seize an *aspis*, which it subsequently dropped. *Aspis* can mean 'asp', but more usually means 'shield'. Xanthias puts the pun to comic advantage: as the *aspis* turns, in Aristophanes' subtle Greek, from snake to shield, so the eagle becomes Kleonymos, who notoriously lost his shield in battle (15–23). The logic of comic repartee dictates that Sosias' dream must outdo that of his comrade; and so it proves. Here it really is imperative to quote an extensive passage from the original Greek, since a translation, even such a brilliant one as that by David Barrett, can only gesture lamely towards Aristophanes' virtuosity (31–51):

> Σω. ἔδοξέ μοι περὶ πρῶτον ὕπνον ἐν τῇ πυκνὶ
> ἐκκλησιάζειν πρόβατα συγκαθήμενα,
> βακτηρίας ἔχοντα καὶ τριβώνια·
> κἄπειτα τούτοις τοῖς προβάτοισι μοὐδόκει
> δημηγορεῖν φάλαινα πανδοκεύτρια,
> ἔχουσα φωνὴν ἐμπεπρησμένης ὑός.
> Ξα. αἰβοῖ. Σω. τί ἔστι; Ξα. παῦε παῦε, μὴ λέγε·
> ὄζει κάκιστον τοὐνύπνιον βύρσης σαπρᾶς.
> Σω. εἶθ᾽ ἡ μιαρὰ φάλαιν᾽ ἔχουσα τρυτάνην
> ἵστη βόειον δημόν. Ξα. οἴμοι δείλαιος·
> τὸν δῆμον ἡμῶν βούλεται διιστάναι.

---

[63] Silk (2000) 239.   [64] Silk (2000) 239.   [65] Silk (2000) 282–6.

Σω. ἐδόκει δέ μοι Θέωρος αὐτῆς πλησίον
χαμαὶ καθῆσθαι τὴν κεφαλὴν κόρακος ἔχων.
εἶτ' Ἀλκιβιάδης εἶπε πρός με τραυλίσας,
'ὁλᾷς; Θέωλος τὴν κεφαλὴν κόλυκος ἔχει.'
Ξα. ὀρθῶς γε τοῦτ' Ἀλκιβιάδης ἐτραύλισεν.
Σω. οὔκουν ἐκεῖν' ἀλλόκοτον, ὁ Θέωρος κόραξ
γιγνόμενος; Ξα. ἤκιστ', ἀλλ' ἄριστον. Σω. πῶς; Ξα. ὅπως;
ἄνθρωπος ὢν εἶτ' ἐγένετ' ἐξαίφνης κόραξ·
οὔκουν ἐναργὲς τοῦτο συμβαλεῖν, ὅτι
ἀρθεὶς ἀφ' ἡμῶν ἐς κόρακας οἰχήσεται;

Sos.   Well, I'd no sooner fallen asleep than I saw a whole lot of sheep, and
they were holding an assembly on the Pnyx: they all had little cloaks
on, and they had staves in their hands; and these sheep were all
listening to a harangue by a rapacious-looking creature with a
figure like a whale and a voice like a scalded sow.

Xan.   No, no!

Sos.   What's the matter?

Xan.   Don't tell me any more, I can't bear it. Your dream stinks like a
tanner's yard.

Sos.   And this horrible whale-creature had a pair of scales and it was
weighing out bits of fat from a carcass.

Xan.   Dividing up the body politic—I see it all. Ghastly![66]

Sos.   And then I noticed that Theoros was sitting on the ground at the
creature's feet, only he had a head like a raven. And Alkibiades turned
to me and said, 'Look! Theowuth hath got the head of a waven!'

Xan.   That'th a vewy accuwate lithp by Althibiadeth!

Sos.   Yes, but isn't that a bit sinister, Theoros becoming (*gignomenos*) a raven?

Xan.   On the contrary, very good sign.

Sos.   Why?

Xan.   Well, first he was a man, then he suddenly became (*egenet'*) a raven:
isn't it obvious what that means? He's going to croak [*literally*: 'go to
the crows'].[67]

Sosias purports to have dreamed that the Athenian assembly was full
of sheep, being addressed by a greedy whale. Unsurprisingly this
turns out to be Kleon ('the tanner'), one of whose devotees, sitting
at the feet of the whale, has the head of a *korax* (crow)—which

---

[66] There is an untranslatable pun in the Greek, on δημόν ('fat') and δῆμον
('populace'), the only difference being in the placing of the word accent.

[67] The translation is in essence that by D. Barrett (1964), though I have made a few
amendments—I hope, in the spirit of Barrett's version.

enables Sosias/Aristophanes to 'turn' the crow into a *kolax*, 'flat-
terer'—because the word is imagined as being pronounced by the
lisping Alkibiades... This kind of irrepressible flight of the imagination confronts us 'at every turn' in Aristophanes.

Not all Aristophanic transformations correspond to our two working categories of metamorphoses-of-gods and metamorphoses-of-
humans-into-non-human-form, nor do they all involve corporeal
change. But they do collectively demonstrate both that Aristophanic
comedy is a world which embraces all manner of imaginings about
drastic change, and that these imaginings are a product, not of
childlike or even childish fantasy, but of a mature and bold artistic
genius, constrained but also liberated by the conventions of the
comic genre.

3

Visual Arts

At all periods of ancient Greek culture, verbal narratives of myths were complemented, supplemented, and sometimes contradicted by visual representations. Images of metamorphosis illustrate how artists faced quite different challenges from those confronting composers of literary narratives. Modern interpreters too face challenges when viewing these images. One recurrent problem involves deciding whether what is being depicted should or should not be regarded as metamorphosis, an issue bound up with the relationship between metamorphosis and hybridity. A point which has been less often highlighted concerns the degree of 'strangeness' to be detected in images of transformation.

Scholars working on images of metamorphosis sometimes distinguish between them according to a threefold typology. In Type A, metamorphosis is represented serially, i.e. as a sequence of several discrete stages; in Type B, metamorphosis is already complete, so that the only way of deducing its previous occurrence is by reference to the context; in Type C, an image of a *hybrid* form *may* need to be interpreted (again this has to be deduced from the context) either as representing an as yet incomplete transformation, or as alluding in some other way to a transformation.[1] In what follows I shall myself sometimes invoke this tripartite scheme, even though the data do not always fall comfortably into one or other of the classes.[2] I shall also

---

[1] For the three types, see Sharrock (1996) 107; the whole of Sharrock's essay is relevant to the subject of the present chapter. Cf. also Frontisi-Ducroux (2003) 80–1.

[2] Frontisi-Ducroux ((2003) 83) gives a subtle account of why it is that the Etruscan vase-painting (**Fig. 9**) of a series of part-men, part-dolphins (the presumed result of Dionysos' transformation of some overbold pirates) is not what it might at first sight appear to be—namely a representation of a sequence of several metamorphoses, each progressively more complete than the last—but rather a representation of just two metamorphic perspectives, each with a separate 'direction': one beginning at the feet, the other at the head.

Figure 9. Men changing into dolphins. Etruscan hydria, *c.* 510–500 BC.

arrange the material according to another and usually less problematic division, that between metamorphoses of divinities and metamorphoses of mortals.

HOW TO VISUALIZE A CHANGING GOD

The most straightforward images of divine metamorphosis are those in which the viewer is given enough contextual clues to read one of the participants in a scene as an already metamorphosed divinity (Type B). A classic example concerns the union of Zeus and Danae. On an early fifth-century krater in St Petersburg (**Fig. 10**) Danae, her face turned skywards, receives a shower of golden rain into her lap. Although our early textual evidence for the myth of Zeus and Danae is not extensive (especially as none of the tragedies composed on the theme has survived), the testimony of the fifth-century author Pherekydes of Athens confirms that by his time the shower-of-gold motif was already established.[3] There can be little doubt that Danae's

[3] F 10 Fowler; cf. Gantz (1993) 299–303.

Figure 10. Danae receives Zeus in the form of a shower of gold. Attic red-figure krater, *c.* 490 BC.

confinement in a bronze (i.e. seemingly impenetrable) chamber, and Zeus' subsequent penetration of both it and her—*metamorphōtheis eis chruson*, 'transformed into gold', is how the mythographer Apollodoros would later phrase it—were familiar enough to remove any ambiguity about the identity of the cascading metal on the St Petersburg vase.[4] Lest there *should* be any doubt, the artist who created the Danae on a late fifth-century silver ring included an eagle to indicate the presence of the father of the gods (**Fig. 11**).

---

[4] Apollod. *Bibl.* 2.4.1.

Figure 11. As well as being present in the shower which falls into Danae's lap, Zeus is symbolized by the bird (presumably an eagle) at the top. Silver ring, *c.* 410 BC.

Equally definite in its mythological reference is a group of frank representations of the copulation of a woman with a swan, a scene which, with or without a clue in the form of an inscription, must have led inevitably to the reading: 'Leda with Zeus/swan' (**Fig. 12**). 'Inevitably' is a strong word, particularly as the extant Archaic/ Classical textual sources are not lavish; but such allusions as that in Euripides' *Helen* (215–16: 'Zeus shining snow-white through the bright air with the wings of a swan') suggest that the story was well known in verbal narratives also.

In the case of Zeus' transformation into a bull before his abduction of Europa, the explicitness of the scene is usually more restrained, though the emphasis on Europa's naked breasts in one image (**Fig. 13**) reminds the viewer of the ultimate purpose of this bull-back voyage, while Europa's touching of the tip of the bull's horn in another (**Fig. 14**) might conceivably be seen as a differently encoded allusion to sexuality.

The images just described do not visualize the *process* of metamorphosis: the transformation has already been accomplished by the

Figure 12. A graphic image of Leda with Zeus-as-swan. Marble relief from Brauron, 2nd cent. AD.

Figure 13. Europa aboard Zeus-as-bull. Below the couple, various sea creatures embellish the Crete-ward voyage; above, Eros bears garlands; to the right a man, presumably a member of Europa's family (Agenor? Phoinix?), watches the astonishing departure. Lucanian amphora, 400–390 BC.

Figure 14. Europa balances herself by grasping the bull's prominent horn. Attic red-figure krater, *c.* 480 BC.

time the viewer is admitted to the scene. There is thus nothing incomplete or transitional about Zeus' appearance: indeed, so far as I am aware, there are *no* ancient representations of the supreme god as *part* shower-of-gold, or *part* swan, or *part* bull. In fact I know of no image of Zeus, either in the Archaic/Classical periods or later in antiquity, which portrays him at a midway stage between forms, and which would therefore assimilate him to hybridity/monstrosity. We

Figure 15. Zeus, in human form, carries off Ganymede. Terracotta group from Olympia, *c.* 470 BC.

Figure 16. Zeus, transformed into an eagle, gathers up Ganymede; the image conveys a fine blend of power and sensuality. Greek bronze mirror cover, *c.* 360–350 BC.

see him either completely anthropomorphic or completely 'other', as in the case of representations of the abduction of Ganymede either by an entirely anthropomorphic Zeus (**Fig. 15**) or by an eagle (**Fig. 16**). There is, that is to say, no ancient equivalent of Correggio's extraordinary *Jupiter and Io*, in which the god is represented half in and half out of the form of a cloud (**Fig. 17**),[5] nor of the near-pornographic, half-anthropomorphic, half-serpentine figure of Jupiter depicted in the *Jupiter and Olympias* by Giulio Romano and assistants (**Fig. 18**).[6] Ancient images of the completely metamorphosed Zeus also stand in a different kind of contrastive relationship to representations of such lesser mythological figures as Pan (**Fig. 19**), centaurs (**Fig. 20**), and satyrs (**Fig. 21**), in all of whom the alliance of animality with anthropomorphism is permanent, rather than being a state which the subject temporarily adopts. Of course, such creatures embody not metamorphosis but hybridity; but metamorphosis and hybridity, which are in one sense opposed, are in another intimately interrelated.[7] It is only viewers with previous knowledge of the mythology

[5] See Bull (2005) 166–9.   [6] See Bull (2005) 157.
[7] Cf. Sharrock (1996), esp. 108–10; Bynum (2001), esp. 28–33; Izquierdo and Le Meaux (2003).

Figure 17. Correggio, *Jupiter and Io*. Oil on canvas, *c.* 1530. The form of Jupiter might even be said to be *triple*: part cloud, part human—and part animal: for does not the god's embracing right hand resemble a bear's paw?

relating to Pan, centaurs, and satyrs who are able to read what they see as hybridity and not as incomplete (Type C) metamorphosis.

A divinity who changes shape serially presents a particular challenge to visual artists, who must adopt different representational strategies from those available to myth-tellers in verse or prose. When Sophokles' Deianeira recalls the three shapes adopted by her admirer the river-god Acheloos, she describes his appearance as

Figure 18. Giulio Romano, *Jupiter and Olympias*. Fresco, Palazzo del Tè, Mantua, 1526–1534. Zeus, in semi-serpentine form, is manifestly ready to take Olympias, wife of Philip of Macedon. The terrified woman shows none of the erotic abandon experienced by Correggio's Io.

having been *successively* that of a bull, a serpent, and a creature 'with a man's body and the front/face of an ox' and with streams of water dripping from his beard.[8] By contrast, in the numerous visual representations of Acheloos, succession is transposed into simultaneity. One painter gives us a genuinely tri-form monster, complete with a serpentine tail, a human upper body topped by a rather ugly human head, and a bovine horn and ears (**Fig. 22**); another imagines an Acheloos who combines the body of a bull with the face, albeit horned, of a handsome, indeed heroically distinguished man (**Fig. 23**); a third represents the god as a centaur (**Fig. 24**).

[8] Soph. *Tr.* 9–14. The text, and therefore the translation, are by no means secure; see Easterling (1982) ad loc.

Figure 19. Goatish Pan amid his devotees. Boiotian black-figure skyphos, 4th cent. BC.

A different kind of simultaneity can be found in images of the sea-nymph Thetis. We are a world away from the anguished, loving mother depicted in the *Iliad*: artists preferred a more visually idio-syncratic area of her mythology, namely her extraordinary wrestling match with her human suitor Peleus. In a desperate attempt to escape the dishonour of marriage to a mortal, the goddess changed herself serially into several dangerous forms—in Apollodoros' words, 'be-coming (*ginomenēn*) now fire, now water, now a wild beast'; other sources specify a lion or a cuttlefish.[9] The analogy between this struggle and those involving Proteus and Menelaos, Nereus and Herakles, and Acheloos and Herakles—all contests in which the elusive god has his home in water—led Frazer to see 'their mutability reflecting as it were the instability of the fickle, inconstant element of which they were born'.[10] Forbes Irving points out, by contrast, that among the many epithets for, and perceptions of, the sea—

---

[9] Apollod. *Bibl.* 3.13.5; see Scarpi (1996) ad loc. Lion: Soph. F 150 Radt. Cuttle-fish: e.g. schol. Ap. Rhod. *Arg.* 1.582.

[10] Frazer (1921) ii. 68. The Nereus/Herakles episode is related in Apollod. *Bibl.* 2.5.11.

Figure 20. Clay centaur from
Lefkandi (Euboia), *c.* 900 BC.

Figure 21. Reclining satyr in a sympotic context. Agate scarab, probably
from Etruria, *c.* 530 BC.

Figure 22. Acheloos in combat with Herakles. The river god is shown in triple form. Attic red-figure stamnos, 530–500 BC.

boundless, unharvested, dangerous, unpredictable, etc.—the idea of a medium which can shift its form is by no means prominent.[11] Frontisi-Ducroux, however, shares Frazer's view, finding a link between the shifting sea, the hybrid nature of some sea divinities, and the capacity of some sea divinities to shift shape.[12] What certainly is the case is that Thetis is not just any sea divinity: she has an iconography all her own. This comprises a set of images in which she seems somehow to be spawning creatures which fall from her body and attack Peleus (**Figs. 25** and **26**). On the face of it—in contrast to the kind of artistic strategy which depicts Acheloos as a hybrid—what we have is a morphologically non-monstrous Thetis *accompanied by* some of her equally non-monstrous metastases. If the viewer interprets these images as representations of metamorphosis, such an interpretation must rest on the interpreter's prior knowledge of the mythological background.

INTERPRETATION AND THE FACE OF HUMANITY

Some of the most intriguing and complex artistic representations of the metamorphosis of mortals relate to the story of Circe. The Homeric account speaks of humans whose physical forms Circe

[11] FI 173–4.
[12] Frontisi-Ducroux (2003) 40. On the problematic category of the 'shape-shifter', see 168–77 below.

Figure 23. Horned, heroic Acheloos, in a context which demonstrates his watery quality: before him is a basin (on which Eros stands), while on his back sits a woman with a water-jar. Campanian amphora, *c.* 340–320 BC.

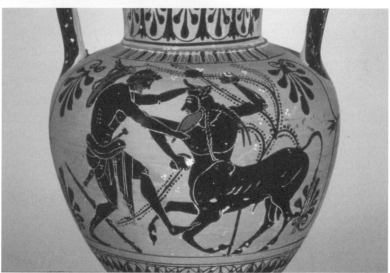

Figure 24. Acheloos as centaur, fighting Herakles. Attic black-figure amphora, *c.* 510–500 BC.

Figure 25. Thetis struggles with her suitor Peleus; the panther and snakes surrounding her stand visually for the forms into which she serially changes in an attempt to elude his clutches. Boiotian black-figure dish, *c.* 500–475 BC.

Figure 26. Another image of Thetis' attempts to repel her would-be lover. As well as snakes there is a metamorphic lion. Attic red-figure kylix, *c.* 510–500 BC.

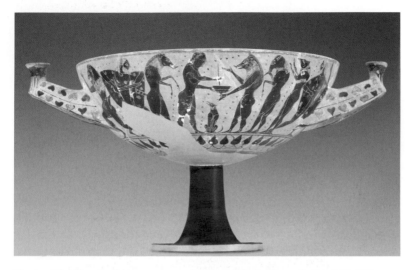

Figure 27. Circe's diverse menagerie. Attic black-figure kylix, 560–550 BC.

transforms *entirely* into those of animals—definitely into pigs, and probably into wolves and lions;[13] the fact that these creatures still retain something of the human is indicated in the text either inferentially (in the case of the wolves and lions) by the description of their untypical, i.e. fawning, behaviour, or explicitly (in the case of the pigs) by the assertion on the part of the narrator (Odysseus) that 'their mind remained as it had been before'.[14] Visual artists must work differently. They evoke the metamorphosis of Circe's victims by imagining them in forms which incorporate a mixture of natural kinds, part human, part animal. Here the artistic tradition goes far beyond Homer in variety: we find Circe surrounded by creatures with the head, and sometimes the tail and legs, of, among other animals, a boar, lion, ram, ox, horse, cock, donkey, panther, and goat.[15] A striking example can be seen on a black-figure cup in Boston (**Fig. 27**). A naked Circe extends a cup (whose contents she simultaneously stirs) to, on the viewer's right, a man with a boar's

[13] 'Probably': see 41 above.

[14] *Od.* 10.214–19; 240. Apollonios of Rhodes gives a quite different account: Circe is surrounded by creatures, neither entirely beasts nor entirely human beings, consisting of an unidentifiable jumble of diverse limbs (*Arg.* 4.672–82; cf. 119–20 below).

[15] Cf. many entries in *LIMC* vi 'Kirke'.

head, behind whom stands another man with the head and front legs of a ram, and a third with the head and front legs of a dog; at the extreme right is an untransformed human—presumably Odysseus' companion Eurylochos—running from the scene. Behind Circe comes first a man with the head and front legs of a boar; then Odysseus, armed, menacing, and entirely human; and finally a lion-headed man making his exit towards the left. Beneath the cup which Circe is holding is a dog.

I want to make two points about this scene. First, the dog. Is this creature, too, the end-result of a metamorphosis, or has it always been a dog? One *might* say that, since the artist seems in all the other cases to have depicted transformed creatures by means of the 'monstrous hybrid' strategy, this dog is, by contrast, just a dog. But that would be to assume that the artist can have had only one method for denoting metamorphosis. That assumption is, it is true, not implausible, especially as many other vases depict Odysseus' transformed companions as hybrids; but it cannot be watertight. What we can say, in any case, is that the painter has stressed the intermediate status of these hybrids by visualizing alongside them the two extremes of form which they combine: the wholly animal (the dog) and the wholly human (Odysseus, Circe, and the man on the far right).[16]

Secondly: has the painter 'photographed' a single, identifiable instant from within the implied mythical narrative? The answer seems to be: no. Since the creature standing before Circe has already been transformed, why is she still apparently in the act of administering the magic potion to him? What we have is not a snapshot but a synchronic dramatization of a diachronic set of events.[17] Not every portrayal of the episode follows so obviously synchronic an approach, however: more than one artist chose to visualize the ominous cup in mid-air, falling from Circe's grasp (**Fig. 28**).[18]

---

[16] This is, I think, the point which Davies is making ((1986) 183 n. 18) when he suggests that 'this genuine animal' (sc. the dog) may have been 'intended as a foil' for the fully human Circe and the metamorphosed companions.

[17] See Snodgrass (1982) and (1998) 58–61, on the 'synoptic' technique of early Greek art and its relevance to this particular cup; cf. also Raeck (1984) 4–5.

[18] *LIMC* vi 'Kirke' 25; cf. also 22 and 26. On representations of 'the instantaneous', see Frontisi-Ducroux (2003) 283 n. 33.

Figure 28. The instant when Circe's potion-bowl falls to the ground. Attic red-figure krater, 440 BC.

Figure 29. Another variation on the Circe–Odysseus confrontation. Chalkidian amphora, 530 BC.

One more image of Circe may be considered. On a black-figure vase from Vulci (**Fig. 29**), Odysseus is about to draw his sword (in other comparable images it is already drawn); as on the Boston cup, Circe's nakedness draws attention to her confident sexuality, but also to her 'strangeness'—no ordinary Greek female would greet a chance

Figure 30. Pasiphae and her unusual baby. Etruscan cup, 400–350 BC.

Figure 31. Centaur and Lapith, from the Parthenon metopes.

Figure 32. Io in cow-form. To the right, enthroned and affectionate, is Zeus; to the left is Hermes, in the act of killing the many-eyed watcher Argos. Attic red-figure kalpis, *c.* 470 BC.

visitor looking like this. Even more remarkable than Circe are the two creatures who quasi-heraldically flank her and Odysseus. Behind Odysseus is the familiar kind of hybrid: a man with the head and forelegs of a boar. Behind Circe, though, is a figure who is, in relation to the extant iconography of this scene, quite exceptional: a boar with a human face—reminiscent of the human-faced Acheloos (**Fig. 23**), except that the man/boar behind Circe is standing on two legs. The painter has done everything possible to achieve compositional symmetry; there are even formal echoes between the stalks of the two plants. In this quest for balance, the artist has not only extended the repertoire of Circe's menagerie, but has also implicitly posed a question for the viewer/interpreter. Is there a significant difference between a hybrid with the face of a human, and one with the face of a beast? A difference, perhaps, in their degree of 'strangeness'? Could it be that creatures with a human face, and hence with the capacity for human facial expression, stand closer to humanity than do hybrids

Figure 33. Hermes prepares to terminate Argos' surveillance over the apparently hybrid Io. Lucanian oinochoe, *c.* 445–430 BC.

Figure 34. The horned Io at her toilette. Lucanian skyphos, end of 5th cent. BC.

Figure 35. Niobe, in the process of metamorphosis, is depicted within a funerary *naiskos*. Apulian red-figure loutrophoros, *c.* 330 BC.

lacking that capacity? On this question it is extremely hard to find something that could count as convincing cultural evidence, and hence it is dangerous for the interpreter to back his or her own instincts: strangeness is in the eye of the beholder. To look sideways once more from metamorphosis to hybridity: it would be a bold interpreter who would be prepared to affirm that the image of a bull-*headed* baby Minotaur being dandled and burped by its mother Pasiphae (**Fig. 30**) would have been perceived as more (or less) 'strange' than a horse-*bodied* centaur (**Fig. 31**).[19]

---

[19] On the Minotaur vis-à-vis a vase depicting Circe with a bull-headed man, see Frontisi-Ducroux (2003) 70–1.

In spite of the difficulty of resolving such questions, it is clear that, in the case of many metamorphoses, artists could choose from a range of possibilities for locating their transformed subject at a more or less great distance from human form. The transformation of Io was sometimes realized visually as already complete (Type B) (**Fig. 32**); in this case the context, in the shape of the unmistakable many-eyed Argos set to watch over Io, removes any ambiguity about the identity of the cow. Alternatively, the image itself may embody its own inter-specific status (Type C), either as a horned, woman-faced cow (**Fig. 33**), or as a horned woman contemplating her changed appearance in a mirror (**Fig. 34**).[20]

In the case of images of Niobe, one can virtually calibrate geometrically her distance from humanity. Having rashly boasted of her own superiority to the goddess Leto in respect of the number of children each had brought into the world, Niobe saw her own offspring slaughtered by the son (Apollo) and daughter (Artemis) of her rival. Her unutterable grief found its natural analogue in stone.[21] Niobe's was a transformation which artists took to occur—like Socrates' imagined, gradual death as described in Plato's *Phaidon* (117e–118a)—from the feet upwards. Sometimes her petrifaction has risen only as high as the shins (**Fig. 35**); sometimes it has already crept above the waist (**Fig. 36**). The effect of this directionality is to allow the human figure to retain, to the very last, its capacity to express emotion with the face and hands, even though the lower part of its anatomy has solidified for ever into immobility. The same effect is achieved in a representation of Perseus' enemy Polydektes, still gesticulating but partially petrified, as his heroic adversary confronts him with the irresistible glare of the Gorgon (**Fig. 37**). A presumably instantaneous metamorphosis is expressed visually through the image of a hybrid of flesh and stone.

On the matter of distance from or proximity to humanity, the most absorbing case is that of Aktaion. Although most later representations in European art focus on the sensuous moment when

[20] There is an error in *LIMC* at this point. The textual entry for the vase illustrating Io-with-mirror is at *LIMC* v 'Io I' 40; but the image is *illustrated* in the corresponding Plates volume as the right-hand image of 'Io I' 43.

[21] One of the great moments from Ted Hughes's *Tales from Ovid* is the phrase: 'And yet this stone woman wept' ((1997) 223).

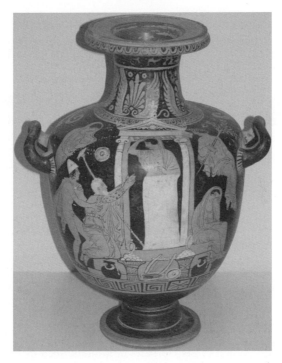

Figure 36. Niobe surrounded by her grieving family. Above right is Apollo, one of the instruments of her doom. Campanian hydria, 350–325 BC.

Aktaion saw the naked Artemis, ancient Greek art concentrates on the young man's punishment.[22] In keeping with the motivational pluralism which characterizes the whole of Greek mythology, the literary sources give a variety of reasons for Aktaion's downfall: either he angered Zeus by wooing Semele, the then object of Zeus' lust; or he incurred the wrath of Artemis, whether by boasting of his superiority to her in hunting, or by seeking to marry her, or by accidentally seeing her when she was naked.[23] Whatever the motive, the same catastrophic outcome recurs: Aktaion is changed into a stag and is torn apart by his own hounds. With the resources of language, nothing is easier for the verbal myth-teller than to combine an

[22] Cf. Frontisi-Ducroux (2003) 98.
[23] See Gantz (1993) 478–81.

Figure 37. At the sight of the Gorgon's head brandished by Perseus, Polydektes begins to turn to stone; Athene contemplates the scene. Attic red-figure krater, *c.* 450–440 BC.

account of metamorphosis with a description of the state of mind of the protagonists before, during, and after the transformation, a description which may exploit the fact that the hunter both 'is' and 'is not' Aktaion. As for the mentality of the hapless victim himself, no surviving Greek source can rival Ovid for ingenuity and delight in paradox ('He longed to cry out: "I am Aktaion! Recognize your own master!", but the words would not come—the air echoed with barking.')[24] But the surviving Greek accounts take a little more interest in the mentality of the hounds. One version preserved by Apollodoros reports that the dogs devoured Aktaion 'without recognizing him';

[24] *Met.* 3.229–31. As I have already stressed (6 above), one of Ovid's classic themes is the change in the *voice* of the metamorphosed individual.

Figure 38. Under the vengeful eye of Artemis, Aktaion succumbs to the jaws of his hounds. Attic red-figure krater, *c.* 470 BC.

Pausanias reckons they were suffering from a kind of rabies, so that they 'would have torn to pieces anyone they came across'.[25]

For the visual artist, the key problem is different: how—and indeed whether—to convey the fact that the hunter has been changed into a stag. Approaches vary.[26] Sometimes Aktaion appears in fully human form, with no explicit allusion at all to the theme of metamorphosis (i.e. none of Types A, B, or C would apply). If the viewer, on the basis of prior mythological knowledge, reads such scenes in terms of transformation, then the metamorphosis must be presumed to have taken place within the minds of the hounds (**Fig. 38**). Equally common, however, are representations of Aktaion with certain physical traits which do allude to his transformation. These traits range from modest little horns (**Fig. 39**) to extremely substantial antlers (**Fig. 40**). Does the choice depend on the degree of distance-from-humanity which the artist wishes to signal? It is, at any rate, extremely uncommon to find an image which dehumanizes Aktaion's *face*—conceivably because, the more Aktaion retains the capacity for human expression, the greater the pathos of his death. An exception

---

[25] Apollod. *Bibl.* 3.4.4; Paus. 9.2.3.
[26] Good comments in Sharrock (1996) 110–12.

Figure 39. This time the hounds' assault on their master is symbolized by the figure of Lyssa, 'Rabid Madness', advancing from the left; above her head there protrudes emblematically the head of a dog. To the right, Artemis presides; to the left, Zeus contemplates the scene. Attic red-figure krater, *c.* 440 BC.

Figure 40. Aktaion's head is now adorned with the most distinctive attribute of a stag. Right and left, two Pan-like figures look on, showing the location of the action in the wild world outside civilization. Red-figure skyphos from Paestum, 350–300 BC.

is a south Italian terracotta from Locri (**Fig. 41**), on which Artemis oversees the rending, by dogs, of a human male with a deer's head. There remains one more way of alluding to Aktaion's transformation. This consists in representing him 'wearing' a deerskin. The entry in *Lexicon Iconographicum Mythologiae Classicae* lists eight such images, of which the most vivid is to be found on a red-figure amphora in Hamburg (**Fig. 42**).[27] The rubric in the *LIMC* article, 'Aktaion vêtu d'une peau de cerf' ('Aktaion clad in a deerskin'), seems at first sight to apply uncontentiously to the Hamburg Aktaion, especially in the light of a remark made by Pausanias describing a spot in Boiotia where the hunter liked to take a rest (9.2.3):

Stesichoros of Himera wrote that the goddess put a deerskin around Aktaion (*elaphou peribalein derma Aktaiōni*) and arranged his death through his hounds to prevent his taking Semele to wife.

But, just as we may legitimately ask what precisely Pausanias implies by the phrase 'put a deerskin around',[28] so the visual imagery of the deerskin also merits reconsideration. For nothing can rule out the reading of images which apparently depict Aktaion (merely) *wearing* a deerskin as 'Aktaion *transformed into a deer*'. It might be objected that we have a mass of images of Herakles wearing a lionskin, and that there is no reason to interpret these as signifying metamorphosis (**Fig. 43**). This is true, although the association between Herakles and monstrous violence might lead one to wonder whether the hero can be quite so completely divorced from his clothing.[29] Again, the Trojan spy Dolon, famously hunted and executed by Odysseus and Diomedes in *Iliad* Book 10, is represented wearing a wolfskin (**Fig. 44**). Once more, nothing in the mythological tradition justifies our reading this as a metamorphosis, though here again there is a degree of assimilation between clothes and wearer: Dolon possesses characteristics (being an outsider; trickiness) regarded by Greeks as typical of his animal analogue.[30] But in any

[27] See *LIMC* i 'Aktaion' 26–33; the Hamburg vase is 27.

[28] FI 199 rightly notes that this is ambiguous as between corporeal transformation and the mere wearing of clothing, although he goes on to say that 'the context makes clear, I think, that a normal transformation is being referred to'. For Frontisi-Ducroux ((2003) 110) Pausanias' text is 'intentionally ambiguous'.

[29] Herakles assimilated to the Nemean lion: see Schnapp-Gourbeillon (1998).

[30] See Buxton (1987) 60–7.

Figure 41. Artemis (left)
watches as the stag-headed
Aktaion is ripped apart.
Fragment of terracotta from
south Italy, *c.* 470–450 BC.

Figure 42. Aktaion 'wearing' a deerskin. Attic red-figure amphora,
c. 490–480 BC.

Figure 43. By donning the skin of the Nemean lion Herakles also takes on that beast's formidable power. Attic black-figure olpe, late 6th cent. BC.

case there is no reason why a specific iconographical trait—in this case, the wearing of an animal skin—should be glued to just one meaning. In the Herakles and Dolon stories it might have one resonance, in the Aktaion myth quite another, especially when the mythological context of the Aktaion imagery so strongly speaks of metamorphosis.

Figure 44. Dolon's wolfish trickiness is no match for the cunning and strength of Odysseus and Diomedes. Attic red-figure kylix, *c.* 480 BC.

Figure 45. Agamemnon is on the point of sacrificing Iphigeneia at Aulis, when she is 'replaced' by a deer. Apulian red-figure krater, 370–355 BC.

One strategy available to Greek myth-tellers was to demythologize their material through 'rationalization'. Is this what has happened with the 'Aktaion wearing a deerskin' images? Could these be rationalizations of metamorphosis, rather than affirmations of it? Or is it the modern interpreter who sees a rationalization here, where an ancient viewer saw none? Finality in such interpretative questions is impossible, given the difficulty of establishing the horizons of expectation of Greek image-makers, their clients, and their viewers. But it may be worth looking sideways at another image, to see if it can teach us anything.

An Apulian krater in the British Museum (**Fig. 45**) has at the focus of its imagery an altar, behind which there stands a bearded man. In his left hand he carries a staff, a symbol of authority; in his right he wields a knife, holding it over the head of a young woman. To the left of the altar, a young man holds a tray; he is evidently assisting in the action which involves the bearded man and the girl. Further to the left is a woman, whose hand is raised, perhaps as a reaction to the scene which she beholds. Contemplating these events from above are Apollo and Artemis (identified respectively by laurel branch and bow). In the space between the divinities hang two *houkrunia*, ox-skulls, marking the central scene as one of sacrifice. One detail remains to be mentioned, a detail which will be crucial in enabling us to identify the episode being represented: around the figure of the girl can be seen the outline of a deer.

It is usually a serious mistake to regard visual representations of Greek myths as mere derivatives of verbal mythological narratives; such a view ignores the independence and distinctiveness of the various artistic traditions. But there are some cases where the key which unlocks the meaning of a puzzling piece of iconography may indeed be found in our written sources. So it is with the Apulian krater. In the course of his description of the events leading up to the Trojan War, the mythographer Apollodoros relates what happened when the Greek fleet was held up by adverse winds at Aulis. Offended by a rash boast on the part of Agamemnon, Artemis demanded compensation: the sacrifice of Iphigeneia. But the sacrifice was never completed (*Epit.* 3.22):

Clytemnestra sent her, and Agamemnon placed her beside the altar and was about to slaughter her, when Artemis carried her off to the land of the

Taurians and established her there as her priestess, having substituted a deer for her (*elaphon ant' autēs parastēsasa*) at the altar.

In the light of this, what do we make of the image on the Apulian krater? The scene depicted clearly belongs within the context of the immediate preliminaries to the sacrifice of Iphigeneia by Agamemnon. The instant isolated by the painter is that of the miraculous substitution of maiden by deer. It would obviously have been possible for the artist to have depicted the moment *before* the substitution; in that case, Iphigeneia alone would have been visible. It would have been equally possible to represent the moment *after* the substitution; in that case there would have been a deer but no maiden. What we actually have is a simultaneity of maiden and deer. But what sort of simultaneity? In the caption to his illustration of the krater, Ioannis Kakridis writes: 'The sacrificer raises the knife, while *behind Iphigeneia*, who is approaching the altar, the deer has already appeared.'[31] The idea that the deer is *behind* Iphigeneia is one way of reading the image, but it is a way which brings us back to the implicitly demystifying approach to Homeric transformations-of-deities-into-birds which reduces strangeness by introducing a punctuating 'disappearance'.[32] A less literal way of viewing the image on the krater would be to see the deer as *being in exactly the same place as* Iphigeneia, in such a way that the two become blended.[33]

If we return to the image of Aktaion 'wearing' a deerskin (**Fig. 42**), we can hardly fail to register a degree of similarity with the deer circumscribed around Iphigeneia, a similarity most marked at the head. But the legs are a different matter: whereas those of the animal on the Iphigeneia image belong to a living creature, the splayed legs on the Aktaion image are part of a hide. The analogy between the two is thus incomplete, and it cannot resolve the meaning of Aktaion's deerskin. While it seems to me that the most convincing reading of the Iphigeneia scene is: 'A deer stands miraculously in the same place

---

[31] Ὁ θύτης υψώνει το μαχαίρι, ενώ *πίσω από την Ιφιγένεια*, *που πλησιάζει προς το βωμό*, *έχει κιόλας εμφανιστεί το ελάφι* (Kakridis (1986–7) v. 28, caption to pl. 18; my emphasis).

[32] See above, 32–3.

[33] Thus Odette Touchefeu (*LIMC* i 'Agamemnon' 30) more persuasively speaks of Iphigeneia's silhouette *beginning to blend into* that of the deer ('Sa silhouette *commence à se confondre* avec celle de la biche'); my emphasis.

as Iphigeneia', the question, 'What did Aktaion "really" look like when the hounds killed him?' is unanswerable in relation to this image. All we can say is that Aktaion is simultaneously a stag and a transgressing human. The artist, exploiting the resources of his medium, has kept both possibilities alive.

'Transformation,' observes Forbes Irving, 'is not a popular theme in classical art, perhaps for obvious reasons.'[34] He presumably means that the difficulty of achieving a satisfactory visual representation of this process dissuaded artists from attempting it. Statistically, there does seem to be some justification for this observation. But what also needs stressing is that even the relatively few images which we do possess display a rich diversity of strategies for evoking transform-ation. Compared with, say, the artists who opted to provide yet one more picture of Herakles' combat with the Nemean lion, the painters and sculptors who tackled metamorphosis were embarking on a journey with fewer landmarks, but with more exciting possibilities for discovery.

[34] FI 200.

4

Hellenistic Transformations

In the period after Alexander's death Hellenistic writers tried to make sense of the radically reconfigured political and cultural present by exploring how it grew out of what went before. Such writers were often drawn to the notion of aitia, *the 'causes' which laid the foundations for the contemporary world. Hellenistic treatments of the theme of metamorphosis exemplify this same fascination. Stories of transformation were held to explain how certain aspects of the present originated. Tellers of metamorphosis myths—which burgeon in this period—regard their great Classical predecessors with respect, but also deliberately diverge from them in a creative play of imitation and innovation.*

THE COLLECTORS

The Hellenistic penchant for the systematization of inherited cultural experience found one of its characteristic expressions in the assembling and organizing of tales of marvellous change, especially tales which narrated the prolongation of mortal existence into forms of the natural environment (in its widest sense).[1] Some of the collectors are little more than names to us: Antigonos of Karystos, Didymarchos, Kallisthenes, Theodoros.[2] Even when we do know a little about the author concerned, as with the scholar and poet Parthenios, our information about his treatment of metamorphosis is extremely

---

[1] Hellenistic collections of metamorphosis stories: Myers (1994) 21–6. Hellenistic literature and 'the marvellous': Fraser (1972) i. 454–5.

[2] See FI 19–20; Cameron (2004) 272.

sketchy.[3] Since paucity of evidence precludes us from giving a detailed account of most collections of metamorphosis narratives of which we are aware, we depend heavily on the *Metamorphoses* of Antoninus Liberalis, a compendium of prose tales probably written in the Antonine period or slightly later.[4] By means of a marginal annotation next to each story, the sole surviving manuscript identifies the source(s) on which Antoninus was apparently drawing when compiling his own version. The authors whom he most often cites as predecessors are the Hellenistic writers Nicander of Kolophon (cited twenty-two times) and Boios (ten times).[5] So far as we can reconstruct their approaches, Nicander and Boios both used tales of metamorphosis in order to offer *aitia* for present conditions. But they did so with differing emphases.

In his *Heteroioumena* ('Transformations'; perhaps third century BC) Nicander seems to have predominantly stressed not the physical process of metamorphosis, but the embeddedness of the stories in local topography and cult.[6] An example is his narrative about Dryope, recorded as no. 32 in Antoninus' collection; the manuscript cites Nicander as the sole source.

Dryope was a maiden who lived near Mount Oita in central Greece; her grandfather was Spercheios, the local river-god. Dryope was a dear companion of the local nymphs; she also caught the eye of Apollo. First the god became (*egeneto*) a tortoise, which the naive girl put inside her dress. Then, changing shape (*metabalōn*), he became (*egeneto*) a snake, causing the nymphs to flee in terror. The inevitable followed. By Apollo Dryope had a son named Amphissos, eventual ruler of the area near Oita. Amphissos founded a temple to Apollo, and it was there that Dryope passed from mortal existence. In the first stage of her passing the nymphs, out of kindness, concealed her in the wood near the sanctuary; in her place they made a poplar rise up, and beside it a spring. After that Dryope 'changed and instead of a mortal became a nymph' (*metebale kai anti thnētēs egeneto numphe*). In recognition of the honour which his mother

---

[3] See Lightfoot (1999), esp. 39–40 and 164–7.
[4] See Papathomopoulos (1968); Sanz Morales (2002) 129–88.
[5] Helpful discussion of these two writers in FI 19–37.
[6] For the date, see Fantuzzi (2000) 898; on Nicander, see Cameron (2004) 298–301.

had received, Amphissos founded a sanctuary to the nymphs, and instituted a competition in running:

Even today (*kai eti nun*) the local people keep this custom of the competition. But it is not proper for a woman to take part in the race, because two girls reported to the local people that Dryope had disappeared (*aphanistheisan*) at the hands of the nymphs. The nymphs were angry with the girls, and changed them into pine trees (*autas anti parthenōn elatas epoiēsan*).

Several aspects of this narrative are worth highlighting. First, it is rooted in the ceremonies and beliefs of one specific part of Greece, where 'even today'—the today of Nicander and/or Antoninus—there is a foot-race which recalls this episode from the mythical past. Secondly, unlike some narratives which we considered earlier, this one really does operate with the notion of disappearance as a precursor to metamorphosis: there is no description of the process of metamorphosis, merely an acknowledgement that it has taken place. Yet this does not necessarily imply that the narrator wishes to demystify his account. The reason why the nymphs punish the girls who betrayed the secret of Dryope's transformation is precisely that that occurrence belonged to the world of the sacred, and should hence have been beyond the vision of mere mortals.

A third point concerns the manner in which the tale contrasts with our other ancient source for this myth, Ovid's *Metamorphoses* (9.327–93). Ovid's version is narrated by Dryope's half-sister Iole. Instead of localizing the transformation in a specific part of the Greek world, or relating it to cultic activities which take place 'even today', the Ovidian emphasis is generic, on a *type* of landscape (334–5):

There is a lake, with banks gently shelving, so that it looks like the seashore, where myrtle groves encircle the water's edge.[7]

Characteristically Ovid also focuses on the detailed narration of physiological changes, and on their psychological effects upon the protagonist and those around her (349–62):

She wanted to retreat, to depart from the spot, after offering prayers to the nymphs. But her feet were held fast by a root and, when she struggled to tear

---

[7] Here and below I adopt, with occasional amendments, the translation by Innes (1955).

them free, she could move only the upper part of her body. Pliant bark, growing up from the ground, gradually gripped the whole length of her thighs. When she saw this, she made to tear her hair, but filled her hand with leaves—leaves covered all her head. The boy Amphissos (for such was the name that his grandfather Eurytos had given him) felt his mother's breasts hardening, and the milky fluid refused to come when he sucked. I stood there, and watched this cruel stroke of fate, and yet I could not help you, my sister. Still, as far as I was able, I delayed the growth of the tree, throwing my arms around the rising trunk and branches, wishing, you may be sure, that I might be buried beneath that same bark.

As usual, Ovid homes in on the anomalous status of the victim as a temporary hybrid, and exploits the possibilities for pathos which this status offers. By contrast with the version in Nicander/Antoninus, the Ovidian Amphissos is not a grown man but an infant. Too young to articulate in words the enormity of what is happening, he senses the weirdness of the event with his little mouth as he feels his mother's breasts grow hard. Dryope herself does, for the time being, retain the power of speech, since her transformation is taking place—we recall Niobe—from her lower limbs upwards (368–72):

Tears sprinkled the leaves that were growing from her wretched body, and while she could, while her lips afforded a passage for her voice, she poured out her misery in such laments as these: 'If there is any truth in the words of the wretched, I swear by the gods that I have not deserved this wicked treatment.'

The thought experiments conducted in Ovid's retellings of mythology habitually explore the limits of language—Ovid's own language, but also the language of his protagonists, who strive to give utterance even in situations of the greatest physical and psychological duress.

Antoninus' second main source, Boios, is even more shadowy than Antoninus himself.[8] The treatise ascribed to him under the name of *Ornithogonia* is undated, and none of it survives. However, given the drift of his stories as they can be reconstructed from Antoninus, it is clear that the collection exemplified the Hellenistic tendency to

[8] See FI 33 for the possibility that the author might have been an author*ess*, Boio (based on Philochoros *FGrH* 328 F 214, from Athen. *Deipn.* 393e).

compile tales linked by a common theme. In this case the theme is that of the origins of kinds of birds: each kind is derived from an original metamorphosis of a mortal into a bird, which is believed to perpetuate the ex-mortal's characteristics.

In their general scope and motivations, Boios' stories all fall within the traditional web of Greek mythology. But frequently the characters involved in Antoninus' Boios-derived vignettes are—or seem to us to be—new additions to the mythological repertory. An example is the story about Hierax, a just and pious man from the land of the Mariandynians in Bithynia (Ant. Lib. 3). In return for founding sanctuaries to Demeter, the goddess gave Hierax abundant crops; but this gift was to lead to his downfall. When the Teukrians (i.e. Trojans) negligently failed to sacrifice to Poseidon, the god punished them by sending a sea monster against them and destroying their crops. The Teukrians implored Hierax for help, and he duly sent them food to alleviate their hunger—thus acting directly against Poseidon's wishes.

But Poseidon was enraged that Hierax was undoing the honours due to him, and so turned the man into a bird (*epoiēsen ornitha*), the bird still now known as a *hierax* (hawk). Having made Hierax disappear (*aphanisas*), the god also changed (*ēllaxen*) his character: whereas before he had been greatly loved by mankind, the god now made him hated by the birds; and whereas formerly Hierax had prevented the deaths of many humans, the god now made him kill large numbers of birds.

This tale, known to us only from Antoninus, gives an unfamiliar ending to a common story pattern. Numerous mythical precedents make it inevitable that Hierax's implied dishonouring of Poseidon will be punished: as Hippolytos, among others, discovered to his cost, it is incumbent on mortals to revere *all* the gods. That Hierax should suffer metamorphosis is one of several possible consequences which might have awaited him. What individualizes the outcome of this particular tale is the nature attributed to the bird into which Hierax is changed. The dénouement ironically inverts the more usual motif according to which a transformed mortal retains intact the disposition which he or she formerly possessed while in human form. The twist in the tale evidently reflects Poseidon's unwillingness to forget his anger even after Hierax's transformation.

Another Antoninan story, again said to derive from Boios, looks back not so much to a common mythical pattern as to a single extraordinarily well-known myth. This tale (Ant. Lib. 5) begins as an everyday intra-familial conflict: when the widow Timandre takes a younger lover (Aigypios), her son Neophron resents the incomer and tries to block his mother's new friendship. However, in the characteristic manner of mythology, the tension is played out in extreme terms. After seducing Aigypios' mother (named Boulis), Neophron treacherously engineers an unwitting sexual encounter between her and her son. While Aigypios is in post-coital slumber, Boulis recognizes the identity of her partner. The story attains its quasi-tragic climax as Boulis and Aigypios momentarily occupy the roles of Jocasta and Oedipus. Boulis threatens to blind Aigypios before committing suicide herself, while Aigypios raises his eyes to the sky in a prayer that 'all people should disappear along with him'. However, unlike the situation towards the end of Sophokles' *Oedipus the King*, the outcome is not suspended in a kind of moral and cognitive limbo without any indication of the gods' attitude or purpose. On the contrary, Zeus intervenes explicitly and conclusively, transforming the protagonists into birds. Aigypios and Neophron both become vultures, but of contrasting colour and size, just as, in their previous human form, they had displayed something of the 'mirror image' in their behaviour. As for the mothers, Timandre becomes a titmouse, while the wretched Boulis turns into a *poynx* (an unidentifiable bird)[9] which allegedly lives off the eyes of fish, birds, and snakes; the narrator explicitly highlights the connection with Boulis' wish to blind her son. Whereas the tale of Hierax involves, unusually, an *inversion* of characteristics between the human and the aviform protagonist, in the case of Timandre and Boulis it is the *continuity* between human and bird which is emphasized: the narrator concludes his tale by observing that the *poynx* and the titmouse are never seen together.

[9] Aristot. *HA* 617[a]8 (here the bird is named the *phōux*); cf. Pollard (1977) 19; Arnott (2007) 193.

DIALOGUES WITH THE PAST

Alongside the movement to systematize and organize material on the basis of thematic similarity, Hellenistic tellers of metamorphosis stories also developed their material in another direction (we already saw traces of it in Antoninus). Myth-tellers conducted a sophisticated dialogue with their predecessors, knowingly weaving in and out of existing versions of transformation tales in a ballet of reminiscence and innovation. I shall examine this process in relation to the work of two poets: Apollonios of Rhodes, and Moschos.

Strange shapes in the *Argonautika*

Apollonios' fundamental poetic strategy—that of echoing Homeric precedents yet simultaneously setting them at a distance—affects, among other things, the representation of marvellous transformation. Though at first sight metamorphoses play only a modest part in the *Argonautika*, when they do occur they throw much light on the interaction of the human and the divine in the world of the poem.

The Homeric epics abound in episodes in which transformed Olympians appear on earth, either by adopting the persuasive guise of a mortal in order to fit snugly into human expectations, or by opting for the more astonishing form of, say, a departing bird. Apollonios offers us nothing comparable to this abundance. His downplaying of interventions by the Olympians corresponds to the overall manner in which action is represented within the *Argonautika*.[10] Space now opens up for lesser divinities, especially nymphs, who possess more modest and localized powers than those of the Olympians: their presence signals one way in which the poem elides the difference between humanity and the natural world. Nymphs of Pelion gazed in amazement (*ethambeon*) at the *Argo* (1.549–52); nymphs of the groves mourned the suicide of Kleite, the grieving widow of honourable King Kyzikos, and their tears still

---

[10] This has been highlighted by some excellent recent literary criticism of the poem, especially by Hunter (1993a) and Knight (1995).

flow as a spring (1.1065–9); nymphs of river, mountain, and wood brought flowers for the wedding of Jason and Medea (4.1143–52). Orpheus and Medea, possessed of contrasting but equally remarkable powers, illustrate the porosity of the boundary between the human and the natural in their own distinctive ways: Orpheus' music bewitches rocks and streams and moves oak trees (1.26–31), and the Argonauts' harmonious singing to his lyre makes the coast rejoice (2.162–3); Medea exercises power over rivers, stars, and moon (3.528–33). Through similes, too, mortals can be assimilated to the natural world: the amorous conversation between Jason and Medea is like the whispering of oaks or tall firs (3.967–72). And at the heart of the poem is the wooden *Argo* itself, able to utter human speech thanks to her plank of sacred Dodona oak (4.580–92).

These examples provide the background to a series of episodes concerned with metamorphosis. The relevant narratives cluster in Book 4, which evokes the *Argo's* return journey, during which the crew are confronted with experiences even more eerie than those which befell them in Colchis. In particular, Jason's treacherous murder of Medea's brother Apsyrtos triggers a series of encounters with the uncanny, encounters which involve several instances of astonishing change.

Tears of amber

Prompted by the enormity of Jason's crime, the *Argo* herself gives voice, warning the Argonauts of the anger of Zeus: the only way for them to be cleansed of pollution is by seeking absolution from Circe. Their route takes them to a far-away part of the river Eridanos where Phaethon, the foolhardy son of Helios, once crashed from his father's chariot into the waters of a marsh after being thunderbolted by Zeus. So intricately does this passage explore the interfusing of the human and the natural that it needs quoting in full (4.599–626):

To this very day (*eti nun*) the marsh exhales a heavy vapour which rises from his smouldering wound; no bird can stretch out its fragile wings to fly over that water, but in mid-flight it falls dead in the flames. Around the lake the unhappy Heliades, encased in their slender poplars, grieve in moaning lamentation. Bright drops of amber fall to the ground from their eyes; on the sand these are dried by the sun, and when the waters of the dark lake wash over the shores, as they are driven by the breath of the groaning wind, then the swelling current rolls all the amber into the Eridanos. The Celts' tale, however, is that it is the tears of Leto's son Apollo which are carried by the whirling currents. He is said to have wept countless tears at the time when he reached the holy race of the Hyperboreans, after leaving glittering heaven in the face of his father's threats; he was angry because of the son whom noble Koronis had borne to him in rich Lakereia beside the streams of the Amyros. This then is how the story goes amongst those people. The heroes desired neither food nor drink, nor did their minds have any thought of delights. The days they spent worn out and exhausted, weighed down by the foul smell which rose from the small branches of the Eridanos as Phaethon's corpse steamed; at night they heard the piercing sound of the Heliades' shrill lamentation. As they wept, their tears were carried on the waters like drops of oil.[11]

On the face of it Apollonios seems to be in his most Herodotean mood, as he provides competing explanations for the creation of amber ('The Celts' tale, however, is that...'). But the competition is not, as it often is in Herodotos, between a 'sacred' and a 'more rationalizing' explanation, but rather between two slightly different but comparably sacred explanations: amber comes from the tears of a suprahuman being, but are they those of Phaethon's sisters transformed into poplars, or those of Apollo grieving at the loss of his son Asklepios? Either way, the episode blends into its local and broader frameworks. First, the fetid atmosphere suits the narrative context: given the pollution currently surrounding the *Argo*, the stench emanating from Phaethon's rotting corpse is symbolically appropriate. Then, the mention of Asklepios echoes the story of Phaethon, even down to the manner in which their hubris is punished: by the thunderbolt. Next, the connection with Helios is thematically relevant, in that Medea is the Sun's granddaughter, while Circe, whom the Argonauts are about to visit, is his daughter.[12] Finally, the landscape is once more represented as numinous, in virtue of the presence of nymphs. As Phaethon exists in an apparently permanent

[11] Trans. Hunter (1993b). In what follows I continue to cite Hunter's translation, with minor modifications.

[12] Cf. 4.727–9: 'the whole race of Helios was easy to identify upon sight, because their eyes threw out into the far distance sparkling rays which glittered like gold.'

state of decay, poised between bodily integrity and dissolution, between anthropomorphism and river water, so his sisters are poised between human and arboreal shape: encased in bark, their bodies ceaselessly break out in all-too-human lamentation.

Phaethon's fall confronts the Argonauts with a coalescing of living and dead, woman and tree, tears and amber, fire and water: where else should such things happen but at the world's end? Yet the next stage of the *Argo's* voyage takes it to an even more remote spot: the (imaginary) confluence of the Eridanos (Po) and Rhodanos (Rhone). Since the Rhodanos rises 'in the remotest recess of the earth, where are the gates and halls of Night' (629–30), the Argonauts run the risk of entering Ocean itself: the point of no return (639). But Hera's solicitude saves them, and they return closer to the known world: known, that is, from Homer. For their next landfall is Aiaia, the home of Circe.

Strange mixtures

Unlike the cool and (initially) dominant Circe whom Odysseus encounters in the *Odyssey*, the Circe of the *Argonautika* is in confusion from the outset: the narrator discovers her in the act of carrying out purificatory rites to neutralize her recent blood-filled dreams. The uncanny state of Circe's dwelling interrupts her first inclination towards all visitors—the urge to transform them (665–7):

All the chambers and courts of her house seemed to drip with blood, and flame consumed all the drugs with which it had been her habit till then to bewitch any stranger who arrived.

Mirroring this perturbation of Circe's normal world is the picture of the chaotic beasts which surround her (672–82):

Her beasts—which were not entirely like flesh-devouring beasts, nor like men, but rather a jumble of different limbs—all came with her, like a large flock of sheep which follow the shepherd out of the stalls. Similar to these were the creatures which in earlier times the earth itself had created out of the mud, pieced together from a jumble of limbs, before it had been properly solidified by the thirsty air or the rays of the parching sun had eliminated sufficient moisture. Time then sorted these out by grouping them into

proper categories. Similarly unidentifiable were the forms which followed
after Circe and caused the heroes boundless astonishment (*thambos*).

This *thambos* is the same astonishment that we meet in countless
metamorphosis narratives; but here the situation is—or may be—
different, because nothing in Apollonios' text makes it certain that
the beasts are the product of transformation. Whereas the unnerv-
ingly tame beasts accompanying the Homeric Circe are real animal
types which have been (on the most plausible reading) transformed
out of human form, the hybrid throwbacks walking around in
Apollonios' text, have, for all we know, always looked like that.[13]
Even if they *are* to be taken as the end-products of metamorphosis, it
is metamorphosis of an intellectually intriguing kind, so that, as
Hunter observes, 'this Circe outdoes her Homeric self by changing
men not to beasts but to the primeval ancestors of beasts'.[14] This
would not be the only time that Apollonios plays with the idea of
different generations coexisting: the bronze giant Talos is later introduced as 'the last survivor of the bronze race of men born from ash-
trees'.[15] It is as if this narrator, so conscious of his role in blending
inherited poetic tradition with present innovation, were mapping the
same characteristic onto some of his mythological material.

The encounter with Circe brings no improvement in the Argonauts' situation. Circe feels pity for her kinswoman Medea, but none
at all for Jason (745–6): 'Leave my house,' she commands Medea, 'go
with this stranger—whoever this unknown man is whom you have
carried off behind your father's back.' There follows a series of
episodes (the Sirens; Scylla and Charybdis; the cattle of the Sun) in
which the *Argo* passes through waters which Odysseus' vessel will
explore, and yet, in another sense, has already explored, thanks to
Homer's narrative: Apollonios' delight in playing with chronology is
again in evidence. Then, when the irregular liaison between Jason
and Medea has at last been formally solemnized on Phaiakia thanks
to Alkinoos and Arete (predictably in the presence of the ubiquitous

[13] Cf. Knight (1995) 188–9.
[14] Hunter (1993a) 165.
[15] 4.1641–2. Cf. Hunter (1993a) 105: Apollonios 'clearly delights in mixing the
temporal levels'.

nymphs: 1143–52; 1196–1200), one last, outlandish trial awaits the Argonauts, in the burning Libyan desert.

Heroines, Hesperides, and the play of invisibility

This voyage into no-man's-land is framed by two encounters with local, female, divine beings. The first occurs when the Argonauts are in their habitual state of helpless indecision; this time they behave as if they are mourning for their own deaths, as they cover their heads with their cloaks (1294–6). At midday—an 'extreme', limiting time, ideal for divine epiphanies—three goddesses appear to Jason, in an episode which Hunter excellently characterizes as 'a kind of cross between an epic dream-sequence and the description of a desert mirage'.[16] The poet describes the goddesses as 'the heroines, guardians of Libya'; their own self-characterization is as 'solitary (*oiopoloi*) goddesses of the land' (1322).[17] When they gently remove the cloak from Jason's head, he reacts with bewilderment (*atuzomenon*, 1317). The goddesses' enigmatic prediction—that the Argonauts' safe return depends on their making fair recompense to their mother for what she suffered whilst carrying them in her belly—is followed by their immediate disappearance (*aphantoi*, 1330): this time the text rules out any possibility that it is merely the modern interpreter who has imported the idea that a divinity has 'vanished'.

Although the epiphany is witnessed by Jason alone, he needs his companions' help to interpret the prediction. When he reports the epiphany to them, they react with astonishment: *ethambeon* (1363). In order for the goddesses' prediction to become intelligible, another prompt is needed, in the form of an occurrence strange enough to count as a portent. This duly occurs when a huge, golden-maned horse appears from the sea and gallops away across the sand. The role of seer is taken by Peleus, who recognizes the horse as one that draws Poseidon's chariot. The direction it has taken is the one the Argonauts should follow, while carrying the *Argo* on their shoulders:

---

[16] Hunter (1993b) 159, n. to p. 129.

[17] Less plausibly—bearing in mind the landscape—the scholiast gives the meaning of *oiopoloi* as 'shepherd' goddesses (the epithet recurs at 1413). Livrea ((1987) 184 n. 55) argues that the word can retain both meanings.

for the mother who has borne them in her belly is none other than their vessel herself.

Having carried her for twelve days and twelve nights, the Argonauts set the *Argo* down in the waters of Lake Triton—a paradoxical destination, then, which is reached on land but by boat.[18] Here they come across a second group of local divinities, in an encounter even stranger than that involving the 'heroines' of Libya. Desperate for water, the Argonauts reach a spot where, up until the previous day, a serpent used to guard the golden apples of the Hesperid nymphs. But the scene is now one of putrid desolation, reminiscent (though the climate is different) of the place where Phaethon's corpse lies rotting; for the serpent has been killed by the poisonous arrows of that former Argonaut, Herakles, and flies lie shrivelling on the carcass.

There now unfolds a sequence of metamorphoses impossible to parallel in Greek mythological narratives (one thinks, rather, of Dante). The Hesperides, who have been lamenting the loss of their apples, become (*egenonto*) dust and earth when approached by the Argonauts (1408); it is as if, in their parched state, the exhausted heroes can find nothing in their world but sand. What is needed is the intervention of a voice powerful enough to convince the Hesperides to reassume a benign and fertile shape: the voice of Orpheus. Persuaded by his mellifluous offer that they will in future receive unlimited libations and feasts, the goddesses send up shoots which in turn become trees, each of which embodies one of their number: a poplar, an elm, and a willow. But the sequence of transformations is not yet complete, for the trees then revert to their earlier, anthropomorphic forms; not surprisingly, the poet calls this an exceedingly great *thambos* (1430). To confirm that they no longer feel hostility towards the Argonauts, the Hesperides reveal the source of a spring, recently created when Herakles kicked a rock: from dryness and dust they have become associated with reviving moisture.

Throughout the *Argonautika* Apollonios plays with the notions of eyes and sight: who looks at whom directly, who looks aside, how the

---

[18] Cf. Calame (2003) 59.

emotions—above all those of love and shame—affect the gaze.[19] In the Libyan desert this theme receives a new twist. What links Jason's encounter with 'the heroines' to the multiple appearances of the Hesperides is the idea of (in)visibility: both groups of goddesses can remove themselves from human sight at will. Hunter's reference to the mirage provides the key here.[20] In the fierce desert heat, at this extreme point of the *Argo*'s southerly journey, it becomes impossible to distinguish real from imaginary, visible from invisible. Precisely the same is true of the last appearance (perhaps) of Herakles in the poem, a few lines later (1477–80): 'As for Herakles, Lynkeus alone at that time thought that he saw him far away across the vast land, as a man sees or imagines he sees the moon through a mist at the beginning of a new month.' This most solid of heroes is reduced to the enigmatic insubstantiality with which the desert invests all of its inhabitants, permanent or temporary.

Final transformations

In spite of the relief afforded by the Herakles-generated spring, the Argonauts' encounters with the perils of the desert continue. Three motifs combined in the episode of Herakles and the apples of the Hesperides—serpent, poison, rotting corpse—recombine in the tale of the death of the seer Mopsos. He is bitten in the leg, at midday, by a deadly snake, one of the brood which sprang from the blood of the Gorgon when Perseus flew over Libya carrying her severed head. This fertilization of the desert is inversely mirrored by the demise of Mopsos, whose body decomposes with incredible speed (1529–31): 'For no time at all was his body to lie exposed to the sun, for at once the poison began to rot his flesh within, and the hair on his body grew moist and fell away.' There are also similarities to, and differences from, the demise of Phaethon. Whereas Phaethon is still rotting, Mopsos' corpse putrefies completely on the spot; yet both receive the lamentation of young women—the Heliades, and the servant girls of Medea, respectively. Another element in Apollonios' intricate play of similarity and difference concerns snakes. The serpent which kills Mopsos is taking a kind of symbolic

---

[19] See Buxton (2000a).   [20] See n. 16 above.

revenge, not only for the snake which Herakles has just violently despatched, but also, by a more exact reversal, for the Colchian snake which Medea put to sleep: whereas Medea's *pharmaka* caused the snake to drop its jaw and fall to the ground in narcotic slumber, in Mopsos' encounter with a snake it was the seer himself who grew numb and collapsed to the ground (156–61; 1526–7). Even in imagery the Argonauts are unable to escape from snakes, or from the desert which snakes inhabit: the *Argo*'s wandering search for a navigable channel out of Lake Triton is compared to the winding path taken by a serpent under a fierce sun (1541–7).

The Argonauts' escape from Lake Triton depends on a divinity who undergoes double metamorphosis. The local god Triton first appears resembling (*enalinkios*, 1551) a personable young man. Then he vanishes (*aphantos*, 1590) into the lake, only to reappear 'as he really was to look upon' (1603), that is, in his true form (1610–14):

From the top of his head to his belly, and all around his back and his waist, his body was exactly like the glorious form of the blessed gods, but beneath his flanks spread in two directions the long, forked tail of a sea-monster.

Like some representations of Acheloos, Triton is a hybrid who is also capable of metamorphosis.[21] Not surprisingly, the Argonauts cry out when their eyes witness the 'dreadful wonder' (*teras ainon*, 1619) of this remarkable god diving into the water.

One last metamorphic story remains to be played out before the *Argonautika* ends, a story linking dream with waking, past with future, earth with humanity, sea with land. When he first appeared, Triton entrusted a clod of Libyan earth to one of the Argonauts, Poseidon's son Euphemos. Near the beginning of the *Argonautika* we learned that Euphemos' fleetness of foot was so great that he could skim over the surface of the sea, thus symbolically converting water to earth—'intermingling the categories of sea and land', as Claude Calame puts it.[22] With the *Argo* back in Aegean waters Euphemos has a dream, the complexity of which rivals Penelope's vision in *Odyssey* Book 19. It is a dream which in its own way points to the mixing of earth and water (1733–45):

---

[21] Acheloos: see above, 85, with Figs. 22–4.
[22] Calame (2003) 59. The description of Euphemos' fleetness of foot is at 1.179–84.

He dreamed that the divine clod was in his arms at his breast and was nourished by white drops of milk, and from the clod, small though it was, came a woman looking like a young virgin. Overcome by irresistible desire he made love to her, but lamented as though he had bedded his own daughter whom he had nursed with his own milk. She, however, consoled him with gentle words: 'I am of the race of Triton, I, my friend, am your children's nurse, not your daughter, for my parents are Triton and Libya. Entrust me to the maiden daughters of Nereus so that I may dwell in the sea near Anaphe. Later I shall go towards the sun's rays, when I am ready for your descendants.'

With Mopsos dead, it falls to Jason to interpret Euphemos' dream. He predicts a marvellous mineralogical transformation (1749–53):

Ah! Most glorious is the fate which awaits you. If you throw the clod into the sea, the gods will fashion from it an island, where the future sons of your sons will dwell, since Triton presented you with this piece of the Libyan land as a gift.

The 'birth' of the island of Kalliste out of the sea will have two eventual consequences: (1) the settlement of the island by Euphemos' descendants, led by its founder Theras, for whom the island will be renamed as Thera (mod. Santorini); (2) the subsequent colonization of Cyrene from Thera. However, this second development—which gives rise to one of the richest of all Greek narratives of colonial foundation, thanks to the elaborations by Pindar, Herodotos, and Kallimachos, among others[23]—forms no part of Apollonios' tale: the latest time to which he alludes is that at which Thera will be settled.[24] But even that lies long in the future. For the moment, all that matters is the emergence out of the deep of Kalliste, 'Very Beautiful': the name inaugurates the happy mood of the last few lines of the *Argonautika*. Driven by favourable winds, amid the sound of rejoicing, and with the ominous on-board presence of Medea passed over in silence, the *Argo* at last sails into her home port of Pagasai, putting behind her all memories of putrefying serpents and transformations in the desert.

---

[23] See Calame (2003) 35–113.
[24] The scholiasts to Apollonios, though, prolong the tale as far as the foundation of Cyrene; cf. Calame (2003) 143 n. 49.

Moschos and the myth of Europa

In the second century BC Moschos of Syracuse wrote a poem in 166 hexameters about the abduction of Phoinix's daughter by Zeus metamorphosed into a bull. Moschos has an impeccable Hellenistic pedigree: he was said to have been not just a grammarian but actually a pupil of the great Alexandrian scholar Aristarchos. His elegant and sexy poem about Europa is the most notable literary account of this myth to survive from antiquity. It breathes an atmosphere pervaded by transformations, of several kinds. The manner in which the poem deals with this theme is typically Hellenistic, in that it consistently alludes to, while subtly departing from, earlier 'classic' mythological narratives.

The narrative

While Europa lies sleeping in her father's house, Aphrodite sends her a 'sweet' dream which prefigures her destiny (8–9): 'She imagined that two continents were contending for her, Asia and the land opposite; their appearance was that of women.' The woman/land-with-no-name 'had the form (*morphē*) of a foreigner, but the other looked like (*eōikei*) a woman of the girl's own country' (10–11); indeed this native woman clung protectively to the girl, claiming to be her mother. Yet when the woman/land-with-no-name laid aggressive hands on the girl, the text tells us that, strangely, this aggression was not contrary to the girl's will—a prefiguration of another act of appropriation which Europa is soon to experience, namely her abduction by Zeus/bull, an act which will itself prove, finally, not contrary to her will.

When Europa awakens, as well as fear she also feels longing for the woman/land-with-no-name (25–6): 'How fondly she welcomed me, and looked at me as though at her own child.' But not only does the strange woman/land stand towards Europa in a relationship of surrogate parenthood; not only does she prefigure Europa's divine lover; she also turns out to be Europa herself; or rather, Europa will become her: no longer, then, without a name.

Europa sets off to join her girl companions, with whom she has always played when arrayed for the dance, or when she has bathed at the mouth of a stream, or picked lilies in the fields. This time her companions come to her with baskets for flowers; together they set off for their usual haunt, the meadows by the sea. Europa's basket, made of gold, represents the myth of Io, a maiden loved by Zeus.

Right on cue, Zeus steps into Europa's story too. The moment he sees her, his desire is stirred. He transforms himself into a bull, simultaneously to avoid Hera's jealousy and to deceive Europa's naïveté (79):

He hid his divinity and transformed his body (*trepse demas*) and became (*gineto*) a bull.

And what a bull: his whole body is blond, except for the white circle which gleams in the centre of his brow; his bright eyes strike with the lightning of desire; his fragrance is heavenly, lovelier by far than that of the meadow flowers. Europa caresses and kisses him, and invites her companions to join her in mounting his back. Just as they are about to do so, the bull bounds up and heads for the sea, with Europa alone on board.

In spite of the marvels surrounding the couple as the bull speeds over the sea's surface—frolicking dolphins, troops of Nereids riding sea monsters, waves smoothed by Poseidon, bridal salutations trumpeted by conch-wielding Tritons—Europa remains hesitant. But the bull reassures her (155–6): 'I am Zeus in person, even if from close to I look like (*eidomai*) a bull.' And he announces her future (158–60): 'Soon Crete will receive you—the land where I myself was raised. That is where your wedding will be celebrated.' As Crete comes into view, Zeus *palin spheterēn anelazeto morphēn*, 'took back his own [sc., we must assume, anthropomorphic] shape again' (163), leaving the poet-narrator to conclude by summarizing Europa's future: the maiden will become Zeus' bride, and the mother of his children.

Strands in the mythical web

Moschos' poem lies at the intersection of many other narratives, some of which bear directly on the theme of metamorphosis. I want to explore this point in relation to two motifs: the fate of Io, and the experiences of certain mythological heroines who were, like Europa, associated with Crete.

Moschos himself alerts us to the parallel between Europa and Io through his twenty-six-line description of Europa's golden basket. Featured in its design is the Argive maiden who, still in the form of a heifer, on wandering feet, crosses the salt paths of the sea like one swimming. So close is the link between basket and context that the metaphor of a mirror imposes itself: Europa and tauriform Zeus, Zeus and bovine Io.[25] Europa holds in her hand a variation on her own history: the history of another girl about to succumb to a god and to become a wife and mother. If this version of the girl-meets-god story is anything to judge by, the outlook for Europa is optimistic: not only is the Io myth bathed in the gleam and glamour of the golden object being described, but also the demeanour of Zeus is gentle, the eventual union entirely anthropomorphic (50–2):

And on it too was Zeus the son of Kronos lightly touching with his hands the heifer, daughter of Inachos, whom by the seven-mouthed Nile he changed back (*metameibe*) from a horned cow into a woman.

The echoes of the Io myth are inter- as well as intratextual. One text which clearly underlies, yet is strongly differentiated from, that of Moschos is *Prometheus Bound*.[26] The tragic Io, unlike Moschos' Europa, remains psychologically close to her father: she tells him her dreams and, when an oracle obliges him to drive her from home, it is against his will as well as hers.[27] The brutality of this separation is represented at the psychological level by Io's madness, and in physical terms by her metamorphosis into a cow. In Moschos, by contrast, Europa's attachment to home is weaker, her departure from that home less traumatic. Whereas Io was made wretched by her visions, Europa's dream is 'sweet', and separation from her father is mentioned only once, as late as line 147. For Europa there is no madness, no real anguish to set beside that of Io.[28]

---

[25] There are close verbal echoes at e.g. 46/114 and 50–1/95.

[26] See above, 53–6.

[27] *PV* 655–7; 671.

[28] Contrast Aesch. *Kares* (F 99 Radt), in which Europa evokes her pain at being separated from her children; cf. Gantz (1993) 210–11.

The second intertextual aspect of Moschos' poem concerns Zeus metamorphosed into a bull.[29] Europa's experience is both like and unlike that of others who interact with bulls in uncanny mythical circumstances.[30] Some bulls are standard opponents for heroes: the Cretan bull defeated by Herakles, the bull of Marathon dealt with by Theseus, the fire-breathing bulls yoked by Jason. But two bulls are more closely relevant, because they are connected with Crete, and in particular with its royal family.

From Europa onwards, Crete's royal women are represented as yearning for that which is strange.[31] Ariadne possesses this gene in a mild form: first she desires Theseus, who is distanced from her by being both a foreigner and an enemy of her father; then she is united to Dionysos, whose 'otherness' is that of an immortal as against Ariadne's (initial) mortality.[32] More unorthodox in her attraction to the strange is Minos' wife Pasiphae, who mates with a (non-transformed) bull by concealing herself in an artificial cow fabricated by Daidalos, and who subsequently gives birth to the Minotaur.[33] The unnaturalness of Pasiphae's act is expressed in the hybrid nature of her offspring, the Minotaur—quite unlike the three corporally integral heroes to whom Europa gives birth.

Phaidra, like her sister Ariadne and her mother Pasiphae, is another Cretan heroine who feels a yearning for that which is off limits, though in her case the object of desire is situated too close rather than (in species terms) too far away: her stepson Hippolytos. In keeping with the consistent *imaginaire* which haunts the Cretan royal family, the agency by which the Phaidra's illicit longings are

---

[29] Not every narrative about Europa represents the bull as a metamorphosed Zeus. Sometimes the bull is simply Zeus' emissary, as in Akousilaos *FGrH* 2 F 29, from Apollod. *Bibl.* 2.5.7; cf. Gantz (1993) 211.

[30] For a full study of bulls in their real-life and symbolic aspects in cultures of the ancient Mediterranean, see Delgado Linacero (1996) and (2007).

[31] For an exploration of this theme in Roman poetry about Cretan women, see Armstrong (2006), esp. ch. 2 ('The Call of the Wild').

[32] For variants, see Gantz (1993) 264–70.

[33] Here too *may* be a variant. According to Porphyry, Pindar related that Zeus turned *himself* into a bull—and into an eagle and a swan—in order to mate with Pasiphae (Pi. fr. 91 SM, from Porph. *Abst.* 3.16). But the text of Porphyry looks corrupt: a plausible emendation would remove all mention of Pasiphae. See Griffiths (1960); Gantz (1993) 260.

dashed is a monstrous bull from the sea, raised by Poseidon in response to Theseus' injudicious curse. In the light of the narrative of the News-bringer in Euripides' *Hippolytos*, we have no reason to regard the bull as a metamorphosed god; but it is certainly uncanny, a 'wild wonder' (*agrion teras*, 1214).

The danger and uncanniness associated with mythological bulls is plain from these examples. In the case of Moschos' *Europa*, this potential is mixed with a frisson of sexual innuendo. The fact that Europa keeps her balance by grasping the Zeus-bull's long horn (126)—a motif which is often reproduced iconographically—is a gesture which may or not be regarded as symbolically appropriate.[34] But some of the poem's other imagery is impossible to desexualize (93–6):

He stopped before the feet of the blameless Europa, and licked her neck, and enchanted the girl; and she caressed him, and with her hands tenderly wiped off the abundant foam from his mouth, and kissed the bull.

Moschos comes teasingly close to depicting bestiality, while simultaneously veering away from such an impression by reminding his readers that this is really an anthropomorphic god in disguise.[35]

Transformations of Europa

Zeus' change of shape—the metamorphosis which Moschos' poem seems most obviously to be 'about'—is only one of the transformations evoked in the poem. For Europa, too, changes. But how?

The name we have been applying to the daughter of Phoinix is the Latinized form of *Eurōpē*, the Greek word used to designate both a mythological heroine and a geographical region. Is this, then, another mythological trajectory enacted by the poem: from woman to continent? Unfortunately for such a reading, the geographical notion of Europe is—excepting only the associations evoked in the maiden's dream—quite simply absent from the poem.[36] This refusal of the

[34] See above, 79.

[35] Campbell's suggestion (1991: n. on line 95) that the 'foam' hints at a *double entendre*—oral sex between Europa and the bull—seems to me unnecessary. Even in such a sexy poem as this, there can be such a thing as interpretative overkill.

[36] For what follows, see Buxton (1992).

poem to fulfil its 'proper' role as geographical *aition* has by no means seemed acceptable to all critics, as the thrust of commentary on the end of the poem makes clear.

The poem's final couplet runs as follows (165–6):

> ἡ δὲ πάρος κούρη Ζηνὸς γένετ' αὐτίκα νύμφη,
> καὶ Κρονίδῃ τέκε τέκνα καὶ αὐτίκα γίνετο μήτηρ.

She who was formerly a young maiden became (*geneto*) forthwith the bride of Zeus. And she bore children to the son of Kronos, and became (*gineto*) forthwith a mother.

The last four words—*kai autika gineto mētēr*—have been felt by some scholars to be weak, especially in view of the repetition of *autika* from the previous line.[37] Valckenaer wanted to delete the whole of verse 166.[38] Wilamowitz, followed by Pasquali, athetized the last four words only, positing a lacuna at the end of the poem in which Moschos would have made explicit reference to the naming of the continent after the heroine.[39] Granarolo found it 'remarkable' that at the end of Moschos' poem there is no allusion to the naming of the land-mass; Hopkinson similarly observed that '[t]he conclusion is abrupt; and one might have expected a poem with this theme [what theme?] to have ended with an *aition* for the name of Europe'.[40] Yet the absence of an *aition* for the continent of Europe is in fact not surprising. In order to see why, we need to step back from the poem.

For the Greeks the geographical concept of Europe was fluid. One could speak, with Hekataios, of a binary distinction between Europe and Asia (in which case Libya, i.e. Africa, counted as part of Asia), or, with Herodotos, of a tripartite division between Europe, Asia, and Libya.[41] But these were far from being the only ways of cutting the cake. The poet of the *Homeric Hymn to Apollo* distinguished between the Peloponnese, the islands, and Europe, apparently using this last concept to designate mainland Greece (250–1; 290–1). More usually, Greece was taken to be a *part* of Europe. Yet Aristotle could *contrast*

[37] However Walther Ludwig ((1961) 186–7) found no inconcinnity in the repetition.
[38] Valckenaer (1781) 352–3.
[39] Wilamowitz-Moellendorff (1906) 100–1; Pasquali (1920) 287 n. 1.
[40] Granarolo (1979) 68; Hopkinson (1988) n. on 165–6.
[41] Hekataios *FGrH* 1, frs. on pp. 16–47 (cf. also Isoc. *Paneg.* 179); Hdt. 4.42.

the peoples of both Asia and Europe with the Greeks, on the ground that the Greeks were in a geographically intermediate—and, it goes without saying, favourable—position between the inhabitants of the other two land-masses (*Pol.* 1327ᵇ). Regardless of such differences of opinion about Europe's frontiers and constituent regions, the point which bears on our present enquiry is that the geographical idea of Europe, and consequently the notion of a European identity, were matters of little concern to most ancient Greeks. It is true that, as Arnaldo Momigliano demonstrated, the sense of 'being European' did for a brief period take on a sharper relevance in the politics of Isokrates, who saw in Philip of Macedon the champion of Europe in face of the threat from the Asiatic King of Persia.⁴² But it did not take long for this perceived political dichotomy to be subsumed under the Euro-Asiatic ecumenisms of Alexander and, after him, of Rome.⁴³ In short, for most Greeks most of the time, 'belonging to Europe' was, if it ever came to mind at all, a matter of minuscule importance compared with the ties which bound individuals to communities closer to home. To be Spartan, to be Corinthian, to be Argive: these were fundamental. To be Hellenic: this too, depending on particular historical circumstances (for example, shared external threats), might be a very significant aspect of one's identity.⁴⁴ But to be *European*?

This general lack of interest in European-ness explains the absence of an ancient Greek foundation myth for Europe. Unlike the origins of Thebes, or Athens, or Cyrene, or Arcadia, or Messenia, or dozens of other citizen-states and regions, the origins of Europe lacked a story from which a group of diverse peoples could derive a feeling of common identity. So far as genealogy is concerned, only a tiny fraction of the population of the Greek world could claim ancestry from Europa through her children Minos, Sarpedon, and Rhadamanthys: she was no Pyrrha, nor even a Pandora—not, that is, a mother-figure at the head of a pan-continental family tree. The only candidate for the status of founding myth was that which highlighted the nominal

---

⁴² Momigliano (1933).
⁴³ Momigliano (1933) 486.
⁴⁴ On Hellenic ethnicity in antiquity, see Hall (1997) and (2002).

link between heroine and continent. The *locus classicus* is Herodotos 4.45; but the historian's attitude is distinctly offhand:

As for Europe, nobody knows if it is surrounded by sea, or where it got its name from, or who gave it, unless we are to say that it came from Europa the Tyrian woman, and before that was nameless like the rest. This, however, is unlikely; for Europa was an Asiatic and never visited the country which we now call Europe, but only sailed from Phoenicia to Crete and from Crete to Lycia. But that is quite enough on this subject...[45]

The passage falls in the middle of the narrative about Darius' invasion of Scythia. Herodotos raises the question of the accuracy of mapmakers in their depiction of the continents of Asia, Libya, and Europe. After making his own observations about this, the historian puts in a brief aside about nomenclature ('Another thing that puzzles me is why three distinct women's names [namely Asia, Libya, and Europe] should have been given to what is really a single land-mass'), to which he appends his sceptical remark about the Europa/Europe etymology. In spite of Herodotos' scepticism, the link between Europe and Europa did continue to be made; but relatively rarely.[46] Myths must serve a purpose if they are to be told and retold. The greater the purpose, the more intensive and frequent the retelling. No such purpose existed to foster the construction of a grand narrative grounding Europe's identity in the world of myth.

There is, then, no need to be surprised that Moschos' tale does not culminate in the naming of a continent, nor do we need to rewrite the last two lines of the poem as if it did. The metamorphosis of Europa which the poem *actually* centres on has nothing to do with geography: it is a transformation which a young woman experiences within herself.

At the beginning of the poem, a girl who is still a virgin is slumbering in her bed in her father's house, a location wholly correct for one who is still defined by her relationship to that father ('the daughter of Phoinix', 7). But this stability is immediately disrupted by the dream sent by Aphrodite. Europa is torn between her familiar, familial past and an uncertain but beguiling future. When she wakes,

---

[45] Trans. de Sélincourt (2003).
[46] See the evidence in Bühler (1968) 39–41.

this insecurity expresses itself through an immediate restlessness and a change of scene to a flowering meadow—the location of numerous erotic encounters for the young women of Greek myth.[47] The fact that the meadow is by the sea shore intensifies the marginality of Europa's condition. But soon she will be marginalized no longer, as she makes an even more decisive (albeit involuntary) move away from her father's side, across the seeming infinity of the sea. All sense of directionality is lost: there is no land, only water, sky—and the bull, itself out of place in the middle of the ocean. But this (unlike the case of Io) is the limit of Europa's disorientation. When the bull reveals his identity, the way is open for Europa to make landfall and to reacquire a social identity, this time the identity of wife and mother. The last two lines of the poem provide not a weak ending, but one entirely suited to the development which the poem has charted. And after that? Europa, like many another mythical heroine, finds that, having given birth to a god's heroic offspring, she has nothing to look forward to but silence.[48]

---

[47] See for example Bremer (1975) and Schrier (1979).

[48] Note though the exceptional fragment of Aischylos' *Kares* referred to above (n. 28), in which Europa is far from silent. The plurality of Greek mythology is inexhaustible.

5

Post-Hellenistic Narratives

With the end of the Hellenistic era we reach a period when, above all with the work of Ovid, stories of metamorphosis narrated in Latin texts began to flourish and eventually to dominate. Yet for several centuries after Ovid composed his Metamorphoses *there continued to be produced a series of Greek explorations of the same cluster of themes, reworking and often innovating on the basis of the tradition whose lineaments I have been sketching. Indeed the range of imaginative uses to which metamorphosis was put became if anything even more diverse. In this chapter I shall attempt to show how metamorphosis was 'good to think with' regarding (1) the credibility of myths, as explored by Pausanias, (2) the debate about whether animals possess reason, as dramatized by Plutarch, (3) the interpretation of dreams, as conducted by Artemidoros. Finally, I shall turn to Nonnos, author of an extraordinary literary extravaganza which places metamorphosis at the heart of its world.*

(DIS)BELIEVING IN TRANSFORMATION

The attitudes of the great traveller and antiquarian Pausanias towards the credibility of myth are characterized by a multiplicity which reflects the demands of the shifting narrative-topographical contexts within which the expression of such attitudes is located.[1] This

---

[1] I draw here on the as yet unpublished findings of my research student Greta Hawes, whose work will significantly advance our understanding of the concept of 'rationalization' in relation to ancient myth-telling.

context dependence is exemplified in Pausanias' various reflections
on the possibility that human beings might be transformed into non-
human shape. At times he is quite prepared to express outright
disbelief, as with the alleged metamorphosis of Kyknos into a swan
(1.30.3: 'It is incredible to me that a bird should come from a man').
In other passages he gives grounds for his disbelief by using the
commonsensical tools of rationalization. Thus Tereus' grave became *the haunt of* a hoopoe, while the lamentations of Prokne and
Philomela merely *resembled the cries of* the nightingale and the
swallow (1.41.9). Elsewhere though, less conventionally, Pausanias
is prepared to accept the veracity of at least *part* of a tale of astonishing transformation, when it suits his argument to do so.
Commenting on the gruesome myth of the cannibal-turned-wolf
Lykaon, he remarks (8.2.4): 'This tale persuades me. It has been
told in Arcadia from ancient times and has likelihood on its side.'
But he is not persuaded by the *whole* of the tale. The parts which do
convince him are those which narrate Lykaon's sacrifice of a newborn
baby on Zeus' altar, and the transgressor's subsequent transformation
into a wolf (*genesthai lukon*) (8.2.3). Why does Pausanias find just
these things credible at *this* point in his narrative? Because they allow
him to illustrate a contrast between 'ancient times' and his own day.
In ancient times people sat with the gods at table and, in virtue of this
proximity, were rewarded for good behaviour and punished for bad.
In such an environment, not only Lykaon's transformation but also
Niobe's might be held to be believable (8.2.5). In Pausanias' own
time, by contrast, 'when wickedness has increased to the last
degree'—as has, by implication, the distance between gods and
humans—the deification of mortals is no longer credible, nor is their
punishment by the gods an immediate prospect. A corollary of the
difference between then and now is the fact that the old myths have
been elaborated out of all proportion: Pausanias gives as examples
the assertions that, in the wake of Lykaon, each year someone turns
temporarily into a wolf at the sacrifice performed for Lykaian Zeus,
and that the stone Niobe on Mount Sipylos still weeps. Pausanias'
conclusion from all this is, for him, unusually outspoken (8.2.7):
'People who enjoy listening to mythical stories are naturally disposed
to add even more wonders of their own (*epiterateuesthai*); in this way

they have corrupted the truth, which they have mixed up with a lot of lies.'

The driving force behind this passage—the then/now contrast—enables Pausanias to express scepticism about deification (and hence, presumably, about the notion of ruler cult). More striking, and perhaps to us surprising, is the fact that the argument does not lead him to disbelieve in the original metamorphoses of Lykaon and Niobe, only in some contemporary ramifications of those metamorphoses. But in fact there is nothing surprising about Pausanias' strategy. From our earliest Greek texts onwards we constantly find writers who reason about myths, discriminating here and there in respect of credibility. Classic cases are Herodotos (on Io, Medea, and Helen (1.5): 'That is what the Persians and Phoenicians relate. As for me, I do not propose to say whether these events happened like this or in another way, but rather I shall rely on what I know'), Thucydides (on the Trojan War (1.11): the expedition was actually less important than it has been—and still is—made out to be by the poets), and Euripides (e.g. *Herakles* 1340–6, where the great hero maintains that stories of divine immorality are 'the wretched lies of bards'). Pausanias is no less capable of exercising his reason. What is significant for us, however, is that, precisely when he is in 'rationalizing mode', he accepts that, once upon a time, humans *did* turn into non-human forms. Anyone tempted to deny that Greeks—intelligent, articulate Greeks such as Pausanias—could sometimes hold the notion of metamorphosis to be credible has the impossible task of disregarding the present passage.

GRUNTER'S REASON

If the credibility of mythology was one of the matters which metamorphosis was used to think about, another was the distinction between humans and animals. This latter question was of course explored in a broad range of contexts at every period of antiquity.[2]

---

[2] See Dierauer (1977); Sorabji (1993); Cassin and Labarrière (1997); Gilhus (2006).

But in the Graeco-Roman world such exploration intensified. One work which makes a novel and wry contribution in this area is Plutarch's smart dialogue *On the Use of Reason by Irrational Animals,* sometimes referred to as *Gryllos* in recognition of its most distinctive character. This work stands foursquare within the metamorphic tradition, yet at the same time its tone sets it at an ironical distance from earlier treatments of the theme. Above all, it rests upon and simultaneously plays with the *Odyssey.* Plutarch's imagined prolongation of the encounter between Odysseus and Circe centres on the trenchantly expressed views of Gryllos ('Grunter'), one of Odysseus' ex-crewmen now transformed into a pig.

The dialogue begins with a spat between Circe and Odysseus in the course of what is evidently a long-running battle of wits between the two. 'Why do we so often have to argue about the same things?', grumbles Odysseus, in response to Circe's complaint that he has spurned a life of agelessness beside her in favour of a wish to return to his ageing spouse in Ithaca. When Odysseus counters by asking Circe to liberate his men from their confinement in animal form, she rejoins that he might at least ask his men whether they *want* to be re-transformed. At the stroke of her wand she lends human voice to one of the porcine ex-humans, so amending in one crucial respect the Homeric relationship between continuity and change in the metamorphic state, as well as implicitly echoing Ovid's perception—and anticipating Kafka's—of the centrality of the human voice to the manner in which transformation is perceived.

Inverting the *Odyssey*'s privileging of the human over the bestial, and showing no deference whatever to his erstwhile leader, Gryllos tells Odysseus that he prefers his current existence to his former life as a man. Is Odysseus right to assume that Circe has affected Gryllos' mind as well as his shape, to induce him to express this preference? The text gives no answer. At any rate, as Gryllos depicts it, a pig's life is far from beastly. His mental capacities are impressive, and his adeptness at sophistical argument makes him more than a match for Odysseus (988d):

And, to sum up, if you think that you are superior in courage to the beasts, why do your poets call the best fighters 'wolf-minded' and 'lion-hearted' and 'like a boar in valour', though none of them ever calls a lion 'human-hearted' or a boar 'like a man in valour'?

Again, striking closer to home (989a):

As for the chastity of Penelope, countless cawing crows will pour ridicule and scorn on it; for every crow, if her mate dies, remains a widow, not just for a short time, but for nine human generations. So your fair Penelope is nine times inferior in chastity to any crow you like to mention.

The dialogue plays with the philosophical tradition about the question: 'Do animals possess reason?'[3] Where does Plutarch himself stand in relation to this debate? It is enormously difficult to get behind the dialogue form to reach what we might crudely call 'Plutarch's views' on the matter since, as Robert Lamberton puts it, 'the dialogue with its polyphony allows Plutarch to present multiple solutions to a given question and to keep them in balance, in tension with one another, without conceding that they are mutually exclusive'.[4] If we do attempt to uncover a Plutarchan attitude, it is likely that Marina Warner has made the best guess in her elegant and shrewd discussion. Advising us against an excessively moralistic reading of *Gryllos* as an attack on man's inhumanity to animals, she more plausibly stresses the ironical tone, characterizing the work as 'an inspired early satire in the great fabric of the literature of folly'.[5] The work is certainly great fun, casting, as it does, Gryllos in the role of a Teiresias figure, able to comment on the merits and demerits of two forms of existence, having experienced both of them (986e). Like Kafka's Gregor Samsa, Gryllos finds that his tastes have changed after metamorphosis: the artificial pleasures of elaborate clothing or gold and silver hold no joy for him; better, and more natural, to relax in deep, soft mud (989e). It is as if he only truly comes into his own after his transformation: significantly, we have no idea of the name he had before he became 'Grunter'.

For all its jauntiness, *Gryllos* is yet one more imaginative work which fosters a sense of the potential continuity between the diverse shapes of being. Such a continuity is not, to be sure, presented as unlimited: specifically, it is confined to animals not plants—at least according to Gryllos, who argues that every tree is identical to every other tree insofar as all are equally insensible and soulless (992d). But

---

[3] See Sorabji (1993); Kindstrand (1998).
[4] Lamberton (2001) 26. [5] Warner (1998) 274.

Gryllos unquestionably forms part of the metamorphic tradition, exemplifying—as Aristophanes had done long before, though in a quite different vein—that comedy is one of the modes in which transformation can be seriously depicted.

DREAMING OF CHANGE

Imagined changes of form unquestionably played a part in the dream experiences of ancient Greeks. In the nature of things we can have no direct access to such experiences, only indirect representations of them, embedded in literary texts with their own generic and specific imperatives. Nor can we say what proportion of dreams had a metamorphic quality. However, texts from different periods and genres preserve accounts of dreams centring on the notion of transformation. I have already analysed Penelope's elaborate and richly symbolic dream in *Odyssey* Book 19, in which the geese-slaying eagle identifies itself as Odysseus.[6] I also discussed the punning exchange between Sosias and Xanthias at the beginning of *Wasps,* in which the two slaves recall a pair of politically charged metamorphic dreams which came to them the previous night.[7] It is not difficult to add other examples. In Euripides' *Iphigeneia in Tauris* Iphigeneia reports a dream in which she imagined the whole of her house collapsing, except for one column, which 'let fair hair fall upon its capital and took on human voice'—the voice, of course, of Orestes (44–58). More amusingly, Socrates dreamed that Plato turned into a crow, which jumped on to his head and pecked at his bald spot.[8] Restlessly intelligent as always, Augustine would try out an explanation for the metamorphic quality of dreams. He suggested that each person has a 'phantom' which, in his imagination or in his dreams, takes on various forms under the influence of varying circumstances.[9]

Were transformational dreams regarded as significant and even, if correctly interpreted, veridical? It is impossible to give a blanket answer.

---

[6] See 44–5 above. [7] See 73–5 above.
[8] Athen. *Deipn.* 507c–d; Riginos (1976) 54–5; Miller (1994) 3.
[9] August. *C.D.* 18.18; cf. Miller (1994) 41–2.

Clearly, *some* Greeks considered such dreams to be empty. In a passage from Plato's *Theaitetos*, people who dream of being winged and of having the ability to fly are dismissed by the Platonic Socrates as delusional (158b). Penelope herself is deeply sceptical about the reliability of the geese-and-eagle dream: it is, she feels, unlikely to have emerged from the 'gates of polished horn', the passageway for true dreams (*Od.* 19.560–9). But at least, on Penelope's reading, *some* dreams *are* predictive. It all depends on the interpreter.

Artemidoros (second century AD) was such a dream-interpreter. This sane, practical, and intelligent man wrote as a practitioner, but he also developed theories of dream classification.[10] In keeping with a dominant assumption in antiquity, he investigated the predictive, future-oriented quality of dreams, while sensibly observing that some dreams (which he called *enhupnia*) are present-oriented: a thirsty man dreams of drinking, a lover dreams of his beloved, and so forth (1.1).[11] Of other dreams Artemidoros posited that they might stand in an allegorical relationship to the future, signifying one thing by another. Dreams about metamorphosis, of which there are many in Artemidoros' book, constitute one type of allegory.

Usually an implicit logic can be discerned in the relationship between the dreamed metamorphosis and the outcome which Artemidoros predicts from it. Sometimes this logic is so common-sensical that it might seem hardly to require the services of an interpreter. Thus a man dreamed that he rose up and flew towards a place which he was eager to reach; then, on arrival, he imagined that he had wings and was flying with the birds; finally he flew back home (1.4). Unlike the Socrates of *Theaitetos*, Artemidoros treats this dream with matter-of-fact pragmatism. 'In real life,' he observes, 'the man emigrated from his homeland, as was indicated by the flight, and, since he got to his destination, he was successful in the business projects which he pursued with great industry.'[12] However, if all interpretations could be read off so easily from dream narratives,

---

[10] See Pack (1955); P. Brown (1978) 38–41; Lane Fox (1986) 155–8; Martin (1991); R. J. White (1975) 7; Miller (1994) 77–91.

[11] Future-oriented: see Price (2004).

[12] Trans. R. J. White (1975). I have borrowed from or adapted this translation in other passages below.

the interpreter would soon be out of a job. Fortunately for him, this is not the case, since sometimes the nature of the presumed allegory is rather obscure (1.20): 'If a person dreams that he has hog's bristles, it portends dangers that are violent and similar to those which the creature itself, the hog, I mean, encounters.' Or it may be more enigmatic still (1.24): 'To dream that one has the ears of an ass is auspicious only for philosophers, because an ass does not move his ears quickly.' Whether or not Artemidoros was speaking tongue-in-cheek in this case, the client will doubtless have felt the fee to be well spent.

When Artemidoros' clients report metamorphosis dreams, his interpretation hardly ever involves an explicit reference to mythology. It is not Artemidoros' style to explain *obscurum per obscurius*, but rather to make robust sense of an apparently extraordinary vision by relating it to features of everyday and contemporary human experience. However, on rare occasions myth is invoked as an explanatory factor (2.12):

A bear signifies a woman. For the authors of the metamorphosis myths (*hoi peri metamorphōseōn muthologēsantes*) say that Kallisto the Arcadian was changed (*metabalein*) into this animal.

But surely citing Kallisto provides not so much an explanation as a further *explanandum*? Doubtless aware of this, Artemidoros adds that dreaming of a bear

also portends sickness because of its savage nature, and movements and travel, since it has the same name as the ever-moving constellation. On the other hand, it prophesies that a man will linger in the same place. For the star always revolves in the same place and does not set.

The explanation remains within the framework of the plausible, while keeping one step ahead of what the non-expert client might have been able to come up with.

Notwithstanding differences of genre, Pausanias, Plutarch, and Artemidoros each use the possibility of astonishing transformation as a vehicle for intellectual appreciation of, and affective engagement with, the world of everyday belief and action. With the final voice in our discussion of post-Hellenistic writers, however, we enter a new imaginative register. Metamorphosis remains good to think with—and above all good to feel with—but the tones and colours are new and more intense. This is a voice like no other.

IS RIPENESS ALL?

The poet Nonnos, author of the forty-eight-book epic *Dionysiaka*, originated from Egyptian Panopolis, and composed in the mid-fifth century AD.[13] Combining an expansive and relentlessly feverish account of the exploits of Dionysos with a retelling of many myths apparently related only tangentially to the central theme, Nonnos' gigantic poem has encouraged critics to employ terms verging on the personally abusive.[14] 'The mythology of the *Dionysiaka*', wrote H. J. Rose in 1940, 'is interesting as being the longest and most elaborate example we have of Greek myths in their final stage of degeneracy.' Rose went on to situate Nonnos at the end of a process which he identified as having begun at the beginning of the Alexandrian age, a process in which 'belief' in the myths had ceased 'among educated people' ('save perhaps as allegories'), leaving only a collection of 'picturesque tales'.[15] What Nonnos produces in his *Dionysiaka* is, in Rose's view, 'a faded and overcrowded tapestry, moving a little now and then as the breath of his sickly and unwholesome fancy stirs it'.[16]

It was inevitable that such a wholesale dismissal would eventually be the subject of reconsideration. This has now become possible thanks to the heroic labour of editing and commentary undertaken by Francis Vian and his research team, and is manifested in, for example, the literary-critical re-evaluations collected in a group of essays edited by Neil Hopkinson, as well as in an earlier chapter by Glen Bowersock.[17] It is certainly true that one of the assumptions

---

[13] For the date, see Vian et al. (1976–2006) i, pp. xv–xviii.

[14] I borrow the notion of fever from Fauth (1981) 115: 'In Nonnos' entire poem there is scarcely a single character who behaves in a "normal", undisturbed manner. Nearly all of them act as if in a fever, with an intense, almost hysterical excitation of the emotions and appetites.'

[15] Rose in Rouse (1940–2) i, p. x.

[16] Rose in Rouse (1940–2) i, p. xii.

[17] See Vian et al. (1976–2006); Hopkinson (1994); Bowersock (1990) 41–53.

underpinning Rose's negative view—the assumption of a progressive decline in mythological belief—would today be regarded as highly problematic: at best it raises as many problems as it solves.[18] Yet when it comes to the more specific question of the evaluation of Nonnos' extraordinary composition, it is less evident that Rose's strictures are without foundation. The *Dionysiaka* continues to present major obstacles for even the most sympathetic of readers.

To get a flavour of these obstacles—which are as much moral as stylistic—we may turn to the poem's final, forty-eighth book. At its characteristically protracted climax Dionysos is shown pursuing and raping Aura, an Atalanta-like companion of Artemis. Thirsty after her exertions as a huntress, Aura gets drunk on a fountain of wine which Dionysos has craftily caused to spring out of the earth; when she is no longer capable of resistance, he ties the legs and arms of his sleeping victim before forcing himself upon her (590–634). Greek mythology is seldom morally uncomplicated, and it is undeniably relevant that Aura is being punished for a rash insult to Artemis, whose breasts she had mocked for their Aphrodite-esque softness and fullness, unlike Aura's own tougher, more Athene-like breasts (349–52); as a result, Artemis has persuaded Nemesis to intervene to sanction Aura's punishment, which is precipitated when Dionysos is shot by Eros' arrow. Even Dionysos' action of tying Aura up is not spontaneous, since he is prompted by the whispered words of a Hamadryad beside whose tree the tired god has sought midday rest (514–26). But it remains true that Dionysos is represented, without a hint of authorial criticism, as carrying out an act of unambiguous sexual aggression for which he shows no remorse, and whose consequences are horrifying: the distraught Aura first tries to provoke an abortion and then, when she is delivered of twin boys, leaves them in a lioness's den to be devoured. Even though a panther, presumably symbolizing Dionysos himself, nurses the two babies, Aura eats one of her offspring herself in a demented frenzy. The life of the other, Iacchos, is preserved by Artemis, whose earlier cruel mocking of Aura's pregnancy does not prevent her from being shocked at Aura's infanticidal brutality.

---

[18] See Buxton (1994) 155–65.

The outcome of this saga appears to resolve matters in ways which echo inherited patterns of Greek myth and ritual (albeit with characteristically Nonnian elaboration). Aura arrives at the traditional metamorphic condition of closure-with-permanence when she throws her bow, her quiver, and finally herself into the River Sangarios (935–42):

and the son of Kronos turned her (*metameipsen*) into a fountain: her breasts were a spring of water pouring from a mountain source, her body was a stream, her hair was flowers, her bow the horn of the finely horned river in bull-shape, the bowstring changed into (*ameibomenē*) a rush and the whistling arrows into vocal reeds, the quiver passed through to the muddy bed of the river and, as a hollow channel, poured its sounding waters.

Aura's son Iacchos achieves the rare distinction of being suckled by Athene, and goes on to be revered at Eleusis alongside his father (955–68). As for Dionysos, his thoughts immediately revert from Aura to an earlier love, in whose eternal honour he brings about a metamorphosis more distinguished than that achieved by Aura: Ariadne's crown is placed in Olympos, 'an everlasting proclaimer of garlanded wedding' (973). Thereafter Dionysos takes his seat on Olympos, drinking nectar beside Apollo and Hermes. On that note the epic ends.

The three protagonists in this domestic drama—mother, father, son—'move on' in their various ways. What is less easy is for the reader, too, to move on. Not that there is a problem about accepting that Dionysos' outrageous conduct can be compatible with his status as an Olympian: in the mythological tradition there are, after all, countless examples of equally reprehensible divine behaviour, for example Apollo's treatment of Kreousa in Euripides' *Ion*. The problem is, rather, to accept that Dionysos' treatment of Aura can deservedly stand as the culmination of Nonnos' universalizing hymn of praise in honour of the god.

One critical strategy for rescuing Nonnos from evaluative oblivion has involved aesthetics rather than morality: namely, to single out the redundancy of the work not for blame but for celebration. Emphasis has often been placed on the compositional keynote struck by the poet himself at line 15 of Book 1, when he describes his work as a *poikilon humnon*, a song characterized by 'diversity'. Complementary to this stylistic trait is one of the centres of poetic energy permeating the whole work, a quality whose importance far exceeds any designation as a mere 'theme': namely the evocation of various types of multiplicity of form.[19] One aspect of this multiplicity is hybridity, as in the case of Typhoeus (2.252–6):

When the monster arrayed himself in all his manifold shapes, there rang out the howling of wolves, the roaring of lions, the grunting of boars, the lowing of cattle, the hissing of snakes, the bold gaping of leopards, the jaws of bears ready to bite, the rabidity of dogs.

Yet it is not hybridity but metamorphosis which dominates the poem. In the Typhoeus episode itself, the monster's disruptive power is shown as extending to the world of vegetation, including laurel, pine, and anemone: the disruption thus causes grief to the former divine lovers of these plants, namely Apollo (Daphne), Pan (Pitys), and Aphrodite (Adonis) (2.81–90). In the same Typhoean context a Hamadryad considers the advantages and disadvantages of escaping from the monster via metamorphosis, following the examples of Philomela, Prokne, Komaitho (turned into a stream), Myrrha, the Heliades, and Niobe (2.130–62).

The prominence of metamorphosis in the *Dionysiaka*[20] is signalled already in the opening invocation to Proteus, which immediately follows the reference to the *poikilon humnon*, and places Proteus' virtuosity of form alongside both Dionysos' own variegated actions and Nonnos' capacity to encompass those variegations poetically (1.16–25):[21]

For if, as a snake, Proteus should slither along his winding trail, I will sing of the divine combat in which Dionysos, with ivy-wreathed wand, destroyed the bristling hosts of serpent-haired Giants. If as a lion Proteus should shake his hairy mane, I will cry 'Euhoi' to Bacchos who, on the arm of burly Rheia, stealthily sucks the breast of the goddess who suckles lions. If as a leopard Proteus should bound up into the air with an impetuous leap of his paws, changing his variable shape, I will hymn the son of Zeus, telling how he

---

[19] For *poikilia* (variegation) in the poem, see Fauth (1981) 20–2.

[20] See Fauth (1981) *passim*.

[21] See Hopkinson in Hopkinson (1994) 10–11, for parallels between Proteus, Dionysos, and Nonnos himself. Fauth ((1981) 37–8) sees the Proteus prelude as anticipating the kaleidoscopic shifts and changes characteristic of the whole work.

slew the Indian race, riding down the elephants with his leopard-drawn chariot...

And so it goes on, with Proteus in the form of boar, water, and tree, and the Nonnian Dionysos capable of effortlessly outstripping any such virtuosity.

Nonnos' prolixity locates him at the opposite end of the stylistic spectrum to the mythographer Apollodoros, whose bare-bones compendium makes no attempt to subordinate the entire world of mythology to just one mythological theme or figure, in the way that Nonnos does. Yet for all their differences Nonnos shares with Apollodoros, albeit implicitly, the aim of integrating the whole mythological web into the fabric of his own composition. The same might be said of Ovid in his *Metamorphoses*, a work which some have seen as having influenced Nonnos.[22] Although that question of influence is unresolved, what is not in doubt is the extent to which Nonnos, far more comprehensively than Apollodoros although evidently less so than Ovid, adopts metamorphosis as one of the foci of his narrative. By looking at some examples, we can see how Nonnos idiosyncratically revisits some of the tales of miraculous change which we have examined earlier in this study.

Book 5 contains Nonnos' account of the transformation and death of Aktaion (whose relevance is that he is a child of Autonoe, one of Dionysos' aunts). The extended account of the process of metamorphosis is further prolonged by an account of the dead hunter appearing to his sleeping father Aristaios as a ghost-dream in the shape of a stag (412–14), and by the lamentations of Aktaion's mother Autonoe, who kisses the hairy lips of her still-cerviform son (548). Such a conceit might be thought outlandish, but one of the effects of Nonnos' poetical style is to remove all sense of the astonishing. Or rather, where *everything* is astonishing, no individual episode stands out as arousing *thambos*. Aktaion's metamorphosis illustrates a basic aspect of the Nonnian poetic universe: not only *can* things change into other things, they usually do.

---

[22] Cf. Fauth ((1981) 17 nn. 47 and 48) for references to bibliography for and against the idea of Ovidian influence. Hollis ((1994) 57) prefers the view that both Ovid and Nonnos were influenced by lost Hellenistic metamorphosis poetry.

Many metamorphoses in the poem involve the self-transformations of the gods, as when, early in Book 1, the poet narrates Zeus'
abduction of Europa. Although this encounter between a god and a
heroine is free from the agony which befell Aura, the maiden speeding on bull-back across the sea is not untroubled: Europa 'trembles
with fear' (56). However, the emphasis is not on her emotions, but
rather on the sight of a partially clothed young woman riding a bull
while gripping its horn, combined with the paradoxical image of a
land animal moving over water, a sight which a passing sailor calls a
thauma (93). Unlike Moschos, Nonnos is unconcerned with portray-
ing the gradual sexual awakening of the adolescent Europa, but he
does elaborate on the sequel to her abduction. Leaving his bovine
shape, Zeus assumes the appearance of a young man, who undresses
Europa and lies with her. As for the bull, it loses neither identity nor
shape, but is transformed into a constellation, as an eternal sign of
the power of self-transformation of the supreme Olympian.

The account of Zeus' liaison with Europa is by no means the only
reference to his metamorphic amours. In order to bed Persephone
and so engender Zagreus, Zeus turns himself into a serpent (5.566;
6.155–68); Zagreus is killed and chopped up by the Titans and then
appears 'in another shape and changed into many forms' (*allophuēs
morphouto polusperes eidos ameibōn*, 6.176), including that of a bull,
in which form the Titans eventually kill him again. But such episodes
are dwarfed by the 800-line treatment of Zeus' relationship with
Semele: nor is this expansiveness surprising, since their son is the
focal point of the epic. As the ancient god of Time, Aion, points out
to Zeus, what is lacking in the human world is a liquid which will heal
sorrow and bring joy (7.55–66). The gods have nectar; but mortals?
Zeus agrees to bring wine into existence; and, in order for there to be
wine, there must first be the god of wine.

Struck by Eros' arrow, Zeus lusts after Semele, whom he spies
bathing in the river Asopos. So begins a sequence of metamorphoses,
although paradoxically this myth turns on the fact that Zeus will, at
the climactic moment, *not* self-transform. First, though, Zeus turns
into an eagle, through whose sharp eyes he inspects his intended
lover (7.210–21). Then, swift as thought, he comes to her bed.
For the love-making which will lead to the conception of Dionysos,
Zeus mitigates his full divinity in a riot of animal and vegetable

metamorphoses which anticipate the natural realm over which the soon-to-be-born divinity will preside (319–35):

At one moment he leaned over the bed, with a horned head on human limbs, lowing with the voice of a bull, the very imitation of bullhorned Dionysos. Again, he put on the form (*dusato morphēn*) of a shaggy lion; at another time he was a panther, like one who sires a bold son, driver of panthers and charioteer of lions. Again, as a young bridegroom he bound his hair with coiling snakes and vine-leaves intertwined, and twisted purple ivy about his locks, the plaited ornament of Bacchos. A writhing serpent crawled over the trembling bride and licked her rosy neck with gentle lips, then slipping into her bosom girdled the circuit of her firm breasts, hissing a wedding tune, and sprinkled her with sweet honey of the swarming bees instead of the viper's deadly poison. Zeus' love-making was prolonged and, as if the winepress were near, he shouted 'Euhoi!' as he sired his son who would love that cry.[23]

As he ejaculates, Zeus shouts out the Bacchic cry of 'Euhoi'—a striking Nonnian *coup* by which the father becomes the son whom he is engendering. Of the feelings of Semele in reaction to all this intimately invasive strangeness, we hear nothing: they are not Nonnos' concern.

Once Semele is pregnant, however, she does become the focus of the poet's attention. As Zeus had become Dionysos during his love-making, so Semele too is transformed by the power of the god whom she is carrying. She roams the mountains like a maenad; she mimics the bellowing of bulls; she dances with Pan; and she attracts the attention of Phthonos ('Envy'). Putting on 'the false *morphēn* of a counterfeit Ares', Phthonos stirs up the resentment of Athene and especially Hera (8.39). Zeus' consort alters her shape (*demas morphouto*, 8.182) to resemble that of an old nurse ('honey-tongued', 181, a very unusual, almost oxymoronic description for an old woman in Greek mythological narrative). In this guise Hera persuades Semele to be dissatisfied if her divine lover comes to her in any less glory than that in which he visits Hera: amid fire and thunder and lightning. Semele reproaches Zeus in the same terms: 'Bridegroom, you who delight in thunder! You go to Hera's bed

---

[23] Here, and on occasions elsewhere, I have adapted the translation by Rouse (1940–2).

with divine appearance (*eidos*), illuminating your bride with the lightnings of marriage in a chamber brilliant with many lights—fiery Zeus! But to Semele you come as dragon or a bull.'[24] In an ultimate act of naïveté, Semele touches the thunderbolt (391). She is incinerated, confirming one of the constant lessons of the mythological tradition, that relations between gods and mortals can normally be conducted only if the mitigating shield of metamorphosis intervenes between the parties. As Zeus had earlier pointed out (362–6):

> I was not wielding the lightning when I took Danae's maidenhood; no booming thunder, no thunderbolts celebrated the wedding of your ancestress Europa, the Tyrian bride; the cow, Inachos' daughter, saw no flame; you alone, a mortal, demand from me what the goddess Leto did not ask.

But at last Semele is translated to the stars, which entitles her to the immortality enjoyed by the Olympians (407–18). Catasterism is yet another of the modes of metamorphosis evoked in the poem.[25]

As well as shifting shape for sexual gratification, as in the myths of Europa and Semele (and also that of Io, where Zeus touches the maiden 'with love-crazed hands', 3.286), the gods of the *Dionysiaka* also self-transform from other motives. Escape is one, as when Apollo evades Typhon by turning into a swan (2.218–20). Again, there are examples of divinities turning into persuasively human shape, a motif which recurs with typical Nonnian expansiveness in Book 4, when Aphrodite, wearing the love-robe of Persuasion, takes on the appearance (*demas ison eisketo*) of the local girl Peisinoe ('Persuade-the-mind') so as to convince Harmonia to go away with Kadmos (72); or when Ares temporarily adopts the guise (terms used are *tupos*, *morphē*, and *mimēma*) of the warrior Modaios, a blood-thirsty human equivalent of the war-god himself (42.165; 170–1).

But it is Dionysos' own transformative powers which dominate the narrative, both when he alters his own shape and when his presence transmutes that which is around him. Like his father he sometimes shifts shape for erotic purposes. At one point he is lovesick for the

---

[24] 8.320 ff.; the same point is made, with small variations, for another twenty-five lines.

[25] See e.g. 3.351–4, where Harmonia's nurse Elektra, one of the daughters of Atlas, entertains the hope of undergoing catasterism along with her sister Pleiades.

Lebanese nymph Beroe, offspring of the union between Adonis and Aphrodite. When Dionysos appears to her in the form of a young and modest hunter, the narrator makes a point of emphasizing that this is not the god's normal mode of transformation (42.140–2): 'Where are your terrifying horns? Where are the green, snaky bindings of earth-nourished serpents in your hair? Where is your deep-booming bellow?' Perhaps it is appropriate that this un-Dionysos-like suit is unsuccessful: Dionysos is in rivalry with Poseidon for Beroe's affections, and at long last loses out. But when Dionysos exerts powers of transformation which more fully express his nature, he is formidably effective. In combat with the Indian king Deriades he adopts a seemingly inexhaustible range of animal and vegetable shapes (36.292 ff.). Another example is his punishment of the Etruscan pirates. Having first lured them into capturing him by taking the false, literally 'bastard', form (*nothēn...morphēn*, 45.120) of a smooth-skinned, jewel-bedecked boy, he explodes into action surrounded by animal and vegetable life (133–43):

Suddenly the lad grew tall with marvellous form (*morphēi*), that of a man with horned head rising up to Olympos, touching the canopy of airy clouds, and with booming throat roared as loud as an army of nine thousand men. The long hawsers were trailing snakes, changed into (*morphōthentes*) live serpents twisting their bodies about; the forestays hissed; up into the air a horned viper ran along the mast to the yard in trailing coils; near the sky, the mast was a tall cypress with a shade of green leaves; ivy sprang up from the mastbox and ran into the sky...

The description continues luxuriantly amid grapes, bulls, and lions, to be rounded off when the pirates leap into the sea as dolphins.

The most emblematic metamorphosis of all is that of Dionysos' favourite, Ampelos. The relationship between the two is intensely sensual: at one point the pair take part in a Lawrentian naked wrestling match (10.330–82). But all good things come to an end, and Ampelos is tossed, trampled, and gored to death by a wild bull. The narrative of his death is framed by abundant examples of the poem's trademark metamorphoses. The goddess Ate disguises herself as one of Ampelos' age-mates in order to persuade him to adopt the rash course of riding a wild bull (11.113–54). Eros comforts Dionysos having assumed the contrasting form of hairy Silenos, the consolatory tale he relates being that of the romantic lovers Kalamos and Karpos, changed after death into respectively the reed and the fruit-of-the-earth to which they give their names (11.351–483). One of the Horai sees, recorded on the astrological calendar which Helios keeps in his house,[26] prophecies of a host of metamorphoses, including those of many-eyed Argos, Harpalyke,[27] Philomela, Niobe, and Krokos[28] (12.70–102). The culmination of all this is the transformation of Ampelos himself, changed into the plant which gives rise to Dionysos' own liquid (12.173–80):

Then a great astonishment (*mega thambos*) appeared to the eyes of sorrowful Bacchos. For Ampelos, the lovely corpse, rose of his own accord, writhing like a snake, and changed his own shape (*heēn ēllaxato morphēn*) into a plant that heals pain.[29] As the dead body changed, his belly was a very long vine-stock, his fingers grew into tendrils, his feet took root, his curls were grape-clusters, his very fawnskin changed shape (*emorphōthē*) into the rich flourishing of the growing fruit.

Usually the word *thambos* is used to designate the reaction of mortals when the sacred bursts in upon them; but here Nonnos uses it to describe Dionysos' own reaction, as if to emphasize that this occurrence *really is* astonishing.

In her discussion of differences between Greek narratives of metamorphosis and those by Ovid, Françoise Frontisi-Ducroux stresses the 'punctual', 'aoristic', duration-free quality which characterizes most Greek accounts, as opposed to the processual accounts by Ovid, which, in her view, anticipate the later conception of time as infinitely gradual.[30] While this generalization holds up to a point, it fails to do justice to Nonnos, who loves to make his readers linger long over changes of shape and state. And he yields first place to no one, not even Ovid, in the luxuriance of his imagination. Of no episode is this truer than that featuring Ampelos, which concludes

---

[26] See Vian et al. (1976–2006) v, n. on 12.30–5.

[27] After being raped by her father, Harpalyke served up the resulting child to him at a meal. She was turned into the *chalkis*-bird (perhaps an owl). See Lightfoot (1999) on Parthen. *Amat. narr.* 13.

[28] See 219 below.

[29] For the word *anthos* as meaning 'plant' rather than 'flower', see Gerbeau and Vian in Vian et al. (1976–2006) vii, on 18.54–6.

[30] Frontisi-Ducroux (2003) 84–93.

with Dionysos squeezing the dark red juices from his former beloved and drinking deeply of them.

My account of Nonnos brings to an end the first part of this book, in which I have examined how metamorphosis was represented within different narrative contexts. In Part II I shall examine a number of cross-contextual themes, not in order to diminish the importance of a contextualizing account, but in order to look for recurrent patterns which transcend the confines of particular modes of expression.

Part II

The Logic of Transformation

6

Shapes of the Gods

We have already noticed many individual cases of the transformation of Greek divinities: gods who change into birds in Homeric epic; multiform Dionysos in tragedy and in Nonnos; contrasting evocations of the transformed Zeus in visual art and in Moschos; self-changing nymphs in Apollonios. In the first half of the present chapter I comment on three more aspects of the relationship between metamorphosis and Greek notions of divinity: namely, the gods' motivation for changing their form, the astonishment generated by their self-changing, and the possibility that certain gods are especially prone to change. In the second part of the chapter I suggest, against the background of some comparative material, how metamorphosis stories can be brought to bear on the question: how anthropomorphic was Greek religion?

A feature of many religious traditions—perhaps of all of them, each after its own fashion—is the quest to explore the relationship between unity and plurality: to look for an underlying pattern of sacred explanation which might account for the boundless diversity of the phenomenal world. In ancient Greece the interplay of unity with plurality in the religious tradition expresses itself in three main ways. (1) There was a tension between, on the one hand, the almost inexhaustible local variations in the identities of various divinities, as manifested in their cult epithets, and, on the other hand, the drive, as evidenced especially by the ambitions of mythological poetry and art, towards a greater degree of panhellenic commonality of perception about the nature and characteristics of the gods. During the ascendancy of structuralist interpretation, much valuable work was done in looking for the unifying factors underpinning the characteristic types of power ascribed to particular gods. At present, however, more emphasis tends to be laid on the enormous degree of variability in local cult. Thus Robert Parker, a leading contemporary scholar of Greek religion, wrote in 2005 that 'Greek polytheism is indescribable... Gods overflowed like clothes from an over-filled drawer which no one felt obliged to tidy.'[1] (2) Certain ancient thinkers attempted to look behind and beneath the plurality of the gods of common belief, arguing that true divinity should be seen as characterized by Oneness. We shall discuss this strategy in more detail in Chapter 9, especially in relation to the Presocratics and Plato. (3) Numerous though the divinities of the Greek polytheistic system may already have been, they were susceptible of further and almost limitless multiplication, at least to the eye of the beholder, since the same divinity might manifest him- or herself in a variety of forms. This phenomenon is at the centre of our concerns in this book.

WHY DO THE GODS TRANSFORM THEMSELVES?

The most notorious motive which prompts the gods to undergo metamorphosis is erotic passion. A useful starting point is the myth of Semele, which encapsulates much that is central to divine/human relations as portrayed in Greek mythological narratives.[2]

Apollodoros' summary goes to the heart of the matter (3.4.3):

Now Zeus had agreed to do whatever Semele asked. Deceived by Hera, Semele asked Zeus to come to her just as he had come to Hera when he was wooing her. Unable to refuse, Zeus came to Semele's bedroom in a chariot along with lightning and thunder, and hurled a thunderbolt.

Semele's explosive fate starkly exposes the incommensurability of the human and the divine. Nothing mitigates Zeus' power; nothing insulates Semele from his electricity.[3] Although Zeus' preliminary

---

[1] Parker (2005) 387. A valuable attempt to balance local with panhellenic considerations is to be found in Price (1999).

[2] See 148–50 above.

[3] Ted Hughes breathes contemporary life (and death) into a related metaphor when he speaks of Jupiter trying to 'insulate and filter the nuclear blast of his naked impact' on Semele (Hughes (1997) 98–9).

wooing could, as we saw in Nonnos, be visualized as involving a series of metamorphoses, at the climax the god's conduct is remarkable precisely because it is *not* mediated by metamorphosis.[4]

Semele's fate is a limiting case. Normally when Zeus unites with a mortal the potential imbalance in energy is reduced, as if by an electrical transformer, through metamorphosis, so that the mortal partner's physical survival is assured, at least for the duration of the act. Danae survives coition with Zeus to see her son Perseus grow up to heroic manhood; Leda emerges unscathed from a similar experience (although mythology records little about her fate after childbearing);[5] neither Antiope (to whom Zeus comes as a satyr), nor Kallisto (Zeus as Artemis), nor Alkmene (Zeus in the more humdrum form of Amphitryon) lead trouble-free lives after they have given birth, but none is destroyed by the act of intercourse itself.

Poseidon's list of lovers is shorter than Zeus', but he too shifts shape when necessary to mitigate the potentially overwhelming power of his divinity: he approaches Theophane as a ram (having first changed her into a ewe), and Tyro as the river-god Enipeus, a less formidable deity than himself.[6] Nor was erotic metamorphosis the preserve of male deities only. In the *Homeric Hymn to Aphrodite*, when the goddess desired Anchises it was into the unthreatening form of a young girl that she transformed herself (81–3):

And Aphrodite the daughter of Zeus stood before him, being in size and appearance like (*homoiē*) an untamed maiden, in case he should be frightened when he caught sight of her with his eyes.

Anchises, unlike Semele, made love with a divinity and survived to tell the tale. However, his tale-telling led, according to different mythical variants, to his being either blinded by Zeus, or lamed by one of his thunderbolts.[7]

---

[4] There is scope for a refined reinterpretation of this on Neoplatonist lines. See Iamb. *Myst.* 2.4 for the sublime impact of the gods' fire; cf. Lane Fox (1986) 126.

[5] See Alcalde Martín (2001).

[6] Theophane: Hyg. *Fab.* 188; Ov. *Met.* 6.117. Tyro: Hom. *Od.* 11.235–59. Ovid adds the manifestations of Neptune/Poseidon as a bull (to 'the Aeolian maiden', i.e. Kanake), a horse (to Demeter), a bird (to Medusa), and a dolphin (to Melantho) (*Met.* 6.115–20).

[7] Anchises' punishment: see Buxton (1980) 31, with n. 47.

What can these erotic metamorphoses tell us about the Greeks' perceptions of sexual liaisons between human and divine? It will be useful to go back to Moschos' *Europa*, which raises the revealing issue of genealogy. Europa's intimacy with the bull is certainly unconventional. Yet what does it lead to? As Zeus-bull foretells, 'to me you shall bear famous sons, and all shall wield the sceptre among mortal men' (160–1)—that is, Minos, Rhadamanthys, Sarpedon, all three fully human in form. Europa's union with Zeus-bull should thus be sharply distinguished from Pasiphae's copulation, from inside the frame of Daidalos' artificial cow, with the bull sent by Poseidon. Europa is an unmarried maiden whose adolescent longings Moschos transmutes into a physical attraction for a strange and uncannily beautiful creature. Pasiphae, by contrast, is a married woman whose desire for the unusual is at the same time a rejection of her husband Minos. Moreover, the bull she longs for lacks the crucial quality of Europa's partner: it is not a transformed Olympian divinity. The fact that Pasiphae has transgressed is spelled out in the language of genealogy: her offspring is the hybrid Minotaur. Europa's act is quite different: Zeus' metamorphosis places their union within a sanctioning, normalizing framework, which is confirmed when Europa gives birth to the three unmonstrous heroes of Crete.

Other liaisons between mortals and transformed deities similarly generate wholly human offspring. Danae's impregnation by the shower of gold produces Perseus, a hero entirely human in form. As we saw earlier, when Apollo desires Dryope, he turns himself into a tortoise, which she playfully puts down her dress; the tortoise then becomes a snake; and yet the outcome of Dryope's intercourse with the doubly transformed god is the strong and thoroughly human Amphissos.[8] As for Zeus' transformation into a swan in order to couple with Leda, it is true that the effect of this change prolongs itself beyond conception through gestation, in that the offspring of the liaison is an egg (which Pausanias saw in a sanctuary in Sparta, 3.16.1). Nevertheless, the children who hatch out are human. Whatever might be said about Helen's morals, she was not regarded as a physical hybrid.[9]

---

[8] Ant. Lib. 32; see 111–13 above.

[9] On the various versions of Helen's conception, including the variants in which her mother is Nemesis not Leda, see Gantz (1993) 318–23; Alcalde Martín (2001), esp. 27–43.

Genealogy enabled Greek myth-tellers to make implied statements about moral and social normality through descriptions of physical form. Monstrous (i.e. hybrid) parents give birth to monstrous offspring; likewise, abnormality in the *manner* of a sexual liaison may also, though it does not always, produce monstrous children. The fact that this is not generally true of the offspring of metamorphosed gods surely implies that these transformations were not felt to be 'essential': as the whole of a god's being was not channelled into, or exhausted by, the temporarily assumed form (swan, satyr, etc.), there was no necessity, according to the logic of metamorphosis, that the god's offspring should partially embody that temporary form.

In discussing erotic metamorphoses of male deities, Françoise Frontisi-Ducroux interprets the phenomenon in psycho-sexual terms:

The sexual act—envisaged of course from the male point of view—does not consist only of the penetration of the body of the other person, but also of an escape from one's own limits and, in the process of mutual linkage, an experiencing of the diversity of living things, even that of the elements.[10]

In other words, metamorphosis is an image for the longing by the male to escape, at the moment of coition, from the confines of his own form. This assertion is both highly attractive and highly speculative. But we can sometimes demonstrate its truth conclusively from a text. A perfect instance is Nonnos' description of Zeus in the act of coupling with Semele, in which the supreme poetic coup—the cry 'euhoi'—marks the instant when the father becomes the son whom he is in the act of engendering: momentarily Zeus not only steps outside himself, but into the next generation of gods.

It is not only *erōs* which drives divinities to self-transform in order to escape. There are other sorts of escape too: sometimes escape not *through* sexual passion, but *from* it. Demeter tried to evade Poseidon's desires by metamorphosing into a mare; he outwitted her by transforming himself into a stallion.[11] To elude the attentions of Zeus, Asteria, daughter of the Titan Koios, changed herself into a quail and dived into the sea; at that place there appeared an island,

---

[10] Frontisi-Ducroux (2003) 177.   [11] Paus. 8.25.5.

Asteria, later called Delos.[12] Nemesis was another who sought to avoid the ineluctable, as recorded in the *Cypria*:

> Over the earth and the dark barren water
> She fled, and Zeus pursued, for in his heart he longed
> To take her. At one time looking like (*eidomenē*) a fish
> Through the waves of the deep-sounding sea
> She stirred the great waters, at another along
> The river of Ocean, and the ends of the earth,
> At another across the fertile mainland; she kept becoming (*gigneto*)
> Such dread beasts as the land nourishes, trying to escape him.[13]

Her final tactic was to metamorphose into a goose; but Zeus, in the form of a swan, outflanked her.[14]

In the preceding examples it is female deities who self-transform in order to escape. Just as mythological females are regularly associated with the practice of deceit, so are they also connected with escape-metamorphosis, a mode of physical deception incumbent on those inferior in power. Male deities, by contrast, are rarely so weak that they have any need to escape at all. On one occasion, however, the Olympians, excepting only Athene and Zeus, self-transformed *en masse* when they fled to Egypt under the onslaught of the fearsome earthborn divinity Typhon. Apollo chose the form of a hawk, Hermes an ibis, Ares a scaly Nile fish, Artemis a cat, Dionysos a goat, Herakles a fawn, Hephaistos an ox, and Leto a field-mouse. Since the most efficient disguise is that which enables one to blend in with one's surroundings, it is no coincidence that the forms of a hawk (cf. Horus), an ibis (cf. Thoth), and a cat (cf. Bastet) recommended themselves.[15]

---

[12] Apollod. *Bibl.* 1.4.1. According to Hyginus (140), the earlier name of Delos was 'Ortygia' (*ortyx* = 'quail'). Kallimachos (*Del.* 36–8) saw the etymology differently: Asteria leapt into the sea 'like a star' (*asteri isē*). For Pindar (*Pae.* 5.42) Delos was 'the body of Asteria'.

[13] Athen. *Deipn.* 334d = *PEG Cypria* F 9.6–12.

[14] Apollod. *Bibl.* 3.10.7. Eratosthenes (*Cat.* 25) agrees that Nemesis underwent multiple changes in order to elude Zeus and preserve her virginity, but reports that her final metamorphosis was into a swan rather than into a goose.

[15] Ant. Lib. 28. For Griffiths (1960), the flight of the gods before Typhon echoes an Egyptian myth. This whole episode was described by Bouché-Leclercq ((1879–82) i. 125) as 'a grotesque fiction', unworthy of true Greek mythology; the proliferation of such metamorphosis tales was due in his view to 'an invasion by oriental legends'. Bouché-Leclercq's study of divination has never been superseded, but aspects of its ideological stance now sound very dated.

In another group of tales the gods disguise their appearance not to escape, but to allow them to interact surreptitiously with humans, either to help or to harm. In the *Odyssey*, a nameless suitor rebukes the rash Antinoos, who has hurled a footstool at the unrecognized Odysseus. Don't you realize, the young man urges, that he might be a god? 'For the gods do undergo all sorts of transformations, resembling (*eoikotes*) strangers from elsewhere' (17.485–6). A routine feature of the Homeric poems is the tactic by which a god appears to a human in a form which is likely to be most persuasive.[16]

In concealing their divinity beneath a mask of ordinary humanity, the gods seek to nullify the effect which their superior authority would otherwise have produced. In Kallimachos' *Hymn to Demeter*, when the goddess intervenes to try to prevent Erysichthon from sacrilegiously felling trees in her holy precinct, she does so first in the form of a mortal, her own priestess Nikippe. To no avail: 'Be off with you,' is Erysichthon's response, 'lest I stick my great axe in your hide' (53). The goddess's retribution—the inflicting of a terrible, burning hunger on Erysichthon—is delivered when she has resumed her full authority along with her original form (57–8):

But Demeter was unspeakably enraged, and became a goddess again (*geinato d' ha theus*): her steps touched the ground, but her head touched Olympos.[17]

The gods often chose self-transformation as a means of punishing their adversaries. When the giants Otos and Ephialtes rashly paid court to Artemis and Hera, Artemis turned herself into a deer on the island of Naxos, and ran between the two would-be suitors; each threw a spear towards the animal, but Otos succeeded only in piercing Ephialtes, and Ephialtes Otos.[18] Dionysos, too, exploited the ability to shift shape as a means of carrying out aggression; indeed he did so more frequently than any other Olympian. We

---

[16] Lane Fox (1986) 106 uses the term 'accommodation' to describe the process 'whereby gods suit their presence to individuals' capacities'.

[17] But the text is maddeningly uncertain. Hopkinson ((1984) ad loc.) accepts Bergk's conjecture of αὖ instead of the MSS ἁ; he prints γείνατο δ' αὖ θεύς, translating this as 'she took on the form of a goddess again'; which makes good sense. Given that the aorist γείνατο is almost always transitive elsewhere, it may be that the intransitive forms γείνετο or γίνετο are to be preferred (so also Hopkinson).

[18] Apollod. *Bibl.* 1.7.4; for variants, see Gantz (1993) 170–1.

have seen one illustration of this in Euripides' *Bacchants*, and numerous others in Nonnos.

The pursuit of *erōs*, the wish to escape, the desire to conceal, the will to punish: these are the gods' principal motives in self-transformation. The effect of these metamorphoses on those around them—particularly on uncomprehending mortals—is usually startling. It is to these effects that we now turn.

ASTONISHMENT

A motif which regularly accompanies Greek representations of divine epiphany—including epiphanies which involve metamorphosis—is the astonishment of mortal bystanders; the word group most often used to express this is the by now familiar *thambos/thambeō*. Consternation is especially great in the absence of mitigation. Just as the depth of the gulf between mortality and immortality entails that a god who wishes safely to bridge that gulf must mitigate the disparity through metamorphosis, so any mortal who comes face to face with the true nature of divinity—as when the temporary veil of metamorphosis is lifted—will usually be awe-struck or dumbfounded.

Given the plurality of Greek storytelling, it is inevitable that this astonishment should be handled differently in different genres. One genre where astonishment is particularly noticeable is the hymn, a context in which, following the logic of *this* genre, the power of divinity appears at its most irresistible.

In the *Homeric Hymn to Demeter*, the goddess at first mitigates her presence among the Eleusinians by sitting at the village fountain with the appearance of (*enalinkios*) an old woman (101). In that guise she covertly expresses her benevolence to the royal household by anointing the royal prince Demophoon with ambrosia, and by placing him in the fire every night, so as progressively to burn away his propensity to age and die.[19] When his mother Metaneira uncomprehendingly discovers what has happened, Demeter withdraws the boon she had

---

[19] The same motif occurs in a version of the story of Thetis and baby Achilles (Ap. Rhod. *Arg.* 4.869–72).

been working at—but not before altering her stature and form (*eidos*), so that she gives off a divine fragrance and a radiant light, telltale signs of the more-than-human. Metaneira's knees are loosed and she cannot speak. The word *thambos* is absent, but the concept is there in full force.

A later *Hymn to Demeter*, that by Kallimachos, narrates a greater offence than Metaneira's, and once more there is a double metamorphosis. As we saw just now, Demeter first warns Erysichthon off in the mitigating likeness of her own priestess, and then, in the face of his frenzied aggression, 'becomes' a goddess again. At this second transformation the bystanders experience a near-terminal attack of *thambos*—they are 'half-dead' (59).

In the *Homeric Hymn to Aphrodite*, the goddess deceptively makes herself like 'an untamed maiden in stature and form (*eidos*)', so that Anchises shall not be terrified when he sees her and so frustrate her objective (82–3).[20] When Anchises wakes up after their love-making, Aphrodite is already dressed and ready to leave; her original, mitigating change of form is no longer needed: 'her head reached the well-made roof-beam' (173–4). Anchises reacts by looking aside and covering his face with a cloak: the glare of unmitigated divinity is insupportable. If you reveal that we lay together, threatens Aphrodite, Zeus' thunderbolt will silence you for ever (286–8). Mitigation by metamorphosis is no longer part of the bargain.

These three hymns present a relatively homogeneous model for the link between epiphany, metamorphosis, and astonishment. But it is not the only model. In the Homeric epics we find situations which are rather more complex. A good point of entry is via the relationship between Achilles and the two goddesses who protect him.

Visual illustrations of Thetis' capacity to self-transform, in a series of virtuoso attempts to elude the clutches of her suitor Peleus, are among the most striking mythological images in Greek art. But not everywhere do we find the goddess to be a self-transformer; and the exceptions are revealing. When Thetis answers Achilles' call in *Iliad* Book 1, there are no barriers to their mutual recognition. The goddess may emerge from the water 'like mist' (359),[21] but when she sits by her

---

[20] See 159 above.
[21] The debate goes on: for Dirlmeier (1967) 27, this is a simile; for Kakridis (1971) 105, it is a metamorphosis.

son and strokes him, he recognizes her instantly. Not only does she not transform herself into a panther or a snake: she does not even change into a mitigating *human* shape. In Book 18, she again comes out of the sea to comfort Achilles, this time without the mediation even of a comparison, let alone a metamorphosis; once more Achilles' recognition is instantaneous: *mēter emē*, 'My mother' (79). Finally, in Book 24, when Thetis prompts Achilles to accept the ransom for Hektor's body, things are no different: there is no suggestion that Achilles' recognition of his mother is anything other than immediate (120 ff.). Usually in Greek mythological narratives, divinities who confront mortals do so through the mediating gambit of metamorphosis, in order to mitigate the effect of the electric energy which they embody—a mediation which typically results in their being recognized only when they leave. And yet not so here: so special is the Iliadic Achilles that neither does Thetis transform herself, nor does Achilles have difficulty in identifying her the moment she arrives, nor is there the slightest sense of an imbalance in energy between the two. Usually in Greek mythological narratives, the appearance of a divinity before a mortal in *un*-metamorphosed form arouses *thambos* in those present. And yet not so here. The unique intimacy of the Iliadic Thetis/Achilles relationship is expressed through Achilles' *lack* of astonishment—unlike the reaction of Achilles when Athene intervenes in the quarrel between himself and Agamemnon in Book 1—*thambēsen d'Achileus*, 'Achilles was astonished' (199). His relationship with his mother is far closer than that between him and any other divinity, even Athene.[22] In the irredeemably pluralistic and context-sensitive world of Greek mythology, few interpretative expressions are more important than: 'And yet...'[23]

---

[22] On Athene's propensity for epiphany, see Loraux (1995) 213.

[23] Note that in *another* context it can be *Athene's* special proximity to her mortal favourites which is highlighted. Thus at the beginning of *Odyssey* Book 15 she appears by Telemachos' head. He is explicitly said not to be asleep (7), yet there is no evidence that she metamorphoses into a congenial form, nor, of course, that she re-transforms herself afterwards when she leaves him, nor does Telemachos express any astonishment during the encounter. All this shows the specialness and maturity of Telemachos at this juncture, that is to say *in this context*.

The reason why Achilles' unastonished recognition of divinity stands out as extraordinary is that the *Iliad* elsewhere so insistently stresses the gulf between mortality and immortality. Occasionally the narrator bestows the capacity to cross the gulf upon another mortal temporarily bathed in the spotlight of glory—like Diomedes, from whose eyes Athene lifts the mist which normally obscures the difference between mortals and divinities, or like Aineias, who sees through Apollo's appearance in the form of the herald Periphas: 'Aineias recognized Apollo the Far-shooter, looking at him face to face.'[24] But this is not the norm. The norm, Iliadic as well as Odyssean, is Odysseus' experience when Athene meets him in *Odyssey* Book 13, likening herself in body to 'a young man, a shepherd, thoroughly delicate' (222–3). But later in the same conversation, when she chooses to be recognized (288–9): 'In body she took on the appearance (*ēikto*) of a woman both beautiful and tall, and knowledgeable in glorious handiworks.' She chides Odysseus with not recognizing her, to which he replies (312–13): 'It is hard, goddess, for even a man of good understanding to recognize you when he meets you, for you liken yourself (*se . . . autēn eiskeis*) to everything.' The norm is for even the most subtle and sensitive of mortals to be able to recognize divinities only after they have made an astonishing departure. With Athene in the form of Mentes, Telemachos is 'far the first to see her'— to see, but not to recognize (1.113). Only after her departure as a bird does Telemachos realize that he has been in the presence of a divinity: 'He was astonished in his heart' (*thambēsen kata thumon*, 1.323).

When a mortal experiences *thambos* in such situations, it is a recognition that a deity's anthropomorphic appearance has concealed the presence of the uncanny, the ultimately uncontrollable. Such is the diversity of Greek mythological representations, however, that astonishment is not a universal accompaniment to metamorphosis, even when the witness lacks the specialness of Achilles. In *Iliad* Book 24, Hermes, for his meeting with Priam, chooses to mitigate the awesomeness of divinity by appearing as 'a young man, a noble, with his beard just growing, the time of the bloom of young manhood' (347–8)—a younger version of the slaughtered Hektor so achingly present in Priam's thoughts. Eventually, his

---

[24] Diomedes: 5.127–8. Aineias: 17.333–4.

mission as guide accomplished, Hermes takes his leave. But although he identifies himself as an immortal god, there is no *thambos*, no miraculous bird-transformation, no disappearance, certainly no levitation, to take the attention. Hermes *just goes* (468–9):

> So saying, Hermes left for high Olympos;
> but Priam jumped down from the horses to the ground.

At the climax of this greatest of all poems, nothing must be allowed to detract from the impending encounter between Achilles and Priam, alone in their all-too-finite humanity.[25]

SHAPE-SHIFTERS?

The *Cypria* Nemesis narrative, which we cited earlier, refers to a sequence of divine transformations; we have met other instances of such seriality. This phenomenon has sometimes been regarded as a defining feature of a particular group of mythological figures, the so-called 'shape-shifters'. P. M. C. Forbes Irving devotes a separate chapter to them, which he introduces with this preamble:

The stories of the shape-shifters, Proteus, Nereus, Metis, Nemesis, Thetis, Periklymenos, Dionysos, and Mestra are quite different from any of the transformation stories we have considered so far. The defining feature of this class of heroes is that they undergo a whole series of transformations rather than a single one. Further, unlike the changes of most human beings these are self-willed and temporary; unlike those of the gods they have strong suggestions of magic.

In fact the language used to describe these transformations shows that they differ in nature from those of the gods. Whereas our early sources normally use words meaning 'seem' or 'appear as' of the transformations of

---

[25] Note also yet another variation on the Homeric man-meets-metamorphosed-god encounter, once more involving Hermes. When, in *Odyssey* Book 10, we hear of the episode in which Hermes, 'looking like a young man' (278), meets Odysseus, addresses him, and gives him the antidote *mōly* with which to outwit Circe, Odysseus *as the narrator* identifies Hermes three times (277, 302, 307), although the god never identifies himself. The distance of recollection has lent Odysseus the retrospective confidence to identify a divinity which even he could never have possessed in the 'real' situation.

the gods the word used in the case of the shape-shifters is *gignomai* ('become')... This difference in language reveals a difference in conception. Whereas the transformation of the Olympians is only a form of disguise under which the god continues to exist and behave as a god, the shape-shifter completely submerges his personality in the thing he becomes. Whereas too the gods generally become only living creatures and advanced forms of life the shape-shifter may turn himself into the lifeless elements fire or water.[26]

There are several serious problems with these remarks. First, to describe all the characters listed as 'heroes' seems incomprehensible: I can only explain it as some kind of slip of the pen. Secondly, to attribute 'strong suggestions of magic' to the transformations of 'the shape-shifters', in alleged contradistinction to what happens to 'the gods', defines *obscurum per obscurius*, and simply asserts without argument that when a non-'shape-shifter' self-transforms this is *not* 'magic'. How, though, is Zeus' self-transformation into a shower of gold less 'magical' than that of Thetis into a panther? Thirdly, to describe water and fire as 'lifeless' does not take account of ways of thinking, and forms of expression, found in various parts of our tradition which ascribe divinity to precisely these as well as other 'elements' (e.g. the views of Thales about water, or the frequent equation, from as early as the *Iliad*, between Hephaistos and fire).[27] Nor, incidentally, is it the case that the non-'shape-shifter' Olympians do not change into 'lifeless elements': Zeus' manifestation as a shower of gold comes to mind.[28]

Finally, Forbes Irving's proposed differentiation based on the presence or absence of *gignomai* just does not work: the linguistic facts are more supple and less tidy than that. The transformations of Nemesis, as described in the *Cypria*, are narrated not only as processes of becoming—*gigneto thēria*, 'she became wild beasts'—but also as changes of appearance—*ichthui eidomenē*, 'looking like a fish'.[29] The same applies to Dionysos, of whom, in one of his *Homeric Hymns*, it is said at one moment that he looked like (*eoikōs*,

---

[26] FI 171.

[27] *Il.* 2.426. Note also Eur. *Ba.* 625: 'Acheloos' = water.

[28] To be fair, though, Forbes Irving says that the gods do not *generally* turn into lifeless elements.

[29] *PEG Cypria* F 9, lines 8–12.

'resembling') a young man, yet at another that he 'became' (*geneto*) a lion.[30] Nor is it hard to find other examples of self-transforming Olympians who temporarily 'become' something other than themselves. Moschos' Zeus 'hid his divinity and transformed his body and became (*gineto*) a bull' (79), even though elsewhere in the poem his taurine quality is evoked through the language of appearance (*eidomai einai tauros*, 'I seem to be a bull', 155–6; *taurōi eeidomenon*, 'looking like a bull', 158). Apollo 'became' successively (*egeneto* twice) a tortoise and a snake in his erotic pursuit of Dryope (Ant. Lib. 32).[31] The resumption of divine appearance by Demeter in Kallimachos' *Hymn* is expressed by the word *gignomai*.[32] In short, there is no philological support for the view that a god simply *seems* to change whereas a 'shape-shifter' *becomes* something else.

In spite of all these difficulties, I think it is worth having another look at the category of 'shape-shifter'. Another comment by Forbes Irving offers a better point of departure:

These [sc. the shape-shifters] are marginal figures: they are opposed to the Olympians in their weakness as old men or women, in their home in the sea, in their antiquity, and in their magical powers and knowledge, and their characteristic story tells how they are subdued by an Olympian or one of their favourites.[33]

I propose first to review each of the main candidates proposed by Forbes Irving, and then to ask whether collectively they exemplify some or all of the characteristics which he mentions—though I shall omit without discussion the unmanageable criterion of 'magic'. I shall add to the names cited in Forbes Irving's preamble the figures of Empousa and the Telchines, who in their different ways stake claims to be classified as shape-shifters, if such a class is to be retained.[34]

Proteus is the elusive Old Man of the Sea whom Menelaos encounters in *Odyssey* Book 4. The range of his transformational repertoire is (of course) extended by Nonnos, who prefaces his

---

[30] *Hom. h.* (7) *Bacch.* 3 and 44.
[31] See 111 above.
[32] See 163 above.
[33] FI 194.
[34] Forbes Irving does twice touch on the Telchines (178, 291), but only in passing.

account with the suggestive phrase 'with his limbs weaving an imitative form/image' (*meleessi tupon mimēlon huphainōn*).[35] **Nereus** is a kind of double of Proteus. According to Apollodoros (2.5.11), 'Herakles seized hold of him while he was asleep and, although he transformed himself into many different shapes (*pantoias enallassonta morphas*), Herakles bound him and would not let him go until he had learned from him where the apples and the Hesperides were to be found.' **Metis**, like **Nemesis**, tried to escape from Zeus' advances by a series of transformations.[36] **Thetis** uses a sequence of metamorphoses to try to elude the embrace of Peleus.[37]

Periklymenos, son of Neleus, was an Argonaut. His grandfather Poseidon conferred a special power on him, so that, in the words of Apollonios, 'whatever he might pray to be in the fight, this he should become in the stress of battle'.[38] A scholiast on this passage fleshes out the bones of the divine gift, citing Hesiod: 'At one time he would appear among birds, an eagle; and again at another he would be an ant, a marvel (*thauma*) to see; and then a shining swarm of bees; and again at another time a dread, relentless snake.' But Periklymenos was a mere mortal, in spite of his powers. With Athene's help, observes the scholiast, Herakles shot him fatally with an arrow.[39]

Dionysos is repeatedly linked with the capacity for metamorphosis, whether of himself or others. Forbes Irving includes him in his category of 'shape-shifters', though with some hesitation.[40]

Mestra, a mortal, was the daughter of Erysichthon, and had the ability to change her shape. Her father, having been reduced to penury as a result of his insult to Demeter, sold Mestra to various buyers, but she escaped back to her father by variously transforming herself. The story is relatively poorly evidenced in Greek sources: one place where it does occur is in the rationalizing account by Palaiphatos (23), who dismisses it as ridiculous.

---

[35] Hom. *Od.* 4.455–8; Nonn. *Dion.* 43.231.
[36] Apollod. *Bibl.* 1.3.6.
[37] See above, 86–8, with Figs. 25–6; 165–6.
[38] Ap. Rhod. *Arg.* 1.156–60.
[39] Hes. fr. 33(a).14–17 MW. Nonnos gives an alternative version: Herakles crushed the 'deceitful imitation of a false bee' between two fingers (*Dion.* 43.248–9).
[40] FI 191.

Metamorphosis can be threatening and perilous, a disruption of normal categories which may terrify anyone experiencing or witnessing it. Such is the effect of an encounter with **Empousa**, one of the nightmare-women of the Greek *imaginaire*. In Aristophanes' *Frogs* Dionysos' slave Xanthias, *en route* for the Underworld, reports to his quaking master an imagined sighting of this changeable female (288–96):

Xan.	By Zeus, I can see a big beast!
Dion.	What sort of a beast?
Xan.	A fearsome one—it keeps becoming (*gignetai*) different shapes. At one moment it's an ox, at another it's a mule! And now it's a beautiful woman!
Dion.	Where is she? Let me go to her!
Xan.	But now she isn't a woman any more, she's a dog.
Dion.	It must be Empousa.
Xan.	Her face is certainly all lit up with fire.
Dion.	Has she got a bronze leg?
Xan.	Yes, by Poseidon. And the other one's made of cow dung—honestly!

Cow dung strikes the authentic note of Aristophanic scatology, but this and other features of his Empousa—a character of whose name comedy was apparently 'full'[41]—can be paralleled extensively outside the steaming compost of Old Comedy.[42] That she had some kind of abnormality in the leg(s) is attested in several sources. Sometimes she is described as having a 'donkey leg';[43] or she has just one leg (whence an ancient etymology of her name, 'One Leg');[44] another variant credits her with a leg made of donkey dung.[45] The idea of Empousa's 'face of fire' seems to be echoed in the ghastly image conjured up in Aristophanes' *Assemblywomen* (1056), where she is 'enclosed in a blood blister'. (In that play, 'Empousa' is the insult thrown by a young

[41] Harpocrat. *Lex. s.v.* Ἔμπουσα.

[42] For Empousa we have a good encyclopedia entry by Waser (1905), and fascinating articles by Borthwick (1968) and C. G. Brown (1991). Borthwick has intriguing things to say about weasels as bad-luck animals (the supposed encounter with Empousa ends with Xanthias' comment: 'I see a weasel', *Frogs* 304); Brown interprets the *Frogs* scene in the light of the terror symbolism associated with the early stages of the experiences of initiands in the Eleusinian Mysteries.

[43] E.g. schol. *Frogs* 293; other refs. in Waser (1905) 2540.

[44] E.g. schol. *Frogs* 293.

[45] See schol. *Frogs* 295; Athen. *Deipn.* 566e.

man at an old woman with whom, under the city's imagined new legal provisions, he is supposed to have sex.) Empousa's association with dogs—in *Frogs*, not so much an association as a temporary identification—receives corroboration from the link between Empousa and Hekate,[46] a goddess whose canine connections are well known. According to a scholiast on Apollonios' *Argonautika*, Hekate used to change her own shape: hence she was known as 'Empousa'.[47]

Empousa's abnormal leg makes her a hybrid. But what concerns us more directly is her capacity for serial self-transformation. Aristophanes is not alone in depicting her as a self-changer.[48] When Demosthenes alleges that the mother of his arch-opponent Aischines was nicknamed 'Empousa', he ascribes this to the fact that 'she did and put up with everything'.[49] For a woman to be called 'Empousa' was hardly a compliment at the best of times, but the point of Demosthenes' gibe was probably to hint that she was a prostitute: the names of other comparable female monsters (Scylla, Charybdis, Hydra, Sphinx, etc.) could certainly carry that implication.[50]

Finally, the **Telchines**.[51] These are tricky, divine craftsmen who for the most part inhabit the margins of our principal sources for Greek mythology. A fairly substantial account of them is, however, to be found in two chapters from the *Universal History* of Diodoros of Sicily (5.55–6). Writing about the ancient history of Rhodes, Diodoros identifies the Telchines as the island's oldest inhabitants. Their marine credentials are impeccable: they are children of Thalatta ('Sea'), and brothers of Halia ('Salt Sea'); along with one of the daughters of Ocean, they looked after Poseidon when he was a baby. Their powers centred on the ability to effect astonishing change. They were, it was said, the first to transform raw material into statues of the gods; they could alter the weather, bringing clouds, rain, hail, and snow; and they could even change their own shapes (*allattesthai de*

---

[46] Empousa is identified with Hekate at Aristophanes fr. 515 KA.
[47] Schol. Ap. Rhod. *Arg.* 3.861.
[48] See e.g. Luc. *Salt.* 19; cf. Waser (1905) 2541.
[49] Dem. 18.130.
[50] See Anaxilas fr. 22 KA; cf. C. G. Brown (1991) 43–4, with n. 12.
[51] See Blakely (2006), esp. 15–16 and 152–7.

kai tas idias morphas). Other sources corroborate Diodoros, notably over the association with the sea (Nonnos calls them 'manic spirits of the deep', 14.42).[52] Another theme often stressed is the Telchines' maliciousness. Their most famous exploit was to poison the territory of Rhodes after they had lost ownership of it: according to one tradition, they inundated the land with the all-destroying water of the River Styx.[53] Less frequently mentioned is their capacity for self-transformation. However, Suetonius, in the course of his now fragmentary treatise *On Insults*, mentions a tradition which characterizes the Telchines as amphibious, handless, and footless, but as possessing webbed fingers, and also as capable of changing their form (*parēl-lagmenous tais morphais*): now divine spirits, now men, now fish, now snakes.[54] Suetonius also records another metamorphic byway, which he found in the Boiotian historian Armenidas: the Telchines were formerly the hounds of Aktaion, transformed by Zeus into human beings.[55]

Do these multifarious figures form a coherent group of 'shapeshifters'? There are certainly some overlaps.

1. *The sea.* Proteus, Nereus, and Thetis are sea divinities. The Telchines have the sea in their bones. Metis was a daughter of Okeanos, even though her mythology can in other respects hardly be said to be marine. One tradition also recorded Okeanos as the father of Nemesis.[56] Periklymenos, a grandson of Poseidon, is described by the poet Euphorion as '*thalassios* ("of the sea"), like Proteus'.[57] Just conceivably, we might apply the same adjective to Empousa, since a group of the formidable, female, Empousa-like 'Donkey Legs' in Lucian's story are also referred to as *thalattioi*.[58] According to Artemidoros (2.38), 'Proteus, Glaukos, and Phorkys [three sea deities], and the divinities who surround them, signify [sc. in dreams] deceptions and tricks because of the ease of transformation (*to eumetabolon*) of their

---

[52] Blakely (2006) 155, with 265 n. 96.
[53] E.g. Strabo 14.2.7–8; Nonnos *Dion.* 14.45–8; other refs. at Blakely (2006) 263 n. 68.
[54] Suet. *Peri blasphēmiōn* 4, *s.v.* Τελχῖνες; text in Taillardat (1967) 54.
[55] Armenidas *FGrH* 378 F 8.
[56] Paus. 1.33.3; 7.5.1; Tzetzes on *Lyc.* 88.
[57] Euphorion fr. 64 (= Powell (1925) p. 42), cited in schol. Ap. Rhod. *Arg.* 1.156–60.
[58] Luc. *Ver. Hist.* 2.46.

appearance.' Even Dionysos performs some of his transformational tricks at sea, though it would be a travesty of the evidence to call him a 'sea-god'.

2. *Knowledge.* Proteus and Nereus have special knowledge which they are literally bound to reveal. Metis is associated with a particular kind of mental craft, which Zeus absorbs into himself when he swallows her. The Telchines possess a lot of savvy too, in their own domain. Thetis knows special things, above all about the future of her doomed child Achilles. But there seems to be nothing distinctively 'knowledgeable' about the other candidates on the list.

3. *Sex.* Thetis, Metis, and Nemesis share a common motivation: resistance to sexual intercourse. Empousa, by contrast, is linked with aggressive sexuality, and may be associated with prostitution (cf. Mestra); moreover, Philostratos' 'Empousai' are sex-mad man-eaters, while when Lucian's 'Donkey Legs' encounter male strangers, they get them drunk, lie with them, then literally devour them.[59] However, nothing links the other candidates distinctively with sexuality.

4. *Marginality.* The problem here is the catch-all nature of the term. Dionysos is a disruptive outsider; Proteus and Nereus are old; Thetis, Metis, Nemesis, and Empousa are female. But, whereas to be an outsider and to be old may perhaps reasonably count, in some contexts, as marginalizing characteristics, the same is hardly true of the femininity of a goddess. (Are Gaia, Hera, Artemis, Aphrodite, and Demeter 'marginal' merely in virtue of their gender?) And what of Periklymenos and Mestra? *Qua* mortals, they are undoubtedly different from all the others; but does that make them marginal?[60]

While there are, then, some patterns which link several of these figures—the connection with the ever-changing sea is by far the most plausible—I believe that in the end little is gained by arguing that they constitute an exclusive club. Once we abandon the attempt to erect a definitional fence around the shape-shifters, we save ourselves

---

[59] Philostr. *VA* 4.25.4; Luc. *Ver. Hist.* 2.46.

[60] The notion that Periklymenos ('The Renowned') was 'originally' a euphemism for Hades (so FI 180, following Fontenrose (1959) 327–30) has to remain highly speculative, and it is in any case unclear how this would qualify him as 'marginal'.

the trouble of trying to decide whether some potential members belong inside or outside the enclosure. Take the sea-god Triton. As Apollonios relates, this divinity can change his shape at will. He appears to the Argonauts first looking like (*enalinkios*) a young man, Eurypylos, and then in his 'true', i.e. marine form:

From the top of his head to his belly, and all around his back and his waist, his body was exactly like the glorious form of the blessed gods, but beneath his flanks spread in two directions the long, forked tail of a sea-monster. The surface of the water was lashed by his spines whose points divided in curving needles like the horns of the moon.[61]

Triton's marine credentials are impeccable, and he states explicitly that Poseidon has made him knowledgeable about the sea (1558–9). But his story lacks any element of 'binding compulsion', nor does his self-transformation have anything to do with sex.

I end this section by citing a poem which will enable me to draw together some strands of the argument, and to reinforce my recommendation that 'shape-shifters' should not be bracketed off into a separate category.

In the *Homeric Hymn to Apollo*, the eponymous god at first mitigates his confrontation with a shipload of unsuspecting Cretan businessmen by 'resembling a dolphin in body' (*demas delphini eoikōs*, 400) as he leaps aboard their ship. The crew's reaction to this 'great marvel' (*mega thauma*, 415) is one of silent terror, as the god/dolphin shakes the boat around. Later he/it leaps off the boat 'looking like a star' (*asteri eidomenos*, 441). Is this 'just a simile', as with the famous image in *Iliad* Book 6 (401) where the toddler Astyanax is likened to 'a lovely star' (*alinkion asteri kalōi*)? But *sparks* fly off this Apolline star/dolphin-like-a-star/god-like-a-dolphin-like-a-star, who/which then passes into the shrine at Delphi to bathe Krisa in light, before shifting shape once again to look like (*eidomenos*) a fine, strong youth (449–50). This unnerving encounter between the Cretans and the shape-shifting Sacred is ultimately smoothed over by Apollo himself when he incorporates the businessmen, by the end of the *Hymn*, as celebrants of Apollo Delphinios. But they have learned

---

[61] Ap. Rhod. *Arg.* 4.1551–61, 1602–3, 1610–16. I borrow the translation by Hunter (1993b).

a timely lesson: that the elusive capacity for serial metamorphosis may belong even to the most paradigmatically anthropomorphic of gods. *All* the gods, Olympians included, have the potential for self-transformation—even serial self-transformation—as one possible weapon in their armoury.

ANTHROPOMORPHISM AND THE CHANGING SHAPES OF DIVINITY

I want now to apply our findings about divine metamorphosis to a question of perennial interest in relation to Greek religion, namely the extent to which it was anthropomorphic. We already touched on this issue in Chapter 1, while reviewing the debate about whether the Homeric poems can *really* have portrayed gods as changing into animal forms, or whether, rather, the Homeric imagination should be seen as standing in the anthropomorphic vanguard of a struggle against theriomorphism.[62] Before returning to the discussion of Greek anthropomorphism I propose to set out some comparative material, so as to illustrate a range of possibilities offered by different religious traditions for anthropomorphic/non-anthropomorphic conceptions of the divine.

As an example of a religious system with a high degree of anthropomorphism we may cite ancient Mesopotamia. Although we sometimes find animals serving as emblems of deities (e.g. the association of the dog with the warrior goddess Gula), the prevailing conception of the divinities themselves—in physical shape as well as in socio-political arrangements—is that of thorough-going anthropomorphism (**Fig. 46**).[63] Cuneiform texts make repeated reference to parts of the gods' bodies—superior to those of humans, of course, but still perfectly recognizable on the human model. For all that the Mesopotamian gods are powerful, radiant, exalted, and awesome in their perception and knowledge, their form is fundamentally human.[64]

---

[62] See above, 32; 34–5.   [63] See Bottéro (2001) 64.
[64] The same is true of the Ugaritic and Hurro-Hittite divinities; cf. West (1997) 107; Wyatt (2007), e.g. 146.

Figure 46. The god Marduk, wholly anthropomorphic, bears the insignia of kingship, and stands imperiously above the dragon which he has quelled. Babylonian cylinder seal, 9th cent. BC.

A tradition which places far more weight on the *non*-anthropomorphic side of divinity is that of Hindu religion and mythology, which abounds both in hybrid animal/human forms of divinity and in deities who self-transform into an appearance entirely or partially zoomorphic. Such beliefs are all of a piece with a holistic-integrative religious tradition in which 'there is no essential

Figure 47. The elephant god Ganesha, from the 12th cent. AD temple of Hoysaleshvara, Halebid, Tamil Nadu, South India.

difference between human beings, animals and plants'.[65] In Hindu art many lesser divine or semi-divine figures appear as hybrids, e.g. '*nagas*, human figures with the lower body and hood of a snake, *kinnaras* and *kinnaris*, human figures with foliated tails and bird claws, and ... Garuda, a youth with wings and a hooked nose'.[66] Other well-known figures are the monkey-faced god Hanuman, and Ganesha, the elephant-headed son of Shiva and Parvati (**Fig. 47**). But the most striking case of the interfusion of the anthropomorphic with the zoomorphic is that of the great god Vishnu,

[65] Dallapiccola (2002) 10.   [66] Dallapiccola (2002) 13.

whose person embodies both hybridity and a particular sort of metamorphosis. Periodically Vishnu returned to the world of humans to redress the balance between good and evil. He did so incarnated in a series of *avataras* whose form was either partially or wholly zoomorphic: *Matsya* (either a fish or a fish/human hybrid), *Kurma* (a tortoise), *Varaha* (a boar), *Narasimha* (a lion-headed human), and so on. No individual avatar in this series exhausts the person of Vishnu; rather, each is his temporary embodiment. More generally, the animal 'vehicles' (*vahanas*) of Hindu deities are an extension rather than an exhaustive incorporation of their nature.

Different again, and if anything even more complex, is the case of ancient Egypt. Although the broad-brush concept of 'animal deity' has come to epitomize the Egyptian religious system in generalized popular perception, the relationship between animals and humans in ancient Egyptian thought is in fact one of enormous subtlety. While it is true that deities had the capacity to appear in a variety of forms, none of these forms was identical or coterminous with the deity, nor did they exhaust the deity's being; rather they were signs or icons which represented merely one aspect of the deity.[67] There was, moreover, no one-to-one correspondence between icon and deity: while the ibis was always and only a representation of Thoth, the same god also appeared as a baboon, an animal which could in turn represent the deity Khons (**Fig. 48**).[68] In these combinations of the anthropomorphic and the zoomorphic, the animal part—usually the head—depicts the god's power or function. When an Egyptian divinity temporarily adopts a particular, non-anthropomorphic guise, it is typically the case that such a form does not exhaust the god's possibilities.

Distinct from all of the above, as well as from each other, are the religious stances of the three 'religions of Abraham': Judaism, Christianity, and Islam.[69] Each of these has engaged at various times with

---

[67] See Dunand and Zivie-Coche (2004), esp. 13–41.

[68] Dunand and Zivie-Coche (2004) 15, and the splendid study by Hornung (1982), esp. 100–42. See also te Velde (1980); Kessler (1986) 572; Quirke (1992), esp. 14–19; Houlihan (2002); Teeter (2002); Gilhus (2006) 95–100.

[69] For the shared link with Abraham, see Bowker (2002) 174.

Figure 48. Enthroned, ibis-headed Thoth, assisted by Rameses II. Temple of Rameses II at Abydos, 19th Dynasty, 13th cent. BC.

the interrelated problems of how—and whether—God can or should be represented, and how God can or should be spoken of.[70]

The Hebrew Bible amply documents the condemnation as idolatrous of the representation of divinity in carved or pictorial form; indeed this is one of the chief differentiations between the worship of Yahweh and that of the divinities (El, the Baalim) whom he displaces.[71] Yet we find no less ample evidence of anthropomorphic

[70] On representations of divinity, and especially the conflict between 'iconophilia' and iconoclasm, see Besançon (2000).

[71] E.g. Exod. 20: 4–6; Lev. 26: 1; Deut. 12: 3; Ps. 115: 3–8; Isa. 46; cf. Bowker (2002) 182–3; Besançon (2000) 63 ff.

language used of Yahweh: 'his lips are full of indignation, and his tongue is like a devouring fire; his breath is like an overflowing stream' (Isa. 30: 27–8). Later Jewish tradition would be much exercised by the alleged qualities of God, anthropomorphic or otherwise. The twelfth-century philosopher Moses Maimonides regarded the attribution to God of humanlike characteristics and capacities as due to the wish of the writers of the Torah to make themselves comprehensible to ordinary people. But in fact God passes understanding: he possesses no other attribute than his essence, which is identical with his perfections.[72]

In Christian thought too there is a strong tradition of the denial of any comprehensible form to God, coupled with a refusal to countenance God's knowability. For Clement of Alexandria, God is One and infinite, 'infinite not in the sense of measureless extension but in the sense of being without dimensions or boundaries, and therefore without shape or name'.[73] For Origen God has no body.[74] What, then, of physical representations of divinity? The matter was hugely controversial, and played a major part in the dispute between Western and Eastern Christianity. One way of resolving the point was adopted at the second Council of Nicaea (AD 787): an icon of Christ might be the object of 'veneration' rather than 'adoration', and through such veneration the faithful were pointed towards God.[75] The debate is rendered even more complex by the paradoxical co-presence in Christian belief of the principle of God's indisputable Oneness with the equally indubitable existence of the Trinity. Given that God is asserted to be without form and yet simultaneously to be incarnate in Christ, to investigate the degree of anthropomorphism in Christian religion is to touch on some of the most fiercely disputed theological questions ever to have been raised in the history of humanity.

Islam too wrestled with the problem of divine anthropomorphism. If Allah is said to sit on a throne (Qur'ān, Sūra 57.4), does it follow

---

[72] Maimonides 1.59 in Pines (1963). However, 'there is one Judaic tradition that had a close brush with anthropomorphism...In the Zohar...because the human form is the perfect form, the macrocosm—the first complete manifestation of God— is the cosmic, or "Kadmon", Adam' (Besançon (2000) 76).

[73] Clem. Al. *Misc.* 5.12.81; trans. in Wiles and Santer (1975) 6.

[74] Origen *Peri Archōn* 1.1–4.   [75] Bowker (2002) 286–7.

that Allah has a body with several parts—thus compromising his Oneness? The question was debated by groups such as the Muʿtazilites, for whom expressions such as God's 'face' and 'eyes' must be understood symbolically rather than literally.[76] But these de-anthropomorphizations of God were opposed by the theologian al-Ashʿari and his followers, according to whom the terms in which God chooses to reveal himself must be accepted 'without asking how'.[77] As in the cases of Judaism and Christianity, the debate in Islam about God's form became intertwined with the problematic status of representational art. Although figurative images are not explicitly forbidden in the Qur'ān, Muslim tradition developed in a strongly anti-representational direction, on the grounds that to portray a created being is to usurp a power which only God possesses.[78]

Inadequate though the above sketch of possibilities may be—and clearly it could be extended almost indefinitely—it at least gives some sense of a range of strategies which developed historically in response to the challenge of relating the concepts of deity and anthropomorphism. Where, then, should we place Greece against such a background?

Let us begin by acknowledging that there were certain tendencies in Greek thought and religious practice which went *against* the attribution of anthropomorphic characteristics to the gods.

One such tendency found radical expression in the writings of philosophers. Xenophanes' scepticism about the gods is reflected in his observation that, if cattle, lions, and horses had hands with which to make images, horses would draw horse-gods, cattle cattle-gods, and so on.[79] Empedokles was another who baulked at ascribing human form to divinity:

For he is not furnished with a human head upon limbs, nor do two branches spring from his back, he has no feet, no nimble knees, no shaggy genitals, but he is mind alone, holy and beyond description, darting through the whole cosmos with swift thoughts.[80]

---

[76] Bowker (2002) 333.   [77] Ruthven (1997) 59.
[78] Ruthven (1997) 34, 44; cf. Besançon (2000) 77–81.
[79] KRS fr. 169. Montesquieu's variant on this was that, if triangles had a god, he would have three sides (*Lettres persanes* 57). Montesquieu was echoing Spinoza (*Letter* 56): if a triangle had the power of speech, it would describe god as eminently triangular, whereas, for a circle, the Divine Nature would be eminently circular.
[80] KRS fr. 397 (trans. theirs).

Pythagoreans had a rather different way of distancing themselves from traditional ways of conceiving the gods, if an anecdote recorded in Plutarch's *Life of Numa* is to be credited. When Numa allegedly forbade the Romans to worship any likeness of man or beast, he was said to have been doing so under the influence of the views of Pythagoras, for whom 'the first principle of being cannot be perceived or felt, is invisible and uncreated and apprehensible only by the mind'.[81] On this view, not only anthropomorphism but also zoomorphism were called into question. As for the sophist Protagoras, he was agnostic about the very existence of gods, and a fortiori about their form.[82] Concerning the religious views of Aristotle and, more especially, Plato, there is of course a huge literature documenting a range of sharply divergent scholarly opinion.[83] But this much at least is clear: both thinkers, at certain points in their writings, distanced themselves from the traditional anthropomorphic view of divinity.

If we turn from the often idiosyncratic views of philosophers to the mainstream of mythico-religious thought and practice, a quite different sort of evidence for the non-anthropomorphic appearance of divinities presents itself. Here it is not a question of explicit, more or less extreme epistemological scepticism about the gods' characteristics, but rather a large quantity of textual and archaeological/iconographical material, which shares an implied sense that some aspects of divinity cannot fully be captured by an exclusively human model of what a god looks like. There is no shortage of documentation for such non-anthropomorphic representations—enough, in fact, to fill 272 pages of M. W. de Visser's 1903 treatise, *Die nicht menschengestaltigen Götter der Griechen.*

De Visser identified four main kinds of non-anthropomorphic representation of divinity: stones, wooden blocks/pillars, trees, and animals. This categorization is still workable, even though the intervening century has brought much new, principally archaeological material to light. Within his four kinds de Visser introduced a further subdivision, according to what he saw as the nature of the link between divinity and its non-anthropomorphic 'substrate'—according, in particular, to whether a god was merely *associated* with the substrate

---

[81] Plu. *Numa* 8.7; cf. P. Borgeaud in Johnston (2004) 411–12.
[82] DK 80 B4.   [83] See 234–7 below.

concerned, or was *partly* assimilated to it (hybridity), or was felt to reside *wholly* within it. Now not every case lends itself to such neat pigeon-holing. For instance, the pyramidal image of Zeus Meilichios at Sikyon, an image which de Visser described as the 'Sitz des Gottes', was interpreted very differently by Farnell: 'not as the god but rather as the emblem of the god'.[84] Nor is this the only case—far from it—in which there is room for reasonable scholarly disagreement about the kind of sacredness to be attributed to a given juxtaposition of the anthropomorphic with the non-anthropomorphic—quite apart from the intrinsically problematic status of such neat discriminations, if we bear in mind that different ancient worshippers/observers will indisputably have experienced the sacredness of a given object in quite different ways. Nevertheless, with all due account taken of fuzzy edges, we may still take de Visser's differentiations as a starting point.

Cases of association are countless. There was the *omphalos* at Apollo's shrine at Delphi; the numinous sceptre—allegedly the one made by Hephaistos for Zeus—kept at Chaironeia;[85] Athene's sacred olive tree at Athens, Apollo's Delphic laurel and Delian palm, the oak of Zeus at Dodona; the eagle of Zeus, the owl of Athene.[86] Such associations are far from trivial: they may take us to the heart of the individuality of a particular divinity. Thus Erika Simon has highlighted the many connections between Hera and cattle: the location on grazing land of some of the goddess's major shrines, both in Greece and in south Italy; the fact that the hill near the Argive Heraion was named 'Euboia' ('Place of Fine Cattle'); the offerings of hecatombs to the goddess at several sites; Herodotos' tale (1.31) of Kleobis and Biton, who piously transported their mother to Hera's shrine by pulling an ox-cart.[87] Combining this evidence with that—almost always underestimated—which links Hera with seafaring (notably the location of several of her shrines near the shore), Simon concludes that Hera has a much broader 'scope' in early Greece than our literary texts might suggest. Whatever their importance for the understanding of the realities of Greek religion, however, such cases of association do not bear precisely on the question of

---

[84] Paus. 2.9.6; de Visser (1903) 72; Farnell (1896–1909) i. 103.

[85] Paus. 9.40.11; cf. Hom. *Il.* 2.100–9.

[86] Sacred trees and plants: Murr (1890); Baumann (2007). Sacred animals: Bodson (1978).

[87] Simon (1998) 39–43.

anthropomorphism. For that we need to look at instances where a divinity's own form is partially or wholly at issue.

Partial anthropomorphism—hybridity—finds its classic exemplar in the herm, the stone surmounted by an anthropomorphic head and equipped with an erect phallus. Usually this was an image of Hermes, a type of representation whose perceived 'age-old' quality is reflected in Herodotos' observation that it had been borrowed by the Greeks from 'the Pelasgians' (2.51.1). We also find many depictions of a hybrid Dionysos, in the form of a post surmounted by a head/mask and robe.[88] More common than hybrids involving stone or wood are the innumerable part-theriomorphic representations of divinities, a staple of mythology as well as cult. The Hesiodic Typhoeus was partly anguiform ('out of his shoulders grew a hundred fearsome snake-heads'), but exhibited an even greater morphological versatility in his voice: sometimes his utterances were 'as if for the gods' understanding', but sometimes they sounded like a bull, or a lion, or hounds; or they hissed.[89] The metaphorical fringes of Olympos are populated by hybrid divinities: centaurs, satyrs, Pan, dog-headed Lyssa, the snaky Erinyes. Nor of course is it excluded that the Olympians themselves may be imagined as partly theriomorphic. According to Pausanias (8.42.4), the Black Demeter of Arcadian Phigalia 'resembled a woman except for the head; she had the head and mane of a horse, with representations of serpents and other beasts growing out of her head; she wore a tunic down to her feet; on one hand she had a dolphin and on the other a dove.' Other examples are a fish-tailed Artemis Eurynome in Phigalia, a horned Selene in Elis, and dog-faced Hekate, as well as numerous horned river gods.[90] Minor theriomorphic traits are also common. On Archaic vases Artemis is typically depicted with wings; Athene sometimes has the same attribute, as do Eros, Himeros, Nike, and many other lesser divinities.[91]

---

[88] See Simon (1998) 237–9, relating this form of representation to surviving examples of clay and marble masks which may have been used in cult.

[89] Hes. *Th.* 824–5; 829–35. Cf. the 6th-century BC Chalkidian hydria depicting Zeus' combat against the hybrid Typhon (winged and with a snaky body from the waist down): Munich, Staatliche Antikensammlungen 596 = *LIMC* viii 'Typhon' 14.

[90] Artemis: Paus. 8.41.6. Selene: Paus. 6.24.6. Hekate: Eustath. on *Od.* 3.274 (1467, 37). River-gods: for Acheloos, see above, 84–5, with Figs 22–4; other refs. and bibliography in Bodson (1978) 149 nn. 199 and 200.

[91] Some examples: Artemis: early 7th-century Boiotian amphora, Athens Nat. Arch. Mus. 5893 = *LIMC* ii 'Artemis' 21; early 6th-century Corinthian alabastron,

Examples of divinity represented in wholly non-human form clearly constitute the strongest challenge to the model of the Greek religious imagination as fundamentally anthropomorphic. Among sacred stones are the unworked *lithos* representing Eros at Thespiai, the stone known as the Magna Mater at Pessinus in Phrygia, the column representing Hera at Argos, and the *lithos* called Zeus Kappotas at Gythion.[92] Among wooden *agalmata* are the unworked image of Artemis on Ikaros, an *amorphos* Leto on Delos, a plank said to have been the earliest image of Hera on Samos, and at Kyllene (the port of Elis) a representation of Hermes as an erect wooden penis on a pedestal.[93] Among trees worshipped as divinities the oak at Dodona took pride of place, but little Boiai on the coast of Lakonia could boast a myrtle bush under whose guise worship was offered to Artemis Soteira.[94] Among divinized animals, the stork in Thessaly, the weasel in Thebes, and the mouse at Hamaxitos in the Troad are just three out of a much larger number of locally revered creatures; more widely known was the reverence paid to Zeus and Asklepios in the form of snakes.[95]

Much of the above evidence was already collected by de Visser. But collection is one thing, interpretation another. In addition to the 'fuzzy edges' question which I mentioned above, de Visser's book raises a more fundamental methodological issue. His perspective, shared by most of his contemporaries as well as not a few of his successors, is that of full-blown evolutionism, resting on a pervasive assumption that at an earlier stage of Greek belief divinity was attributed to stones, blocks of wood, trees, and animals, whereas at

Delos Arch. Mus. B 6191 = *LIMC* ii 'Artemis' 25; Attic krater ('the François Vase') *c.*570, Florence Mus. Arch. 4209 = *LIMC* vi 'Artemis' 21, 25, and 33. Athene: early 7th-century terracotta pithos, Tinos Arch. Mus. = *LIMC* ii 'Athena' 360. For Eros, Himeros, and Nike, see the respective entries in *LIMC*.

[92] Eros: Paus. 9.27.1. Magna Mater: Herodian *Hist.* 1.11; Livy 29.11.7; other refs. at de Visser (1903) 56–7. Hera: *PEG Phoronis* F 4. Zeus: Paus. 3.22.1. See Frischer (1982) 112; Kron (1992); Marcattili (2005). Simon (1998) 55–7 fascinatingly suggests a link between the columnar imagery of Hera and the column, heraldically supported by two lions, over the great gate at Mycenae.

[93] Artemis and Hera: Clem. Al. *Protr.* 4.40; Arn. *Adv. nat.* 6.11. Leto: Athen. *Deipn.* 614b. Hermes: Paus. 6.26.5; other refs. at de Visser (1903) 115–16.

[94] Paus. 3.22.12.

[95] Stork: Aristot. *Mir. ausc.* 23; Clem. Al. *Protr.* 2.34. Weasel: Clem. Al. *Protr.* 2.34. Mouse: Ael. *NA* 12.5. For snakes, see Bodson (1978) 68–92.

a later stage anthropomorphism made major inroads upon such beliefs, though without ever quite triumphing. On the evolutionary march, images such as those of a piece of wood with a human head, or a being which is half-human, half-animal, stand at what is, conceptually but also historically speaking, the mid-point of the journey.[96] But does the assumption of an evolutionary march stand up to scrutiny?

One of the bases on which belief in a progression from non-anthropomorphism to anthropomorphism has traditionally rested relates, not to all forms of non-anthropomorphism, but specifically to theriomorphism. The case here depends on an inference from tales of metamorphosis, an inference summarized by A. B. Cook like this: '[W]ithin the bounds of Hellenic mythology animal-metamorphosis commonly points to a preceding animal-cult.'[97] Such transformational tales as those of Artemis' devotee Kallisto, and Hera's priestess Io, reflect, it has been felt, an earlier stage of religion at which Artemis was revered *as a bear* and Hera *as a cow*. However, this assumption has been effectively demolished by Forbes Irving, who has convincingly shown the circularity of the argument from metamorphosis to preceding cult. In his trenchant formulation, 'the chief evidence for the existence of an animal-cult is the very metamorphosis story that such a cult is supposed to explain'.[98]

To find a second reason for questioning, not just the theriomorphic aspect of the alleged progression from non-anthropomorphism to anthropomorphism, but the whole of that progression, it is enough to turn the pages of de Visser's book. A large proportion of his textual examples come from two sources: Pausanias, and Clement of Alexandria. Now it is perfectly true that each of these authors had his own furrow to plough. Pausanias was always on the lookout for local cultic details which might intrigue his readers; ancient relics with an uncanny and eerie form clearly had a special appeal within his narrative. Clement, for his part, was bent on highlighting just those aspects of pagan religion which most obviously offered themselves for ridicule—and what could be more ridiculous, as an object of worship, than a stone or a log? And yet to disregard all these testimonies as merely the product of the grinding of two personal axes is

---

[96] De Visser (1903) 35.   [97] Cook (1894) 160.   [98] FI 49.

quite unconvincing. Nor will it do to pension off the beliefs they report as 'survivals'. If the material preserved by Pausanias and Clement (and of course not only by them) is to be given any credence at all, then we have to conclude that beliefs in non-anthropomorphic gods were alive and flourishing well into the Roman imperial period. Instead of the 'triumph of anthropomorphism' model, therefore, it is preferable to use a model stressing the *coexistence* of multiple forms of divinity. Even at a late stage in its development, the language and practice of Greek religion could *simultaneously* exploit *both* anthropomorphic *and* non-anthropomorphic modes of representation.

The aim of my discussion of Greek anthropomorphism has been to place it against the background of other religious traditions. Where, in this regard, have we got to? Although we came across a variety of evidence, in philosophical speculation, cult, and myth, for non-anthropomorphic conceptions of divinity in ancient Greece, it remains true that the *predominant* mode of imagining the gods, whether expressed in texts or in iconography, was in terms of the human form. De Visser himself had no hesitation in observing that 'nowhere did anthropomorphism achieve a greater state of completeness than among the Greeks'.[99] Even stronger was the formulation of Martin Nilsson: 'Anthropomorphism is the distinguishing mark of Homer and all later Greek religion'; and he went on to refer to 'the specifically Greek anthropomorphism'.[100] The idea of Greek specificity has to be qualified in view of what we know about, for example, Near Eastern religious systems.[101] Yet it is enough to peruse the thousands of images in the *Lexicon Iconographicum Mythologiae Classicae*, under the entries for major and minor divinities alike, to be compelled to recognize that, while anthropomorphism is not *specifically* Greek, it *is* Greek: such counter-examples as horse-headed Demeter and serpentine Zeus Meilichios constitute only a small proportion of the extant evidence.

Now the present book is centrally about, not anthropomorphism, but metamorphosis. So one question remains: do the stories of divine metamorphosis constitute another exception to the predominance of anthropomorphism? My answer is that they do not. Insofar

---

[99] De Visser (1903) 52.   [100] Nilsson (1952) 142, 143.
[101] See 177 above.

as Greek gods have a representational 'home base', this must in most cases be taken to be anthropomorphic, even if it is a larger, more fragrant, and more radiant representation than the human norm. When metamorphosis narratives describe the gods *resuming* their shape, that shape is usually, either explicitly or by implication, anthropomorphic. There is a classic case in Moschos, when Zeus 'again took back his own shape' (*palin spheterēn anelazeto morphēn*, 163) before coupling with Europa. Again, in descriptions of serial shape-shifting each ending of the sequence typically involves the resumption of anthropomorphic form; an example is Proteus in *Odyssey* 4.421.

However, lest by banging the traditional drum of anthropomorphism (even if not the drum of anthropomorphism as *specifically* Greek) I seem to be over-domesticating Greek religious experience and neutralizing its strangeness, let me re-emphasize a point I made earlier. Narratives of divine metamorphosis often demonstrate that the gods were imagined as having the potential to shock and alarm mortals by suddenly bursting out of the confines of the expected, to create *thambos*. John Gould insightfully characterized the Greek concept of divinity as a combination of the human and the incommensurable-with-the-human.[102] The gods are bound to human beings by ties of reciprocity, yet at any moment they are liable to step out of the role of partner and into that of terrifyingly strange, unpredictable, and alien power. Greeks constructed all manner of frameworks by which to attempt to control their dealings with that kind of power. Ritual is the most obvious of these frameworks, with its panoply of procession, libation, sacrifice, prayer, votive offering, each mode implying respect for the gods, combined with a constantly renewed affirmation of the ties which bind mortals to gods in a network of mutual obligation. But the message of mythology is very often that, in spite of all precautions, the power of divinity may break out, to the benefit or for the destruction of mortals. Stories of divine metamorphosis express this sense of danger and promise with literally astonishing force.

[102] Gould (2001) 203–34.

7

The Human Aetiology of Landscape

Self-transformations of the gods are endlessly repeatable whenever a divinity should wish it. But another type of metamorphosis represents a unique and pivotal moment within a linear narrative about genesis and aetiology, a moment which radically demarcates After from Before. Such a narrative describes how a mortal's existence can be indefinitely prolonged through transformation, becoming literally re-incorporated into what, from the perspective of ancient myth-tellers, is the present. According to this perspective, it is not that the world has 'evolved'; rather, the world owes certain aspects of its present condition to a series of one-off transitions which took place in the mythical past. This chapter and the next will look at two examples of this kind of transition.

Most people living in the contemporary, industrialized world would, I imagine, hold the belief, among their other beliefs, that there is a gulf between the animate and the inanimate: that a stick or a wall is one kind of thing, a dog or a lily quite another. There are, it would be conceded, marginal cases, such as coral; there are differences between cultures as to where exactly to draw the line;[1] and there may be disputes about such matters as the precise instant at which an organism may be said to die, i.e. to pass from the animate to the inanimate state. But about the general validity of the assumption that a gulf exists there would be widespread agreement. Nor would such an assumption need to be just a matter of common sense: there seem to be entirely persuasive scientific grounds for stressing the divide

---

[1] See Hatano et al. (1993), on differences between the beliefs of North American, Israeli, and Japanese *children* in respect of the animate/inanimate distinction; cf. G. E. R. Lloyd (2007) 46.

between the animate and the inanimate, if one bears in mind the profound difference between the kinds of uniformities which physicists and inorganic chemists ascribe to substances in the inanimate world, and the inexhaustible diversities and uniquenesses which biologists find characteristic of living things, from cells to the most complex life-forms.[2]

But the assumption of a sharp dichotomy between the inanimate and the animate is by no means the only one in play. I imagine that most people who assume the existence of that sharp dichotomy also believe, on the strength of broadly diffused scientific knowledge, that the first living organisms on this planet sprang from a lifeless, chemical proto-soup—a belief which implies a *continuity* between the inanimate and the animate. And there are further complications. According to another presumably widespread assumption, the life lived by a rose differs radically from that lived by a cat, a difference enshrined in contemporary law, which does not stipulate punishments for people who prune (their own) flowers, but does for those who ill-treat their own (or other people's) pets. So from some points of view—for instance, whether or not a given entity is believed to be capable of feeling pain—certain sorts of living organisms can be perceived as in some senses closer to *in*animate objects than to other, perhaps more 'highly developed', living organisms. This is another kind of blurring of the animate/inanimate opposition.

It would seem, then, that beliefs between which there is at least a degree of incompatibility can be held simultaneously, even on such a fundamental issue as the nature of life. Nor is there anything surprising about this. The more we reflect on the nature of belief, the more it becomes evident that not only groups but also individuals can simultaneously feel allegiance to heterogeneous and even contradictory beliefs: for one of the most basic features about beliefs is that their holders do not necessarily hold them systematically. Contrasting and perhaps conflicting approaches, assumptions, attitudes, and hunches surface and find expression in a variety of contexts; they all constitute, in context, 'authentic' beliefs in terms of their significance for the choices and judgements which inform human conduct.

This is true, in particular, about beliefs relating to the animate/inanimate distinction. Take the example of geology. The discovery of

---

[2] This point runs throughout Mayr (1982).

the workings of plate tectonics has introduced a hitherto undreamed-of dynamism into our view of the past, present, and future of the Earth; research into the interaction between the formation of rocks and the living organisms which populate the planet has transformed assumptions about ecology. This new understanding depends in part on our having learned to read the mute testimony of rocks with greater insight, and in part on breakthroughs in thermodynamics. Yet alongside such investigations, inhabitants of the modern, developed world still tell themselves stories about the landscape which depend on quite different assumptions—the assumption, for instance, that some parts of the landscape have an 'organic' genesis in an absolutely literal sense. In spite of the fact that such narratives conflict with current geological methods for deciphering the landscape, the stories continue to be narrated, and to be evoked in the visual arts (**Fig. 4**, p. 14) because they have their own kind of validity, a validity which is, of course, exactly what explains the continuing transmission of the stories.

In the Dolomites of northern Italy, they tell the tale of a little girl called Misurina and her father, the giant Sorapìs. Misurina is the apple of her father's eye; he can refuse her nothing. She grows up ever more spoiled, ever more intolerable—except to Sorapìs; whatever she demands, he finds a way of getting for her. Then one day she hears of a wonderful object which she says she *really* wants: a mirror called *tuttosò* ('I know everything'); whoever looks into it, knows all. The problem is that the mirror belongs to the Fairy of Monte Cristallo. Misurina doesn't give a fig: 'If you don't get it for me, I'll die!', she cries to her distraught father. Poor Sorapìs cannot bear the thought of this, and, reluctantly, he goes to visit the Fairy.

'Well,' says the Fairy of Monte Cristallo, 'let me offer you a bargain. Up here on Monte Cristallo I have no shade; but if I had another mountain in front of me, I'd have some respite from the sun's rays. I'll give you my mirror; but in return, you must be transformed into a mountain.' Sorapìs sadly agrees; but then the Fairy takes pity on him. 'Listen. Go home with the mirror, and tell Misurina that she can keep it—but only on condition that her father is turned into a mountain. If she finds the prospect of that shocking, just return the mirror to me, and the bargain will be off. But if she accepts the condition—well, don't blame me.' Misurina is overjoyed with the wonderful mirror. 'Come now,' she consoles her father, 'don't be downhearted. As a mountain you'll be covered with nice meadows and woods, and I'll be able to enjoy myself playing there.' So Misurina kept the mirror. But Sorapìs grew, and grew, and grew, till he became the mountain which still stands in front of Monte Cristallo. As for Misurina: she found herself perched on ground which suddenly rose vertiginously into the air, while she continued to gaze into the eyes of her father, as they faded into lifelessness. Then all at once, dizzy from the altitude, she plunged headlong, still clutching her precious mirror. Sorapìs, bereft now of his daughter, wept without ceasing, till his tears made a lake below—the lake known as Il Lago di Misurina. And still today, Mount Sorapìs is reflected in the crystal-clear water of the lake, as the father searches in vain for his dead child.[3]

In the form in which I have told it, this is a tale told by grown-ups to children, to socialize them into a world where they cannot have everything. But the narrative of Misurina is not one which a child can simply grow out of. It also has a message for fathers, reminding them that they should not be over-fond—a particularly poignant message in a tale which surely derives from a period of high child mortality. Mountains have their geological history, but families and communities have histories too. For the families and communities whose lives are framed and whose livelihoods are governed by the characteristics of mountains such as Sorapìs and Cristallo, it is too simple to say that a geological narrative in terms of plate tectonics and vulcanology is just 'true', and that the tale of a doting giant and his capricious daughter is just 'false' (**Fig. 49**).

In our contemporary world, then, we find strongly contrasting and highly context-dependent ways of perceiving the relationship between a landscape's past and its present. As we look back at Greece, we again find a plurality of beliefs, but the characteristics of that plurality differ from anything familiar to us today. In particular, at no period in antiquity, not even during the heyday of the Alexandrian Museum, did what we might refer to as 'scientific' speculation enjoy a social cachet, an institutional power, or a cultural prominence remotely comparable with that attained by the sciences today. From

---

[3] The full story is narrated in Ballario (1995) 22–8.

Figure 49. Man as mountain, mountain as man. Joos de Momper the Younger (1564–1635), 'Anthropomorphic Landscape'. Oil on panel.

time to time, it is true, idiosyncratic individuals hazarded more or less informed guesses about the Earth's past. Noting that shells have been found inland and that impressions of fish and seaweed have been found in rock, the Presocratic philosopher Xenophanes inferred that the Earth had once been covered with mud; more generally he argued that a cyclical process is in operation whereby

a mixture of the earth with the sea is going on, and . . . in time the earth is dissolved by the moist . . . All mankind is destroyed whenever the earth is carried down into the sea and becomes mud; then there is another beginning of coming-to-be, and this foundation happens for all the worlds.[4]

But such opinions were formulated against a background of traditional and surely far more widely held views, such as those of Hesiod (*Th.* 126–33):

And first of all Earth (Gaia) bore one equal to herself, starry Heaven (Ouranos), so that he should cover her completely, to be a secure, eternal dwelling-place for the blessed gods. And she bore the long Mountains, delightful haunts of the goddesses, the nymphs who dwell in mountain

---

[4] KRS 184.

glens. And she bore also the unharvested Sea with its furious swell, without love's sweet union.

Sometimes the Xenophanean and the Hesiodic styles of approach are juxtaposed within the works of a single author, even within a single passage, as in alternative accounts preserved by Diodoros of Sicily about the origins of Rhodes. Diodoros' preferred ('true') explanation is that 'while, in the original forming of the world, the island was still muddy and soft, the sun dried up most of its moisture and caused the earth to produce living creatures' (5.56.3). But he also relates a *muthos* about the same process. On this view, Rhodos was a daughter of Poseidon, after whom the island was named. When, as a consequence of the Great Flood, most of the island lay under water, Helios the Sun God fell in love with Rhodos and caused the water which had engulfed her island to disappear.

It was, in fact, an enormously prevalent feeling in antiquity that the landscape was permeated by an immanent, living, divine power. Rivers were gods as well as being water; springs were nymphs; mountains were deities (there had once, people said, been a contest between Kithairon and Helikon).[5] One way in which this immanence was expressed was through narratives about metamorphosis: the remarkable, past fate of a named individual might enjoy a special sort of continuing existence in the present. I shall illustrate this by looking at four features of the landscape: rivers; springs; mountains and rocks; islands.

Despite their drastic seasonal fluctuation in volume, Greek **rivers** were commonly thought of as being ever-flowing and constantly self-renewing—and hence as partaking of the sacred.[6] This self-renewability was not, however, eternal: that is to say, it had not always been so. For belonging to the sacred did not imply being outside time: on the contrary, Greeks normally regarded that which was sacred as having had a specific genesis.

One way of imagining such a genesis was to see it as the product of sexual union: the all-encompassing River Okeanos was, according to

---

[5] See the fragmentary poem by Korinna (*PMG* 654), with Veneri (1996).

[6] Brewster's brief study (1997) of the potentially fascinating topic of Greek mythological rivers has some beautiful photographs, but is less strong on interpretation.

Hesiod's *Theogony*, the child of Gaia and Ouranos (133), while Okeanos' coupling with his sister Tethys led to the birth of lesser but still mighty rivers, from Acheloos and Haliakmon to Peneios and Strymon (337–45). Sometimes, though, a river was believed to owe its origin to a transformation. Pausanias tells a tale about the river Selemnos, near the north Peloponnesian city of Patrai (7.23.1–2):

The local people tell a story about it, that Selemnos was a handsome shepherd lad working there, and that Argyra [the name both of a nearby town and of its spring] was one of the sea nymphs: they say that she fell in love with Selemnos, and that she used to come up out of the sea to visit him and to sleep with him beside the river. But it was not long before Selemnos no longer looked so handsome, and the nymph did not want to visit him any more. So Selemnos lost his Argyra and died of love, and Aphrodite turned him (*epoiēsen*) into a river.

Pausanias goes on to re-emphasize that this is what the locals at Patrai relate; he thus avoids committing *himself* to the veracity of the tale, yet still lends his narrative the ring of authenticity which comes from local particularity. He then adds two codas. First he observes that, even in the form of water, Selemnos was still in love with Argyra: 'so Aphrodite gave Selemnos another favour: she made him forget Argyra.' This leads to the second coda, which, with a wry smile playing on the narrator's face, brings the story up to date:

I did hear another story about him, that the water of Selemnos is good for men and for women as a cure for love, since if they wash in the river they forget their passion. If there is any truth in this story, the water of Selemnos is worth more to humankind than a great deal of money.

Here, as in the story of Misurina, we find a non-geological, all-too-human truth embedded in a narrative of fantastic transformation.

The tale of Selemnos forms part of a much wider pattern according to which Greek rivers were felt to represent a continuity between the present and the remote past. *On Rivers*, a treatise unreliably ascribed to Plutarch, derives the names of numerous rivers (Hydaspes, Ismenos, Hebros, Phasis, Strymon, Eurotas, and so on) from the eponymous mythological figures who allegedly leapt into their respective waters and drowned. This story pattern represents a more highly rationalized approach than that implied by the story told at Patrai: there is no corporeal transformation, only a change of nomenclature. But both *On Rivers* and the tale of Selemnos imply that rivers link the contemporary world with that of the heroes. Although, in the famous opinion of Herakleitos, a river is never identical from one moment to the next, on a less sophisticated but surely more commonly held view it was indeed possible to step into 'the very rivers' into which Selemnos, Eurotas, and Strymon had been transformed.[7]

Springs renew themselves perpetually, a quality which, as with rivers, marks them out as sacred.[8] But, once more as with rivers, perpetual self-renewability does not imply eternal existence. Springs can be created; and the creation of a spring is surrounded by a sense of the numinous, for it necessarily belongs to the Before—the time about which myths are told. A blow from Pegasos' hoof brought forth a fountain of water (Hippokrene, 'Horse Spring') from a rock on Mount Helikon; on Mount Kithairon, maenads wielding the Bacchic *thyrsus* caused water to gush from rock, and wine and milk to spurt from solid ground.[9]

Another way in which springs were said to arise was through metamorphosis, an event typical of the Before. For the modern reader the exemplary case is Ovid's narration of the transformation of the nymph Arethousa. To elude the amorous pursuit of the river-god Alpheios, Arethousa successfully implores the aid of Diana (Gk. Artemis), who alters the maiden's form to that of flowing water (*Met.* 5.632–6). When Alpheios shifts his temporarily assumed human shape in order to mingle liquid with liquid, Diana cleaves the earth in order to enable Arethousa's waters to plunge deep underground, eventually to rise again as the Syracusan spring which bears her name. Pausanias was to relate a rather different version, in which the ardent Alpheios no longer appears as the Don Giovanni portrayed by Ovid (5.7.2):

And there are other tales about Alpheios: that he was a huntsman, and that he fell in love with Arethousa, herself a huntress with hounds. But Arethousa

---

[7] Herakleitos: KRS 214.

[8] See the catalogue in FI 300–7. On real-life and mythological springs, see Buxton (1994) 109–13.

[9] Pegasos: Ant. Lib. 9.2; other refs. in Papathomopoulos (1968) n. 15 on p. 89. Bacchants: Eur. *Ba.* 704–10.

did not want to marry, and they say that she crossed over to the island opposite Syracuse called Ortygia; there out of human form she became (*genesthai*) a spring, and Alpheios, for love, underwent the change (*allagēn*) into a river.

The gentle pathos of Pausanias' vignette strikes a note echoed in other tales whose dénouement is metamorphosis into a spring. To become that which is eternally fluid and restless is a fate which befalls several hapless mortals whose lives are distilled, first into tears, and then into a spring. Kleite was the wife of the magnificently hospitable Kyzikos, whom the Argonauts murdered as the result of a terrible error. Inconsolable, Kleite hanged herself. Apollonios relates the sequel (1.1065–9):

The very nymphs of the groves mourned her death, and from all the tears which dropped to the earth from their eyes the goddesses fashioned the spring which men called Kleite, the ever-renowned name of the unhappy bride.

Peirene, eponym of the still-visible fountain at Corinth, was another mortal woman who literally dissolved in sorrow: she became (*genoito*) a spring, grief-stricken after her son's accidental death at the hands of Artemis (Paus. 2.3.2). As for Byblis, her grief had a more transgressive origin: she fell in love with her twin brother Kaunos, but her feelings were not reciprocated. Our sources agree that, in some way or other, Byblis was 'replaced' by a spring; but the details are variously recounted. According to Antoninus Liberalis (30, following Nicander), Byblis attempted suicide by throwing herself from a mountainside; but the nymphs changed her (*ēllaxan*) into a nymph; the water which still runs down the rock-face is called 'the tear of Byblis'. Ovid's version brings us closer to Pausanias' story of Peirene, for it describes Byblis being consumed by tears and turned into a spring (*vertitur in fontem*), which 'still now' (*nunc quoque*) issues forth (*Met.* 9.663–5). Nonnos likewise reports that Byblis, drenched by tears, changed her body (*demas morphōsato*) and became a fountain (13.560). Other sources opt for a weaker form of replacement: Byblis first commits suicide (cf. Kleite), and then, from her tears, a spring is formed.[10]

---

[10] E.g. Konon *FGrH* 26 F 2; cf. Parthen. *Amat. narr.* 11, with Lightfoot (1999) ad loc. For more refs., see FI 300.

For a feature of the landscape to be credited with an origin in metamorphosis, that feature needed to possess a certain particularity—once upon a time, after all, it had been a human individual. Such individuality was felt to reside in **mountains and rocks**, each with contours and outlines unlike those of any other formation.

One of the most intricate of all the geologico-mythical complexes is that concerning Atlas. Early mythological traditions speak of a Titan of that name who 'holds' the world, or a part of it.[11] In the *Odyssey* he is said to 'hold the tall pillars which keep earth and heaven apart' (1.52–4). According to Hesiod's *Theogony* (517–20):

Atlas, under strong constraint, holds the broad sky, at the limits of the earth, in front of the clear-voiced Hesperides, standing, with his head and tireless hands, for this is the lot which shrewd Zeus assigned to him.

Different again is the image presented by Prometheus of his brother Titan in *Prometheus Bound* (348–50):

in the far west
He stands, pressing the column of sky and earth
Onto his shoulders, a burden hard to bear.

Each of these individual passages poses problems for those who seek to visualize exactly what image is being conjured up; a fortiori, anyone trying to reduce all the variations about Atlas to a single image is going to be disappointed.

The Atlantean tradition takes on a further twist with a passage from Herodotos. In the course of his description of the vast North African region which he calls 'Libya', he refers to a great mountain and the people who live in its shadow (4.184):

Once more at a distance of ten days' journey there is another hill, of salt, and a spring, and men dwell around it; adjoining the salt hill is the mountain called Atlas. The mountain is slender and conical, and so high that, so they say, the top cannot be seen, because neither in summer nor in winter is it ever free of cloud. The local people call it The Pillar of the Sky. They take their name from the mountain: they are called the Atlantes. They are said to eat no living creature, and never to dream.

---

[11] See West (1966) on Hes. *Th.* 517; Griffith (1983) on *PV* 347–50; S. West in Heubeck, West, and Hainsworth (1988) on *Od.* 1.52–4.

Far from holding the pillar, Atlas is here identified with it. Although Herodotos' account contains something of the astonishing—the idea of people who do not dream is an amazing, not to say a terrifying one—the emphasis this time falls on Atlas as a geographical feature.[12]

These contrasting traditions about Atlas illustrate different ancient ways of imagining the relationship between the mental compartments which *we* label as 'mythology' and 'geography'.[13] So far, of course, we have not been dealing with metamorphosis; but the tradition has another trick up its sleeve. According to Johannes Tzetzes's twelfth-century commentary on Lykophron's recondite Hellenistic poem *Alexandra*, a tale about the *transformation* of Atlas was circulating already in the late fifth/early fourth century BC, in a composition by the poet Polyidos:

Polyidos the dithyrambic poet represents [Atlas] as a shepherd who was visited by Perseus. Perseus, Polyidos relates, was asked by Atlas who he was and where he came from, but Atlas did not believe his answer. So Perseus was obliged to show Atlas the Gorgon's face—and turned him to stone. This is the origin of the name of Mount Atlas.[14]

This tale, which Ovid would elaborate in due course (*Met.* 4.627–62), is far from unique in asserting that solid rock had once been flesh and blood. The most famous example is Niobe, whose petrifaction perfectly symbolizes the speechless immobility to which grief has reduced her. Although transformed into a rock on Mount Sipylos in Lydia, however, she does not altogether lose contact with her previous existence. Unlike the blissfully amnesiac River Selemnos, she retains her memory of what has transpired; or at least, she seems to do so, for water everlastingly courses down the face of the rock, as a passage in *Iliad* Book 24 poignantly evokes (614–17):

And now (*nun*) somewhere among the rocks, in the lonely mountains, in Sipylos, where they say are the resting places of the goddesses, the nymphs,

---

[12] For the most telling account of Atlas as *combining* the geographical with the anthropomorphic, we must turn to Virgil (*A.* 4.246–51).

[13] The authoritative third edition of *The Oxford Classical Dictionary* (1996) includes an article on 'Atlas' devoted to the mythological Titan in literature and art, and a separate article—by different authors—on 'Atlas mountains'.

[14] *Etym. Magn.* 164.20 = Tzetz. ad Lyc. *Alex.* 879 = *PMG* 837. On Polyidos, see Riemschneider (1952).

who dance beside the Acheloos, there, stone though she is, she broods on the sorrows that came to her from the gods.

The 'now' referred to is the present time of the Homeric narrator; but Niobe's tears were no less actual in the second century AD, as witnessed by Pausanias (1.21.3):

I myself have seen this Niobe when I was climbing up Mount Sipylos. From close up it is a rock and a cliff, which does not offer the visitor an image of a woman either grieving or otherwise; but if you go further off you will seem to see a woman downcast and in tears.

As we have seen, a similar tale was told of a rock near Miletos which 'until now' (*achri nun*) could be seen shedding Byblis' tears (Ant. Lib. 30).[15] And 'until now' (*achri nun*) there was another rock, called 'The Lookout of Battos', the end-product of the metamorphosis of the countryman who rashly betrayed the secret of Hermes' theft of Apollo's cattle (Ant. Lib. 23). 'Until now': all these places signify, through the still-visible evidence of transformational genesis, the living persistence of the mythological past.[16]

One of the most distinctive features of the landscape of the Hellenic world is its proliferation of **islands**, from countless half-submerged rocks to major sub-regions of the Mediterranean such as Crete, Cyprus, and Sicily. Rough Ithaca, lush Corfu, barren Delos, breath-taking Santorini: as remarkable as their multitude is their diversity. Indeed, the definition of 'island' is far from straightforward, as Christy Constantakopoulou's fascinating book *The Dance of the Islands* demonstrates. For present purposes I shall borrow her spare, working definition: a 'piece of land completely surrounded by water'.[17]

In myth and cult islands play a manifold role. Though no ancient traveller has left us an account of the religious antiquities and beliefs of the islands to set beside Pausanias' guide to the mainland, we can piece together a reasonable picture from disparate sources. Crete was Zeus' birthplace and the home of Minos and Daidalos; on Sicily Persephone caught the eye of Hades; the 'Lemnian deed', by which

---

[15] See 199 above.
[16] For excellent remarks on petrifaction, see Frontisi-Ducroux (2003) 179–220.
[17] Constantakopoulou (2007) 12.

that island's women systematically massacred its entire male population, figured among the most lurid mythical *exempla* of dangerous female behaviour; Naxos (or Dia) witnessed the betrayal of Ariadne by Theseus, and her consolation by Dionysos; Delos claimed to be the birthplace of Apollo; Kythera and Cyprus (especially Paphos) sang to Aphrodite, who came ashore at one spot or another on emerging from the foam; Samothrace was, and still is, difficult of access, and so was ideally situated to be the home of Mysteries for gods whose very names were secret.

One way in which myths expressed not just the interplay but the identity of geology with the sacred was by representing islands as themselves partaking of the divine. A theme of Pindar's lovely *Seventh Olympian* is the emergence of Rhodes into the light of the sun. When the earth was allotted to the immortals, Rhodes still lay hidden beneath the sea. Now it happened that, during the apportionment, Helios was absent; so he received no share. When he returned, Zeus offered to draw the lots again; but Helios saw no need (61–8):

> For he said that in the grey sea
> He saw swelling up from the bottom
> A land with much food for men and friendly to flocks.
> Straightway he told gold-veiled Lachesis
> To lift her hands and not betray
> The great oath of the Gods,
> But, with Kronos' son, to grant
> That, when it was sent to the bright air,
> It should be his special gift henceforward.

Rhodes emerged from the deep: an island and at the same time a desirable maiden (71–6):

> There on a day [Helios] lay with Rhodes, and begat
> Seven sons, who inherited wisdom
> Beyond all earlier men.
> One of them begat Kamiros,
> And Ialysos for firstborn,
> And Lindos. They portioned their father's land
> In three, and kept their separate share of cities,
> And their places are called by their names.[18]

---

[18] Trans. Bowra (1969), slightly adapted.

A similar blend of landscape with divinity is found in the *Homeric Hymn to Delian Apollo*. Alone among lands, the tiny island of Delos was willing to allow Leto to give birth to Apollo upon its/her territory. But Delos was anxious (70–8):

> Therefore I greatly fear in mind and spirit that, as soon as he sees the light of the sun, he will scorn this island—for truly my ground is stony—and will overturn me with his feet and thrust me down in the depths of the sea; then will the great waves wash above my head deeply for ever, and he will go to another land, whichever pleases him, and will establish there his temple and wooded groves. So, octopuses will make their lairs in me, and black seals their secure dwellings, because I lack people.

Yet Leto swore an oath that Apollo would revere Delos above all other places; and Delos was persuaded.

Both stories emphasize the instability of an island's existence: Rhodes had once lain beneath the sea; Delos might some day subside once more beneath the waves. The precariousness of Delos was further demonstrated by the fact that it had, it was said, originally been a *wandering* island, before it was eventually fixed in its central location in the Aegean.[19] And to all this we must add another sort of precariousness, that which goes with being on a boundary between two states of existence. For some islands had once been living beings.

In a sense this idea is just an extension of the notion of metamorphosis into a mountain or rock, for many Greek 'islands' are nothing more than rocky outcrops surrounded by water. Rockiness is certainly an attribute of Aigina. Pausanias calls it 'the most unapproachable island in Greece; all around it there are rocks underwater or just at the surface' (2.29.6), and Aigina is an island whose origin lay, according to mythology, in metamorphosis, of one kind or another. One tradition held that the only thing to be transformed was the island's *name*: Aigina was one of the innumerable nymphs on whom Zeus' lustful eye fell, and the isle to which he took her in order to lie with her was named in her honour.[20] But an isolated variant, recorded in a scholion on the *Iliad*, explained that Zeus transformed (*metemorphōsen*) Aigina into an island, while he himself was changed (*meteblēthē*) into a stone, so as to trick the nymph's father, the river-

---

[19] Call. *Del.* 51–4.   [20] Apollod. *Bibl.* 3.12.6.

god Asopos.[21] The island into which Aigina was transformed had been uninhabited when the transformation took place: perhaps the notion of a nymph transformed into a *populated* island would indeed deserve the epithet 'astonishing'.

The greatest river of central Greece is the Acheloos, which flows into the sea near the ancient town of Oiniadai in Akarnania. A little way offshore lie the islands known as the Echinades, the 'prickly' or 'spiky' ones; the name is related to *echinos*, 'hedgehog'. Classical writers stress the islands' impermanence. Herodotos notes that deposits from the Acheloos have already joined half the islands to the mainland (2.10). Thucydides describes the alluvial process by which these 'uninhabited' islands are formed (2.102). In fact he roots this process in mythology: the polluted matricide Alkmaion was told by an oracle that he could only settle in a place which had not existed as land at the time when he committed his dreadful crime; the land recently generated by the alluvial deposit of the Acheloos was the answer to the conundrum. Pausanias would later make the ecologically shrewd observation that the reason why the anticipated joining of islands to mainland has not in fact taken place is that the Aitolian territory through which the Acheloos flows remains uncultivated (8.24.11).[22] Alongside all these observations there circulated a myth of transformation. At least according to Ovid—we cannot trace the tale back any earlier[23]—the Echinades were originally nymphs who made the fatal mistake of failing to pay proper honour to the river-god Acheloos, and were transformed into islands as punishment (*Met.* 8.573–89). But metamorphosis was as often an avenue of rescue for the hapless innocent as it was an indictment of transgression by the guilty. Ovid's narrative goes on to tell of a mortal girl called Perimele who, so far from shunning Acheloos, had been his lover. Her father discovered the affair and hurled his daughter into the sea; but Poseidon changed her into an island.

Though our Greek sources are once again patchy compared with the Latin ones, there was almost certainly a similar story told of Lichas, the henchman and herald of Herakles. According to Sophokles' *Women of Trachis*, after Lichas had brought his master the robe

---

[21] Schol. *Il.* 1.180.   [22] See Hordern and Purcell (2000) 312–14.
[23] Cf. FI 308.

sent, in ignorance of its lethal effect, by his wife Deianeira, Herakles at last found himself in a trap from which there was no escape. He lashed out at Lichas, throwing him into the sea from the north-western tip of Euboia.[24] Thus originated the Lichades islands, still so named: they lie below the mainland settlement of Lichada, on the western slope of Mount Lichas.[25]

If the Hellenic ancestry of these myths about island metamorph-oses cannot be traced with exactness, there is no doubt that they correspond to a general pattern of thought going back at least to Homer. The *Odyssey* narrates the petrifaction of a whole ship, crew and all. The vessel is that in which the Phaiakians convey Odysseus back to Ithaca. Frustrated in his desire to eliminate Odysseus, Posei-don proposes to work out his anger by petrifying the ship on its return to its home port and, into the bargain, piling a mountain on top of the Phaiakians' city. Zeus vetoes the more extreme reprisal, but allows the milder one (13.159–64):

When Poseidon the Earthshaker heard him, he went off to Scheria, where the Phaiakians dwell. There he waited; and the sea-going ship came close in, lightly pursuing her course. And the Earthshaker came close up to her, and turned her to stone, and rooted her there to the sea's bottom with a flat stroke of his hand.

The reaction of the ordinary Phaiakians is one of perplexity and astonishment in face of the strangeness of this event—*thambos*, though the word itself is absent (165–70). But their king, Alkinoos, more than ordinarily perceptive, detects the presence of an Olympian (just as Nestor had done when Athene flew off at Pylos). Recalling an ancient prophecy which predicted the metamorphosis, Alkinoos without delay sets in train a choice sacrifice to Poseidon so as to avoid the impending risk (to which the prophecy also alluded) that the Phaiakians' city would be annihilated by having a mountain piled upon it.[26]

Stories about metamorphosis from human to landscape rested on assumptions embedded in religious cult. Mountains were places of

---

[24] Soph. *Tr.* 777–82; cf. 787–8.
[25] For the name of the little islands, see Strabo 9.4.4.
[26] Compare Zeus' petrifaction of a snake in the *Iliad*; see 48 above.

danger and reversal, where divinities might be encountered at any time, and where certain divinities, notably Zeus, received worship; rivers were revered as gods, and springs as nymphs.[27] Certain features of the landscape thus already had about them an air of the uncanny, expressed in ritual practice; the idea that metamorphosis had once played a part in their genesis was merely an extension of such perceived sacredness. Yet such considerations are in themselves insufficient to enable us to answer the tremendously difficult question: how far were Greek metamorphosis narratives—in this case, narratives about the landscape—actually 'believed'?

All the testimonies which bear on this question are second-hand: we cannot interrogate the original myth-tellers or their audiences and readers. This already limits the sorts of answer we can give to the question about belief. But one important theme runs through our material, from many historical periods throughout antiquity: Greeks themselves were perfectly well aware that belief in myths was *variable*. Different people, in different contexts, might hear the same stories with a variety of reactions ranging from total scepticism to absolute credulity. Numerous ancient witnesses could be cited to demonstrate this awareness; it will be sufficient to single out one memorable and moving example from the fourth century BC: a passage from Plato's *Phaidros*.

Although it contains no specific reference to metamorphosis, the passage does deal with the numinous quality of a landscape, and with the kinds of attitude which might be adopted towards the myths associated with that landscape.

Socrates Lead on then, and look out for a place where we can sit down.
Phaidros You see that tall plane-tree over there?
Socrates To be sure.
Phaidros There's some shade, and a gentle breeze, and grass to sit down on, or lie down if we like.
Socrates Then lead on.
Phaidros Tell me, Socrates, isn't it somewhere about here that they say Boreas seized Oreithuia from the river Ilisos?
Socrates Yes, that is the story.

---

[27] Cf. Buxton (1994) 80–113; (2004b) 178–91.

Phaidros   Was this the actual spot? Certainly the water looks charmingly
pure and clear; it's just the place for girls to be playing beside the stream.

Socrates   No, it was about a quarter of a mile lower down, where you cross
to the sanctuary of Agra; there is, I believe, an altar dedicated to Boreas
close by.

Phaidros   I have never really noticed it; but pray tell me, Socrates, do you
believe that story to be true?

Socrates   I should be quite in the fashion if I disbelieved it, as the clever
people (*hoi sophoi*) do: I might proceed, in sophisticated vein (*sophizome-
nos*), to maintain that the maiden, while at play with Pharmakeia, was
blown by a gust of Boreas down from the rocks hard by, and that, having
thus met her death, she was said to have been 'seized by Boreas': though it
may have happened on the Areiopagos, according to another version of the
occurrence. For my part, Phaidros, I regard such theories as no doubt
attractive, but as the invention of clever, industrious people who are not
exactly to be envied, for the simple reason that they must then go on to tell
us the real truth about the appearance of centaurs and the Chimaira, not to
mention a whole host of such creatures, Gorgons and Pegasoses and
countless other remarkable monsters flocking in on them. If our sceptic,
with his somewhat crude wisdom (*sophia*), means to reduce every one of
them to the standard of probability, he'll need a deal of time for it. I myself
have certainly no time for the business: and I'll tell you why, my friend. I
can't as yet 'know myself', as the inscription at Delphi enjoins; and, so long
as that ignorance remains, it seems to me ridiculous to inquire into
extraneous matters. Consequently I don't bother about such things, but
accept the current beliefs about them, and direct my inquiries, as I have
just said, rather to myself, to discover whether I really am a more complex
creature and more puffed up with pride than Typhon, or a simpler, gentler
being whom heaven has blessed with a quiet, un-Typhonic nature. By the
way, my friend, isn't this the tree we were making for?

Phaidros   Yes, that's the one.

Socrates   Upon my word, a delightful resting-place, with this tall, spreading
plane, and a lovely shade from the high branches of the agnus: now that
it's in full flower, it will make the place beautifully fragrant. And what a
lovely stream under the plane-tree, and how cool to the feet! Judging by
the statuettes and images I should say it's consecrated to Acheloos and
some of the nymphs.[28]

Four points are worth making about this delightful passage. (1)
Like every other ancient text which touches on the question of belief,

---

[28]   *Phdr.* 229a–230b; trans. based on Hackforth (1952), with amendments.

this one is embedded in a context with its own implied agenda. What Socrates is here concerned to counter is *not* generally held beliefs either about the abduction of Oreithuia or about other extraordinary mythical creatures or occurrences, but rather the 'sophisticated' theories being advanced by his contemporaries in order to undermine such beliefs. It is not that Socrates anywhere expresses his own adherence to these generally held beliefs; rather, because the rationalizing sceptics constitute a rival style of speculation to his own method, they must be tackled head-on, whereas the credulous believer is evidently regarded as unthreatening to the position which Socrates is defending. (2) It is significant that the myths which are singled out as requiring the services of sophisticated experts, in order to make sense of them through rationalization, are those involving hybridity: centaurs, the Chimaira, the Gorgons, Pegasos the winged horse. The shoe of comprehensibility pinches with special acuteness when what is at issue is *strangeness of form*, even if it is a question of hybridity rather than metamorphosis. (3) Even amid his self-distancing elusiveness over the question of belief, Socrates makes his point using the image of the monstrous Typhon. Myths are a shared currency of expression even among those who disagree about their literal veracity. (4) Regardless of his attitude toward those whom he suggests are credulous, Socrates does nothing to undermine respect for the examples of *cult* here referred to—in this case, worship of Acheloos and the nymphs.

Few Greeks, to be sure, could have expressed themselves on the subject of the numinousness of the landscape with the subtle artistry of Plato. What kinds of opinions will have been more commonly held on this topic? One thing is certain: such opinions will have been extraordinarily varied. It is indeed impossible to rule out, either that there will have been individuals who believed in the literal truth of every ancient account of the transformation of human beings into landscape, or that there will have been individuals who regarded every such story as an absurd fabrication. Most people presumably held views which fell somewhere between the extremes, those views being, as usual, dependent on the context within which people narrated, read, and listened to accounts of such astonishing matters.

8

Plants, Trees, and Human Form

Tales of the transformation of human beings into features of the land-scape suggest that the heroic-mythological past could be perceived, at some level and in some contexts, as living on within the present world of the myth-tellers. The same may be said of stories which narrate the transformation of human beings into plants or trees. However, narra-tives of unmediated metamorphoses into plants or trees are quite rare. In order to locate such narratives, we need to set them against the background of other Greek beliefs about the permeability of the bound-ary between plant life and the life of anthropomorphic beings, whether human or divine. According to such beliefs, plants and trees could be variously regarded as (1) being identified with anthropomorphic beings, or (2) having generated such beings, or (3) having grown from such beings via an intermediate bodily fluid which dripped onto the earth. After considering these three types of belief, I shall move finally to discuss the view that (4) human beings could turn into plants or trees through unmediated metamorphosis.

THE IDENTITY OF A NYMPH

Each tree, it was widely assumed, possessed its own sacred individu-ality. A detailed articulation of this assumption can be found in the *Homeric Hymn to Aphrodite*. After making love with the handsome shepherd Anchises, Aphrodite lulls him to sleep. When he wakes up, she reveals what lies in store for Aineias, the child who will be born from this unequal union between goddess and mortal. As befits the product of such disparate parents, Aineias will be looked after in the wilds by beings who are themselves neither mortal nor immortal. In the words of Aphrodite (256–73):

As for him, as soon as he sees the light of the sun, the deep-breasted mountain nymphs who inhabit this great and holy mountain [sc. Ida, near Troy] shall bring him up. They belong neither with mortals nor with immortals. They live long, and eat divine food, and tread the lovely dance with the immortals, and with them the Silenoi and the sharp-eyed Slayer of Argos [sc. Hermes] couple lovingly in the depths of pleasant caves. At their birth fir trees or high-topped oaks spring up with them upon the fruitful earth, beautiful, flourishing trees, towering on the high mountains, and people call them precincts of the immortals, and no mortals cut them with the axe. But when the fate of death is near at hand, first those lovely trees wither where they stand, the bark shrivels around them, the branches fall off, and the life of the nymph and that of the tree leave the light of the sun together. These nymphs shall keep my son with them and rear him.

Myths record the names of many such coeval tree nymphs. The epic poet Pherenikos told the story of Hamadryas, daughter of Oreios ('Mountainous'): she mated with her brother and had children called Karya ('Nut'), Balanos ('Acorn'), Kraneia ('Cornel-cherry'), Morea ('Mulberry'), Aigeiros ('Poplar'), Ptelea ('Elm'), Ampelos ('Vine'), and Suke ('Fig').[1] According to another tale, this time recounted by Apollonios, the mother of the centaur Cheiron was the nymph Philyra ('Lime')—though this was of little relevance to the form of her offspring: more to the point was the fact that Philyra's mate Kronos, caught in adultery by his wife Rheia, leapt up from beside Philyra and galloped away in the form of a stallion.[2]

Other traditions incorporate complexities which belie the seemingly transparent etymology which derives 'hamadryad' from *hama*, 'together with', and *drus*, 'tree' or 'oak tree'.[3] In Kallimachos' *Hymn to Demeter*, when the foolhardy Erysichthon fells a tree sacred to the goddess it is not just Demeter who is pained (37–9):

---

[1] Athen. *Deipn.* 78b.

[2] Ap. Rhod. *Arg.* 2.1231–41. Philyra was also an island (1231)—a further indicator of the symbolic density which mythical logic can attain.

[3] For tree nymphs, see Larson (2001) 73–8. For nymphs in an Indo-European context, see West (2007) 284–92.

There was a poplar, a huge tree reaching to the sky, *near* which the nymphs used to play at noon. This was the first tree struck, and it shrieked miserably to the others.[4]

Neil Hopkinson, whose translation I borrow, renders the Greek preposition *epi* as 'near', and supports this by citing other passages where *epi* takes the dative case and where 'at' or 'around' are reasonable translations.[5] Yet the tree which is struck, and which shrieks, clearly *is* a nymph. So in one and the same passage nymphs can be simultaneously separate from and coextensive with 'their' trees.

Slightly different in emphasis, and no more straightforward, is a passage from Kallimachos' *Hymn to Delos*. When pregnant Leto was searching for a place in which to give birth, among those who fled from the anger of Hera was the nymph Melie ('Ash'), pale of cheek, 'panting for'—that is, presumably, longing to be re-assimilated to— the tree which was coeval (*hēlix*) with her (79–81). The poetic narrator goes on to imply his own uncertainty about the exact nature of a tree nymph's being, and appeals to the Muses for guidance (82–5):

My goddesses, Muses, tell me, did the *drues* truly come into being at the same time as the nymphs did? The nymphs rejoice when rain makes the *drues* grow, and again the nymphs lament when there are no longer leaves on the *drues*.

The concept of the coeval nymph recurs in a speech from Apollonios' *Argonautika*, in which Phineus recounts what happened to the father of his assistant Paraibios. Once upon a time a hamadryad had unsuccessfully begged this man not to fell 'the coeval (*hēlix*) oak *in* which she had always lived her long life' (2.479–80; my italics). Here I adopt the translation by Richard Hunter, who takes the preposition *epi* this time to mean, not 'near', but 'in' the tree. This interpretation might seem to be corroborated by the presence of the word *hēlix*, though to be coeval is not necessarily to be physically coextensive with one's material 'partner': when Aischylos applied the word *hēlix* to the wooden log to which the life of Meleager was fatally linked, he was presumably not implying that the doomed hero *was* the log, only that, when the log burned up, his life would be consumed too.[6] If one

---

[4] Trans. Hopkinson (1984); my italics.   [5] Hopkinson (1984) on line 38.
[6] Aesch. *Cho.* 608.

of the essential aspects of nymphs is their intermediate status between mortal and immortal, another is their variable relationship to
the physical medium in which they have their being.[7]

HUMANITY FROM TREES

The indeterminate nature of tree nymphs implies that the boundary
between the plant world and the anthropomorphic world is, or may
sometimes be, porous. The same implication is present, albeit
differently so, in the belief that human beings were originally generated from trees. In Hesiod's *Works and Days* the Bronze Race, third in
time after those of Gold and Silver, is said to have been created by Zeus
ek melian, 'from ash trees' (143–5). Apollonios drew on a similar
tradition when he described the bronze giant Talos as 'the last
survivor of the bronze race of men born from ash trees' (4.1641–2).[8]
Other sources refer the aetiology of humanity either to *drues*, (oak)
trees, or to *meliai*, ash trees, or to *pitus*, the pine.[9] Parallels have
been sought and found in, for example, ancient Iran and in the
Norse *Edda*, and the conclusion has been drawn that this is a case of
the adaptation into a Greek context of a traditional Indo-European
belief.[10] There is probably no way of confirming this, but it is worth
noting that the idea that humans *originated* as trees is relatively
seldom attested in Greece, as compared with the extensive evidence
for the belief that humans could *generate* plants and trees. Perhaps
the wish to establish the existence of those Indo-European roots (the
pun is perhaps not inappropriate) has sometimes led scholars to

---

[7] On all aspects of nymphs, see the excellent treatment by Larson (2001).

[8] On Talos, see Buxton (2002b).

[9] *Drues*: e.g. schol. *Od.* 19.163. *Meliai*: e.g. Palaeph. *Peri apist.* 35; schol. *Il.*
22.126–7. *Pitus*: Nonnos *Dion.* 12.56. The sources are helpfully discussed by
Seeliger (1924–37) 500–1. See also West (1966) on *Th.* 35 and 187; (1978) on *WD*
145–6. Ancient commentators were prompted into discussing the humans-from-
trees issue by two enigmatic, proverb-like expressions which seemed to demand
explication. One was in Hesiod ('But what is all this round (oak) tree or rock?', *Th.*
35), the other in Homer ('You were not born from any legendary (oak) tree, or a
rock,' *Od.* 19.163). See West (1966) on *Th.* 35.

[10] Seeliger (1924–37) 501; West (2007) 375–6.

overemphasize the prevalence in Greece of the belief that humans came originally from trees.

MILK, TEARS, AND BLOOD

The notion that plants and trees could grow indirectly from anthropomorphic beings, whether mortals or gods, is clearly related to the idea of direct metamorphosis. But I want to consider it separately in order to highlight the generative role attributed to particular bodily fluids.

Milk

I begin with an example which, although untypical as regards the fluid involved, nevertheless illustrates how Greek beliefs about plants were integrated into a wider network of thought. According to a passage in the tenth-century AD Byzantine compilation known as *Geoponika* (a collection of ancient writings on agricultural matters), a white lily grew from the place where Hera's milk continued to flow out onto the ground, after she had finished suckling baby Herakles; on the other hand, the milk which flowed into the sky—we presume she was suckling the baby on celestial Mount Olympos—became the Milky Way (11.19.2). Aptly for a plant associated with the goddess of marital union, the lily could be seen as standing in symbolic opposition to Aphrodite, whose province was sexual pleasure enjoyed outside as well as inside marriage. Such was Aphrodite's antipathy towards the chaste flower that in mockery she endowed it with a rampant yellow pistil.[11] So the lily has something of Hera and something of Aphrodite. Given that Herakles, the child at Hera's breast, was himself the product of Zeus' adultery, the link between the lily and chastity becomes even more double-edged.

---

[11] Athen. *Deipn.* 683d–e = Nic. *Georg.* fr. 74.25–30; cf. Nic. *Alex.* 405–9. See Murr (1890) 251–2.

Although the generative power of breast milk might seem to be close to self-evident, the motif of plants generated by milk is in fact uncommon. More frequent are myths involving two fluids common to male and female: tears and blood.

Tears

One mythical figure to shed generative tears was Helen. When she cried at the death, from snakebite, of Menelaos' steersman Kanobos, from her tears there grew the plant known as *heleneion* (elecampane).[12] Less well known is the tradition according to which Lykourgos, the legendary, Pentheus-like opponent of Dionysos, was once brought to tears when bound fast by the Dionysiac vine. On the spot where his tears fell there grew a *krambē* (cabbage)—whence originates the ongoing antipathy between that vegetable and the vine (exemplified, as Aristotle noted, by the fact that the juice of boiled cabbage is a sovereign cure for a hangover).[13]

The pain-induced tears of Lykourgos may be grievous; the tears of Helen, shed for the death of a friend, can hardly be less than affecting; but neither can compare for pathetic intensity with the tears of a bereaved, divine lover. When Aphrodite's mortal favourite Adonis was gored to death by a wild boar, the goddess was stirred to tears. Divinities do not often weep, especially over mere mortals;[14] in Euripides' *Hippolytos* Artemis even describes it as 'not *themis* (proper order)' for gods so to shed tears (1396). When they do, the motivation must be powerful. Usually the cause is the actual or anticipated loss of one's child: Thetis bewails the impending fate of her doomed son Achilles; Demeter laments the abduction of Persephone; Apollo grieves for the loss of Asklepios and sheds teardrops which turn to amber; Zeus, more extraordinarily, cries tears of blood in sorrowful anticipation of the death of Sarpedon.[15] But in Aphrodite's universe

---

[12] *Etym. Magn.* 328, 16; Nic. *Ther.* 309–19.
[13] Schol. Aristoph. *Knights* 539; *Geop.* 12.17.16–17; Aristot. *Prob.* 873[a–b].
[14] See Reed (1997), n. on Bion *Adon.* 64.
[15] Thetis: *Il.* 1.413–18. Demeter: Call. *Cer.* 17. Apollo: Ap. Rhod. *Arg.* 4.611–18. Zeus: *Il.* 16.459–61. Those tears of blood are exceptional. Whatever their other bodily differences from humanity—*ichōr* in the veins; ambrosia in the digestive tract—the gods seem normally to cry on the same physiological basis as mortals do.

no sentiment takes precedence over sexual love: Adonis means as much to the goddess of *erōs* as do Achilles, Persephone, Asklepios, and Sarpedon to their respective divine parents. So, in the words of the Hellenistic poet Bion in his *Epitaph for Adonis* (64–6):

The Paphian goddess sheds as many tears as Adonis sheds drops of blood; on the ground all become (*ginetai*) flowers: his blood gives birth to the rose, her tears to the anemone.[16]

Instead of making an offering at Adonis' grave, Aphrodite produces from within her own body a substance whose effect will be simultaneously to celebrate and to mourn the young man she has lost. Annually, perpetually, the flowering of the anemone will mark his death, and her love.

What are we to make of these stories, which, by invoking the generative power of tears, link an emotional event from the mythical past to a contemporary feature of the natural world? In our discussion of springs we noted a number of cases in which tears (in spite of their saltiness) were prolonged into ever-flowing sources of fresh water.[17] But the alleged capacity of tears to generate new plant life is something different.

In order to investigate the mythical logic behind this, we need first to ask whether any generally perceived properties of tears in the Greek world can throw light on our stories. One of the very few scholars to have taken an interest in this topic is R. B. Onians, in the course of his remarkable and still enthralling study of the interrelationship between mind and body in ancient perceptions.[18] Onians begins by pointing out that, in a number of Homeric texts, especially in the *Odyssey*, there is an association between the notions of existence (*aiōn*), melting (*tēkesthai*), flowing ((*kat-*)*eibein*), wasting away (*phthinesthai, phthinuthein*), and tears. For example, a person's *aiōn* can be spoken of as being wasted, or as flowing away in lamentation, under the pressure of an intense yearning for a loved one. One classic instance is the tearful melting of Odysseus when he hears

---

[16] For an alternative version, according to which the anemone was generated by Adonis' blood, see Reed (1997) n. on line 66. See also 219–20 below.

[17] See 199 above.

[18] Onians (1951) 200–5.

Demodokos' song about the Trojan horse, a reaction which the narrator compares to the distraught keening of a widow, her cheeks wasted with grief, as she lies over the corpse of her slaughtered husband (*Od.* 8.521–31). Another example is Penelope's wish to die, in order to escape from the tearful longing which she feels for her absent husband, as her *aiōn* is wasted (18.202–5). Above all, there is the image of Odysseus alone on the shore of Kalypso's island: his sweet *aiōn* flows out of him in lamentation as he longs for Penelope (5.151–8). Onians's compelling conclusion is that one's *aiōn* can be imagined as in some sense a liquid, which may flow out of the body in the form of tears.

But there is more. Onians goes on to note another nexus of images, which links wetness and melting with sexual desire as located in the eyes. Euripides expresses the connection in *Hippolytos*, when the chorus invokes the god Eros, who 'drips desire down over the eyes' (525–6).[19] The link gains the support of Aristotle-the-physiologist when he argues that 'of all the parts of the head, the area around the eyes is the most productive of sperm (*spermatikōtatos*)', a point elaborated elsewhere when he speaks of the contraction of the eyes during sexual intercourse as having the effect of forcing out the moisture which collects around the brain.[20] Putting all this together, Onians argues for an identity, evidenced in texts from many diverse areas of Greek thought, between the tears which come from the eyes, and a fluid which may be thought of as a distillation of the human *aiōn*.

In my view Onians has convincingly shown that in ancient Greece tears could be felt to be both central to the 'stuff' of life and potent in the regeneration of that life. What seems to be happening in the myths which we looked at earlier (Lykourgos; Helen and Kanobos; Aphrodite and Adonis) is that the culturally acknowledged idea of the centrality and potency of tears reaches a special degree of intensity as a result of the pathos created by the myth-tellers' narratives. What had been potential becomes actual: mingled with earth, tears actually generate a new form of life.

---

[19] W. S. Barrett (1964) ad loc. rightly observes: 'That sexual desire manifests itself in the eyes is a commonplace of Greek poetry.'
[20] *GA* 747^{a}13–14; *Prob.* 876^{b}8–10.

It is not difficult to find parallels outside Greece for a generative power ascribed to the tears of *divinities*. In ancient Egypt, human beings were said to have been born from the tears of Ra, and aromatic resins to have been generated from the tears of Horus. According to Japanese belief, when the primordial goddess Izanami died, her brother/husband Izanagi shed tears of grief, from which sprang other divinities. The tears of the Hindu god Prajapati caused the generation of the earth.[21] In a more general sense, the shedding of tears by divinities may have the capacity to bring the dead back to life, as in the tales of Anat and Ba'al, or Isis and Osiris.[22] Within that comparative framework, the fecund tears of the goddess Aphrodite need little explanation.

What distinguishes the Greek accounts, though, is that they feature not just the tears of a divinity, but those of a hero and a heroine. (Helen was a daughter of Zeus; Lykourgos' parentage was less august, but still impressive: his father was usually said to have been Dryas, '(Oak) Tree Man', but a variant made him the son of Ares himself.[23]) Now heroes and heroines were believed to possess powers greater than those of ordinary mortals. What could be more congenial to Greek assumptions about the sacred, than that the tears of a hero or heroine should also possess a special potency?

Blood

The genesis of plants from blood is a theme which runs through several Greek myths. Below I set out the principal and most characteristic examples.[24]

1. **Hyakinthos** was a handsome youth loved by Apollo. When the two were indulging in a session of field sports, it happened that a discus cast by the god struck Hyakinthos on the head and killed

[21] Cf. Canney (1926) 53.

[22] See Lutz (1999) 34.

[23] With typical prodigality, Nonnos gives us both versions: son of Ares (20.217; cf. 149) and son of Dryas (21.159).

[24] For what follows I have drawn on Murr (1890), Piccaluga (1966), and Ribichini (1983).

him.[25] Where his blood fell to the ground, there sprang up the flower known as *huakinthos*, said to bear upon it the letters AI AI, a lament in remembrance of Apollo's grief.[26]

2. **Narkissos** was another handsome lad for whom passion led to an early death. Stories varied: he fell in love with his own reflection, or else, in a variant which Pausanias (9.31.7–9) found more plausible, he fell in love with his twin sister, after whose death he consoled himself by gazing at his own reflection in a mountain pool, imagining that he was looking at her. According to the mythographer Konon, Narkissos' self-love was a punishment for his having callously rejected a (male) lover, who then committed suicide.[27] Narkissos, in his turn, killed himself—by the sword, we are to infer; for the people of Thespiai in Boiotia believe, so Konon reports, that an eponymous flower grew where the young man's blood fell to earth. Pausanias, for his part, makes the shrewd observation that this cannot have been the *first* such flower, if one believes the lines of a poet who 'was born many years before Narkissos' and who spoke of Persephone's gathering of that flower just before her abduction by Hades.

3. **Krokos**, like Hyakinthos, died when struck by a discus; this time the unlucky thrower was Hermes. From the young man's blood there grew the *krokos*; according to a variant, however, it was the spilt blood of Herakles which generated the flower.[28] In yet another version of the myth, Krokos' fate was linked to that of a maiden named Smilax, who was herself turned into the plant (bindweed) which bore her name.[29]

4. The downfall of **Adonis** was not athletics, but hunting. As we saw earlier, in Bion's poem the blood of Aphrodite's young favourite produced the rose; in a variant, the bloom generated was the anemone.[30] In a third version, what was at stake was the *colour* of the rose,

---

[25] E.g. Eur. *Hel.* 1469–73; Apollod. *Bibl.* 1.3.3; 3.10.3; Nonnos *Dion.* 10.250–5.

[26] Luc. *DDeor.* 16; other refs. in FI 280–2. See also Mellink (1943); Sergent (1984) 97–123; Amigues (1992); Moreau (1999).

[27] *FGrH* 26 F 1, 24.

[28] Gal. *De comp. medic. sec. loc.* xiii. 269 K; Dioscor. *De mat. med.* 1.26.

[29] Nonnos *Dion.* 12.85–6 (though the text is enigmatic); Ov. *Met.* 4.283. Discussion of the variants by Piccaluga (1966) 240–1 n. 37.

[30] Nic. fr. 65 = schol. Theoc. 5.92; see Reed (1997) on Bion *Adon.* 66.

which allegedly owed its origin to the spattered blood of Aphrodite, who tore her flesh on thorns as she rushed to her dying beloved.[31]

5. The pomegranate (in Greek, *sidē* or *rhoa*) was said to have grown upon the graves of **Menoikeus** and **Eteokles**, two warriors who died defending their Theban homeland from the expedition of the Seven.[32] In view of the blood-red juice which the fruit's seeds exude, it is eminently logical that other narratives also ascribe its origin to spilt blood, either that of **Dionysos** torn apart by the Titans, or that of the heroine **Side**, who committed suicide on her mother's grave in order to escape her father's incestuous advances.[33]

However, the most complex aetiology of the pomegranate, in a myth preserved by the rhetorician and Christian convert Arnobius (second to third centuries AD), ascribes the fruit's origin to **Agdistis**.[34] Agdistis was a hermaphrodite. In myth, such an abnormal creature can never be born by chance, but must originate through an irregular conception. The progenitor in this case was Zeus, the mother being Gaia/Earth. Zeus had shed semen during the night; where this dripped onto the ground, the creature Agdistis was born. Such a monstrous hybrid offended the divine order: at any rate, the gods intervened violently so as to prevent Agdistis from reproducing him- or herself. Arnobius attributes the intervention to Dionysos, who castrated the creature; where the blood fell to earth, a pomegranate grew. (According to the variant recounted by Pausanias (7.17.9–12), it was the gods collectively who were responsible for castrating Agdistis; from the blood of his severed member there grew an almond tree.) Nor does the equation: 'blood + earth = growth of new plant' stop there. Arnobius goes on to relate that Nana, daughter of the River Sangarios, became pregnant because she had placed a pomegranate seed in her lap. Since the seed bore within it something of the abnormality of Agdistis, the tale of abnormal procreation inevitably had further to run. Nana's pregnancy culminated in the birth of a lovely boy called **Attis**; but his erotic career was no more

---

[31] Aphthon. *Prog.* 2; Philostr. *Epist.* 4.
[32] Paus. 9.25.1; Philostr. *Im.* 2.29.
[33] Dionysos: Clem. Al. *Protr.* 2.19.3. Side: Dionys. Perieg. *Ixeut.* 1.7.
[34] Arn. *Adv. nat.* 5.6.

orthodox than that of Agdistis.[35] He was loved both by Agdistis and by the goddess Kybele. On the day of Attis' wedding to Midas' daughter **Ia**, the sudden appearance of Agdistis in a jealous frenzy drove Attis himself mad: in a replay, with variations, of the fate of Agdistis, he castrated himself. Kybele buried the severed penis, from which there grew flowers called *ia* ('violets'), also said to originate from the blood of the hapless Ia, who did away with herself now that her would-be groom was a complete man no more.

6. The plant named *promētheion*, which formed part of Medea's pharmacopoeia as a drug which conferred temporary invulnerability, grew first, according to Apollonios, from the *ichōr* of **Prometheus**, where it dripped to the ground from the wound repeatedly dealt him by the lacerating talons of the eagle.[36]

7. *Selinon*, a word which the Greeks used to denote both 'celery' and 'parsley', enjoyed more than one sanguinary origin. According to Clement of Alexandria—ever keen to mock a pagan mythological detail which combined the immoral with the absurd—two Corybants (male devotees of the Great Mother Goddess Kybele) once slew a third, their brother; from the blood of the dead man there grew *selinon*.[37] The explanatory intention of the myth is clear enough: apparently Corybants did not allow *selinon* to be placed on their table.[38]

Equally aetiological is an alternative mythical origin for *selinon*. The plant was used to wreathe victors at the Nemean Games, and a myth was told to justify the custom. That myth concerned the child Opheltes/Archemoros.[39] King Lykourgos of Nemea had been warned not to put his son Opheltes on the ground before the infant could walk. Unfortunately his nurse Hypsipyle *did* put him on the ground, while she was showing the whereabouts of a spring to the Seven against Thebes, who were passing through Nemea at the time. A snake killed little Opheltes. Amphiaraos, one of the Seven, and a

---

[35] The myth of Attis is analysed with characteristic acumen in Bremmer (2008) 267–302.
[36] Ap. Rhod. *Arg.* 3.843–68; cf. Moreau (2000).
[37] Clem. Al. *Protr.* 2.19.2–3.
[38] Clem. Al. *loc. cit.*; Arn. *Adv. nat.* 5.19.
[39] See Simon (1979); Pülhorn (1984).

seer, interpreted the occurrence as a bad omen for the expedition; Opheltes was renamed 'Archemoros', 'The Beginning of Deadly Fate'.[40] But what of *selinon*? According to a detail preserved by a scholiast on one of Pindar's *Nemean Odes*, the plant germinated where Archemoros' blood fell onto the ground.[41]

8. The remarkable plant *mōly* was said to have been generated where the blood of the giant **Pikoloos** fell to ground. The story went that he had fled from Zeus during the war between the gods and the Giants, had arrived at Circe's island and tried to drive her out, and had been killed by her father Helios who came to his daughter's defence.[42]

It would be unjustifiably reductive to regard all these narratives as exemplifying a single pattern. For one thing, among those from whose blood (or *ichōr*) plants grow there figure not only mortals but also gods (Dionysos, Prometheus): to the emotional vulnerability implied by divine tears there corresponds the physical vulnerability expressed by divine bleeding. But there is a theme common to a *majority* of the narratives: that of a young mortal whose violent death leads to the genesis of a flower. If we wish to contextualize and so to make sense of this theme, an intriguing place to begin is with a pair of articles by Sergio Ribichini and Giulia Piccaluga.

Ribichini's article begins by referring to several Christian tales (collected in two previous discussions by Mircea Eliade) which trace the origin of certain plants to the exact spot where Christ's blood fell upon the ground from the Cross.[43] True to their genesis, these plants were believed to have beneficial qualities, either medicinal or spiritual. In other tales the Saviour's blood was said to have been transformed into wine, and his sweat into myrrh; comparable transformations were ascribed to the blood of the Virgin Mary and of the apostle John.[44] Ribichini suggests that this Christian motif was a reworking of the notion, exemplified in several cultures of the

---

[40] E.g. Apollod. *Bibl.* 3.6.4; other refs. in Bond (1963) 147–9; Pülhorn (1984) 472–3.

[41] Schol. Pi. *N.* 6.71. Hyginus (*Fab.* 74) gives a more prosaic account: baby Opheltes was placed in a spot where there was a lush patch of *apium* (=*selinon*).

[42] Alexandros of Paphos, in Eustath. on *Od.* 10.277 (1658, 48 ff.); cf. Ribichini (1983) 241.

[43] Ribichini (1983), citing Eliade (1939) and (1940–2).

[44] Ribichini (1983) 234–5.

ancient Mediterranean, that the primordial sacrifice of a supernatural being is the prerequisite for the fertilizing of the earth. When it comes to the Greek evidence, however, there is, as Ribichini points out, a problem. It will not do to see these myths—that of Hyakinthos, say, or Adonis—as narrating the theme of 'sacrifice for the greater good of subsequent humanity', since, first, several of the deaths are accidental and therefore hardly examples of sacrifice, and, second, the plants generated are not—it would seem—of primary importance for human survival.

This last observation leads Ribichini to a discussion of the kinds of plants which are the end-product of sanguinary metamorphoses. In Ribichini's view the important point about these plants is that they fall into the category of 'the gathered', as opposed to 'the cultivated'; that is, they belong to a stage of humanity before the introduction of cereals. The possible objection that such plants as *narkissos, krokos,* etc. have nothing to do with humanity's *alimentary* development can be satisfied, in Ribichini's view, by invoking a consideration which Piccaluga's article (to which we turn in a moment) addresses in detail, arguing as it does that what for a modern Westerner may seem merely decorative might for an ancient Greek have played a role in daily diet, whether as vegetable, salad, or condiment. But in the world of cereal agriculture such a role would have become marginalized; and this, according to Ribichini, is a major aspect of the meaning of these myths. In his opinion, it is in the *Homeric Hymn to Demeter* that this meaning becomes most clearly visible. There, the plants which Persephone gathers are, precisely, the *narkissos, krokos,* etc.; yet by the end of the narrative Persephone's mother—now definitively separated from her daughter—will have introduced into the world the cultivation of cereals. Demeter's gift is thus at once in opposition to, and a replacement for, the plants which her daughter was gathering. The blood-into-plant metamorphoses are to be seen, on this interpretation, within a mythical perspective which reflects humanity's alimentary development. In his conclusion Ribichini returns to the Christian stories from which he began. Tales about Christ's blood turning into a great variety of plant species—medicinal, ornamental, comestible—illustrate how Christians attempted to go one better than their pagan predecessors, by presenting Christ as literally incorporating both the world of Demeter and that of the plants which Persephone picked.

Piccaluga's article pre-dates Ribichini's and anticipates it methodologically at several points, especially in the importance ascribed to the contrast between pre-cereal and cereal alimentation. Piccaluga's starting point is a discussion of the precise types of flowers which Persephone gathers before her abduction. These blooms were, Piccaluga demonstrates, linked in various ways to Persephone and her mother: in a procession in honour of Demeter Chthonia at Hermione, children wore garlands woven from flowers which Pausanias identifies with the *huakinthos*; the *ion* might be thought of as wreathing Demeter; one kind of *narkissos*, the *damatrion*, could be used in garlands for Demeter and Persephone; the *krokos* was associated with Demeter and/or Persephone in several ritual contexts in different parts of the Greek world.[45] But, as Piccaluga herself acknowledges, such ritual connections do not explain why these particular plants were linked with these goddesses; they simply extend the field of that which is to be explained.

Piccaluga's next step is to identify Persephone's flowers. When contemplating such identifications it is, as Piccaluga rightly argues, vital not to forget the hundreds of intervening years of plant hybridization, the aim of which has been to use selective breeding in order to adapt, in the interests of the market, the botanical characteristics of the plants which are, nevertheless, still called by names inherited from the Greeks: narcissus, hyacinth, crocus, and so on. If, though, we focus not on the modern but on the ancient environment, then, for example, the *rhodon* is, according to Piccaluga, to be identified with *Rosa canina*, the dog rose, which appears in January/February (Piccaluga's perspective is, as it should be, Mediterranean); again, the *huakinthos* is not to be confused with the blooms, of varied colour, in today's markets, but is actually a wild flower of bright red colour.

After identifying the contents of Persephone's anthology, Piccaluga turns to the characteristics of the flowers. One such is that all the

---

[45] *Huakinthos*: Paus. 2.35.5. *Ion*: Bacchyl. 3.2. *Narkissos*: Soph. *OC* 681–4, with schol. ad loc.; Hesych. *s.v.* δαμάτριον. *Krokos*: Soph. *OC* 684–5, with schol. on 684; Aristoph. *Thesm.* 138; Strabo 9.5.14; other refs. and discussion in Piccaluga (1966) 234–5.

flowers are late winter or early spring blooms found widely in Mediterranean regions. Another is that all have medicinal properties. Finally, and for Piccaluga most crucially, all the gathered flowers play a role in *diet*, whether in virtue of their fruit (*rhodon*) or their bulbs (*krokos, huakinthos, narkissos*).[46] Her conclusion is very similar to that which Ribichini reached later: as one dimension of its meaning, the *Homeric Hymn to Demeter* is concerned with the replacing of pre-cereal alimentation—notably, the consumption of bulbs—by the cultivation of grain.

What do we do with this kind of approach? Piccaluga and Ribichini give us useful pointers, but on some issues I believe we ought to move in a different interpretative direction from theirs.

We may begin with the ingenious observation that several of the blood-generated plants are bulbous—that is, they contain their own sources of regeneration. This property is indeed highly appropriate to tales about young men who are cut down prematurely, their potential as yet unfulfilled: Narkissos, Krokos, and Hyakinthos incorporate enough life-stuff to prolong their existence and to sustain it indefinitely in another form. Moreover, Piccaluga notices, with fiendish ingenuity, that (a) bulbous plants are characteristically described as *kephalorrhizos* ('with a root like a head'), and that (b) both Hyakinthos and Krokos are killed by blows of a discus *to the head*. From *jeunesse dorée* to bulbous perennial.[47] *Non omnis moriar.*

Edibility, however, is a very different matter. In principle I am thoroughly in favour of trying to recover apparently 'strange' aspects of the way in which Greeks thought with plants: such defamiliarization is exactly what is needed if we are to register the cultural differences between ourselves and the ancient Greeks. But, if we consider the crucial fact about blood-generated plants to be their edibility, then, rather than listening to the testimony of the mythical narratives we are dealing with, we are interrupting it. Several of those narratives centre upon the violent, unexpected deaths of young men;

---

[46] See Olck (1899); also Piccaluga (1966) 239, for the eating of *krokos, huakinthos,* and *narkissos* bulbs.

[47] *Kephalorrhizos*: Thphr. *HP* 1.14.2; 2.2.1; etc. Blows to the head: schol. Nic. *Ther.* 903; Luc. *DDeor.* 16.2; Philostr. *Im.* 1.24; Galen, as cited in n. 28 above.

upon beauty and fragility, and the pathos brought about by the loss of those qualities; upon soft petals and delicate fragrances.

His dark blood drips down over his snowy flesh...; the rose flees from his lip... Cruel, cruel is the wound which Adonis bears in his thigh, but greater is the wound which Kythereia [Aphrodite] bears in her heart... Flowers turn crimson from pain... His blood gives birth to the rose... Strew him with garlands and flowers... Sprinkle him with Syrian unguents, sprinkle him with perfumes.[48]

As we listen to these lines from Bion's luxuriant, antiphonal, emotionally fulsome *Epitaph for Adonis*, one characteristic of the rose which the poet makes *no* effort to evoke is its taste. Similarly, the plants referred to in the stories of Hyakinthos, Krokos, and Narkissos are never represented as good to snack on.[49]

A more promising way of making sense of the tales of blood-generated plants is to focus on the perceived qualities of the substance which all the tales have in common. The essence of these narratives is *blood*: it is the fluid which links two different forms of life. The majority of the stories are about young males who die violent and bloody deaths. Now according to Greek belief, bloodshed caused by violence, whether deliberate or accidental, generated pollution. As Robert Parker has definitively demonstrated, Greek ways of understanding and coping with such pollution—coping legally, ritually, mythologically—were extraordinarily complex.[50] The concepts of 'contestation' and 'negotiation' have become desperately overworked in recent scholarship, but in the present instance they serve a sound interpretative purpose: reactions to the religious danger occasioned by *miasma*—for example, whether intention is a mitigating factor or not—were indeed both contested and negotiated.[51] Our list of examples of blood-which-generates-plants includes cases of both intentional and unintentional homicide, but all have in common an act of bloodshed, introducing disorder and hence pollution. Significantly, however, when this pollution is transmuted through metamorphosis, it does not continue to exercise a

48 Bion *Adon.* 9–10, 11, 16–17, 35, 66, 75, 77.
49 Persephone, it is worth recalling, was gathering blooms, not bulbs.
50 Parker (1983).
51 Intention: Parker (1983) 111.

destructive or malevolent effect. The plants generated from blood are, so far from being baneful, seen as useful and/or beautiful features of the living world. The inference is clear: although the social context *temporarily* turns blood into a pollutant, when that context becomes inoperative, so does the blood's capacity to harm. Pollution resides in the context, not in the intrinsic qualities of the blood.

However, it is not just that blood in these stories is non-destructive: it is actually seminal. While this characteristic is of course, within these narrative contexts, a mark of an exceptional occurrence, it is at the same time merely an extension of a recognized attribute which ancient medical writers ascribe to blood: its connection with generation. According to certain theories, what makes up a new being is blood, when collected in the uterus or refined into semen. This was not the Hippocratic view, which evidently drew on Anaxagoras' 'pangenetic' approach, according to which sperm was composed of minuscule quantities of all the different parts of the body.[52] But the haematic origin of sperm does seem to have been affirmed by, for example, Parmenides, and by Diogenes of Apollonia, for whom an animal's sperm is the foam (*aphros*) of its blood; it was also a view attributed, rightly or wrongly, to Pythagoras.[53] In the light of such a medical theory, tales of blood-generated vegetation acquire an intriguing logic. Most of the young males whose blood generates plants die before marriage. More than that: their life-stories oppose them in various ways to the normative pattern which consists of heterosexual relationships within marriage. Hyakinthos and Krokos die in the midst of homoerotic play with the gods; Narkissos' sexuality is dammed up by self-regard; Attis goes mad just as he is about to marry; although Adonis' relationship with Aphrodite is nothing if not heterosexual, it has no chance of leading to marriage. These young men are at the height of their sexual potential, but they die before that potential can be converted into generative power within a formalized sexual relationship with a woman. The young heroes' blood is at its seminal height: even when shed, it remains powerful enough to

---

[52] Duminil (1983) 156–7.

[53] Parmenides: Cael. Aurel. *Chron. pass.* 4.9 (= DK 28 B 18). Diogenes: Clem. Al. *Paed.* 1.6.48 (= DK 64 A 24). Pythagoras: Aetius *Plac.* 5.3.2 (Diels (1879) 417, 6); cf. Duminil (1983) 163–4. Compare also Tert. *Apol.* 50.13: '*semen est sanguis Christianorum*', on which see E. G. Clark (1998) 109.

generate new life.[54] Doubly so in the case of Attis: his penis, having been cut off on his wedding day, was as potent, *mutatis mutandis*, as that of Ouranos. But divine potency is incomparably greater than human. Whereas the severed member of Ouranos gave rise to the cosmic power Aphrodite, that of Attis produced violets: beautiful, but transient.

UNMEDIATED METAMORPHOSIS

An aside by Forbes Irving offers one way into this topic: '[G]ods never transform themselves into trees as they do into animals and birds.'[55] The logic here may be that the immovability and, literally, rootedness of a tree or plant would represent an unacceptable degree of constraint or limitation upon divine power. Whether or not this is so, one of the recurring modes of transformation of *human beings* into plants or trees has to do with a sense of rootedness. This is certainly the burden of a tale related by Antoninus Liberalis (31) about some young Messapian shepherds who claimed to be able to outdance the local nymphs. The boys became (*egenonto*) trees 'where they stood', and *eti nun*, 'still now', it is possible at night to hear voices from their tree-trunks 'as of mourners'.

The association between mourning and trees is also to be found in the tale of the sisters of Phaethon, whose lamentations were perpetuated when they turned into poplars which weep tears of amber.[56] Cognate again is the fate of Adonis' mother Smyrna, alias Myrrha, whose scandalous love for her father placed her outside the realm of the human. Her tears, like those of Phaethon's sisters, are still productive: ever since Zeus transformed her (*metabalōn epoiēse*) into a tree, she 'weeps' myrrh every year (Ant. Lib. 34). Similar too are the fates of Elate and Platanos, sisters of the Aloades (the Giants who

---

[54] It might seem that Opheltes/Archemoros is an exception, in that our literary sources represent him as a baby. But in iconography he can appear as a youth: see *LIMC* ii 'Archemoros' 8 and 10. Of 8, a vase in St Petersburg, Erika Simon ((1979) 37) remarks that Archemoros 'is almost an ephebe already'.

[55] FI 263.

[56] See 117–19 above on Apollonios; other refs. in FI 269–71.

threatened to storm Olympos). After their brothers had been killed for their presumption, the sisters found their mourning—and their height—prolonged indefinitely when they turned into, respectively, a fir tree and a plane tree.[57]

Other accounts of unmediated metamorphosis concern cases where a god's divine lover turns into a plant or tree or flower which will enjoy, in its new form, a perpetual association with the divinity in question. Pitys, pursued by Pan, gave rise to the pine tree; Syrinx, another who attracted Pan's lust, became the reeds which the god made into his trademark pipe.[58] But the myth which the post-classical tradition has elevated to iconic status is that of Daphne. When she rejected Apollo's suit and implored Zeus that she be released from the state of humanity, she turned into the laurel, sacred to Apollo.[59] The catalyst for the later burgeoning of interest in Daphne is Ovid, whose splendid account in *Metamorphoses* culminates in the image of Apollo placing his hand on the trunk of the newly formed tree, so as to feel the still-beating heart beneath the bark (1.553–4). By contrast with such poetic riches, our Greek sources are thin. The main accounts are in Parthenios (a scholar and poet of the first century BC) and Pausanias, both of whom link the Apollo-and-Daphne myth with a tale of the nymph's pursuit by a mortal, Leukippos: since Daphne thought only of hunting with her girl companions, Leukippos dressed as a girl in order to join them, but was exposed as a fraud when the group decided to strip for a bathe. Pausanias makes no mention of Daphne's transformation; Parthenios refers to it briefly at the end of his narrative.[60]

One quality which marks off some plant metamorphoses from others relates to the difference between the generic and the unique. *Every* example of a *daphnē*, wherever it grows, and however often it is depicted in art as Apollo's attribute, is a kind of prolongation of the existence of the transformed nymph; by contrast, the metamorphic 'destination' of the Messapian shepherds is 'one-off'. Whether generic or unique, however, these associations are one more facet of the

---

[57] Liban. *Prog.* 2.38; Niceph. *Prog.* 12; FI 273–4.

[58] Pitys: Liban. *Prog.* 2.4; FI 273. Syrinx: e.g. Ach. Tat. 8.6; FI 277–8.

[59] Iconic: see the catalogue in Reid (1993) i. 325–35.

[60] Parthen. *Amat. narr.* 15, cf. Lightfoot (1999) ad loc.; Paus. 8.20. Detailed discussion of the sources at FI 261–3.

metamorphic tradition, a tradition which stresses as a living reality the interaction between myth, religion, and everyday existence.

Some of the stories we have been reviewing in this chapter are at first sight astonishing: the notion that a man's tears may generate a cabbage will seem counter-intuitive to most readers of this book. Yet if our investigations have shown anything it must be that such a story, and many others like it, forms part of a complex network of belief and practice which, seen in its totality, is capable of conferring imaginative and emotional credibility upon even the 'strangest' narrative details. Moreover, each of the four categories of tale which we have analysed makes its own contribution to an implicit debate about the location, and the flimsiness, of the border between the anthropomorphic world and the world of plant life. All this, coupled with the fact that the medium for the link between human and plant form is Gaia, the earth, should resonate powerfully with those who today seek to rediscover a holistic view of the living, natural world. *Eti nun*, 'still now': perhaps some Greek myths may be good not just to think with and to feel with, but also to live by.

9

Challenges to the Metamorphic Tradition

As this book has sought to demonstrate, for well over a millennium there existed in Greek antiquity a strong and rich tradition of the telling of metamorphosis stories. Yet this tradition did not pass unchallenged. It sometimes provoked scepticism, or scorn, or outright hostility, among advocates of a variety of philosophical-religious positions. Even when such thinkers did not engage with the metamorphic tradition explicitly, they often expressed views about change, identity, and form which may be seen as standing in implicit dialogue with that tradition. The two major types of metamorphosis tale, relating to transformations of gods and transformations of mortals, provoked varying and sometimes vigorous reactions from these thinkers. I shall discuss each type in turn.

CAN A GOD CHANGE?

The first openly critical engagement with the idea that a god can change shape comes in the works of the Presocratic philosophers. We may be confident that the views attributed to these men did not typify everyday Greek assumptions about the world; and yet such untypical views formed no less a part of the ineradicable plurality of Greek thought than did more mainstream opinions. Establishing exactly what the Presocratics' views were about the form of the gods (or about any other topic) is, however, fraught with difficulty, since the fragments of their writings are virtually always embedded in the texts of later writers who, consciously or unconsciously, massaged the alleged opinions of their predecessors so as to bolster their own philosophical standpoints. Nevertheless, among the assertions which can plausibly be ascribed to this or that Presocratic thinker are several which bear on divine metamorphosis.

According to Xenophanes, whereas mortals commonly believe that 'the gods are born, and that they have clothes and speech and bodies like their own', the true situation is quite different: in reality there is 'one god, greatest among gods and men, in no way similar to mortals either in body or in thought'.[1] Not only in form but also in (lack of) mobility is this special Xenophanean deity unchanging:

Always he remains in the same place, moving not at all; nor is it fitting for him to go to different places at different times, but without toil he shakes all things by the thought of his mind.[2]

Although Xenophanes does not explicitly contrast his own conception of deity with the metamorphic tradition, that conception looks to be incompatible with at least *some* mythical narratives in which divinities are said to self-transform, namely those in which the gods allegedly assume the shapes of human beings, moving here and there in order to intervene in the affairs of mortals.

Xenophanes was not 'typical' of Presocratic thought. The Presocratics were individuals; none more so than Herakleitos. And for Herakleitos, metamorphosis was *not* incompatible with divinity—provided that both divinity and metamorphosis were understood on strictly Herakleitean lines:

God is day night, winter summer, war peace, satiety hunger ... he undergoes alteration (*allioioutai*) in the way that fire, when it is mixed with spices, is named according to the scent of each of them.[3]

While there is nothing of the anthropomorphic in this conception of god, to affirm that the divine persists as a unity through change amounts to an assertion, albeit an idiosyncratic one, that the capacity to undergo alteration is essential to the divine. How far can the same be said of other Presocratics, in particular those who posit the existence of a single principle underlying all that is? Is this, in their view, a *divine* principle, susceptible of self-transformation into all the

---

[1] Frs. 167 and 170 KRS (I borrow their translation here and subsequently).
[2] Fr. 171 KRS.   [3] Fr. 204 KRS.

phenomena of the world as we know it? If so, are these thinkers in effect arguing that the world is pervaded by a process of continuous divine metamorphosis? To address this question in detail would entail a full examination of the thought of these philosophers; we have space here only for the briefest sketch.

For Thales, the world was permeated by a divine power. Aristotle ascribes to him the view that 'All things are full of gods,' though the precise significance which we should attribute to this assertion is beyond recovery.[4] Furthermore, Thales' opinion that the unitary principle underlying the world was water *may* have equated to a sense that water was not only the world's source, but also its essential constituent.[5] Thus water *may* have been, for Thales, both that into which and from which all things transform, and something divine. But there are too many imponderables in this chain of reasoning for us to be sure that we can include Thales in the list of those who stood in dialogue with the tradition of divine metamorphosis.

About Anaximenes the evidence is a little less cryptic. That he argued for both the underlying and the originary quality of air seems undeniable.[6] Also firmly documented are his beliefs in the capacity of air to change into all things by becoming finer or denser, and in the divine quality of air. In the words of the theologian Hippolytos (second to third centuries AD):

Anaximenes ... said that infinite air was the principle, from which the things that are becoming, and that are, and that shall be, and gods and things divine, all come into being, and the rest from its products.[7]

But we find no explicit evidence that Anaximenes rejected the traditional gods, with or without reference to the notion of metamorphosis. Augustine, at any rate, observed of him that he 'did not deny that there were gods or pass over them in silence'; Anaximenes' point, according to Augustine, was that it was air not the gods which had priority (it was the gods that arose from air, rather than vice versa).[8]

---

[4] Aristot. *De an.* 411^{a}7–8 = Thales fr. 91 KRS, with their commentary at pp. 95–8.
[5] Fr. 85 KRS, with their commentary at pp. 89–95.
[6] Frs. 140 and 141 KRS.
[7] Hippol. *Ref.* 1.7.1 = Anaximenes fr. 141 KRS.
[8] August. *C.D.* 8.2 = Anaximenes fr. 146 KRS, with their discussion at pp. 150–1.

In the extant fragments of Anaximander we find no explicit rejection of the traditional gods, who, however, were hardly at the forefront of his views of 'the divine'. For him the originary substance was *to apeiron*, 'the indefinite', which, immortal and indestructible, underlay all things, and which was, at least according to Aristotle, *to theion*, 'the divine'.[9] As with Anaximenes, we can argue here for a *kind* of relevance to divine changeability.

Presocratic enquiries into the interplay between change and permanence in the working of the cosmos constitute, then, one area in which we can find at least a modest degree of overlap between some of these thinkers and the metamorphic tradition. There is, however, another area in which we can point to an important, even if usually implicit, difference of emphasis between the Presocratics and the tellers of myths of divine metamorphosis: namely, astonishment. One way of reading the distinctiveness of the Presocratic enterprise is to see it as attempting to explain natural phenomena in such a way as to remove the consternation which they arouse in virtue of their unpredictability.[10] According to an anecdote recorded by Plutarch, Anaxagoras aimed to dispel superstitious *thambos* regarding the phenomena of the heavens, by annulling that reaction thanks to the reasoned, causal explanations offered by natural philosophy.[11] Demokritos was even more explicit in his repudiation of *thambos* in his dictum that 'wisdom which does not allow itself to be astonished (*sophiē athambos*) is worth everything'.[12] There is thus a clear contrast between, on the one hand, the astonishment regularly highlighted in stories of divine metamorphosis in virtue of their depiction of the irruption of the sacred into the everyday, and, on the other hand, the type of unastonished explanation preferred by philosophical enquirers.

For a more sustained engagement with traditional notions of divinity, however, an engagement which, moreover, involves a specific rejection of myths about divine metamorphosis, we must turn to Plato. Now any investigation into Plato's opinions on religion

---

[9] Aristot. *Ph.* 203^{b}13–15 = Anaximander fr. 108 KRS.
[10] Babut (1974) 6–7.
[11] Plut. *Per.* 6.1.
[12] 68 B fr. 216 DK; cf. frs. 4 and 215 (*athambiē* in both fragments). See Babut (1974) 6.

is beset with difficulties as acute as those concerning the Presocratics. As W. J. Verdenius observed several decades ago, the attributes 'god' and 'divine' are applied so widely in Plato that one might be forgiven for thinking that, on the Platonic view(s), 'the divine' is quite simply everywhere.[13] At all events, what is clear is that we are dealing with a conception of divinity very different from that enshrined in the complex of myths and rituals which constitutes the Greek religious system.

At *Republic* 380d Socrates enquires:

'Do you think the god is a kind of magician who can appear at will in different forms (*ideais*) at different times, sometimes becoming (*gignomenon*) them himself and changing his appearance into many shapes (*allattonta to hautou eidos eis pollas morphas*), at other times misleading us into the belief that he has done so? Or is he without deceit and least likely of all things to depart from his proper form (*ideas*)?'

Faced with initial puzzlement on the part of his interlocutor, Socrates clarifies his position by invoking a view of the gods which contrasts sharply with that to be found in mainstream Greek mythology:

'But the state of the god and the divine is perfect.'
  'Certainly.'
  'And therefore the god is least likely of all things to take on many forms (*morphas*).'
  'That is so.'
  'Then would the god change or alter himself (*hauton metaballoi an kai alloioi*) of his own volition?'
  'If he does undergo change (*alloioutai*), that must be how he does.'
  'So does he change himself (*metaballei heauton*) in the direction of the better and finer, or the worse and more shameful?'
  'If he changes (*alloioutai*) it must be for the worse. For we shall not accept that the god can be lacking in any respect in what is fine or excellent.'[14]

That point being conceded, the argument is clinched: stories of gods disguising themselves to walk among mortals, or of the transformations of Proteus and Thetis, must be banned from the state. Tales of divine metamorphosis are dangerous: children, above all, must not

---

[13] Verdenius (1954) 241. On Plato and the gods, see now Bordt (2006).
[14] Trans. Lee (1955), with amendments.

be exposed to them (381d–e). In the event, of course, the kind of benevolent dictatorship of the right-minded advocated by the Platonic Socrates came to nothing. The glamour and enchantment of myths of divine metamorphosis ensured that the narrative voices which preserved them would effortlessly drown out the complaints of the censors—thanks, first, to the sustenance offered by allegorical interpretation in the medieval and Renaissance periods;[15] then, to the enthusiastic embrace of artists and writers during and since the Renaissance;[16] and, last but not least, to the imaginative approaches of modern interpreters such as Bruno Bettelheim and Marina Warner, who have emphasized not the moral threat but rather the therapeutic benefit to be found in tales of metamorphosis, especially when told to children.[17]

Ancient philosophical reflection upon the gods' capacity to change did not, of course, stop with Plato. Aristotle does not tackle the topic head-on, but at various points he discusses both the nature of divinity and the nature of change. Whatever Aristotle the man may have believed about the gods, as philosopher he adopts a standpoint which distances him from most of his contemporaries. He praises as inspired the view of 'our ancestors in the remotest ages' who transmitted myths celebrating the divinity of celestial bodies, but disparages subsidiary traditions such as those which attribute anthropomorphic or zoomorphic appearance to the gods (*Metaph.* 1074^{b}1–14). Even further from conventional views is the ascetic Aristotelian concept of the unmoved mover, the unchanging source of change (*Physics* Book Θ). But perhaps most intriguing for our present argument is what Aristotle has to say about astonishment. In his *Metaphysics* (982^{b}12–13) he argues that not only is the notion of *thauma* not to be *opposed* to wisdom (contrast the view of Demokritos mentioned above), it is, rather, to be situated at the very heart of philosophical activity:

For it was through a sense of being astonished (*to thaumazein*) [or 'wondering'—'a sense of curiosity' is too weak a translation] that men first began and still continue to philosophize.[18]

[15] Seznec (1953).   [16] Barkan (1986); Bull (2005).
[17] Bettelheim (1976); Warner (1994a, 1994b, 1998).
[18] Cf. also *thaumasantes*, 14; *thaumazōn*, 17–18.

However, although in the same passage Aristotle notes that 'even a lover of *muthoi* is a lover of wisdom, since a *muthos* is composed of astonishing things (*thaumasiōn*)', the kinds of astonishing events retold in myth are far removed from the centre of Aristotle's concerns. What of post-Aristotelian philosophical views about gods' propensity for metamorphosis? Stoics and Epicureans adopted contrasting positions. According to Balbus, the advocate of Stoicism in Cicero's *On the Nature of the Gods* (2.70), narratives ('old wives' tales') which ascribe to the gods the shape, clothing, relationships, and behavioural frailties of human beings are idiotic, futile, and frivolous. It follows that the countless tales of gods who adopt precisely such an appearance are to be discarded.[19] Rather different is the position of the Epicureans. In their opinion the gods exist, and they are anthropomorphic. To cite Cicero once more (*N.D.* 1.46–9): according to Velleius, the spokesman for Epicureanism, the view that 'the gods have no other than human shape' is supported by natural conviction and by reason. What the gods do *not* do, however, according to Epicurus, is intervene in human affairs, either to reward or punish.[20] It must follow that the countless stories of the gods' divine self-transformations, undertaken in order to further their own purposes amongst mortals, cannot be regarded as credible.

To conclude this brief review of those who engaged critically with traditions about divine metamorphosis, I want to mention a Christian writer whom I have often cited already as a source for myths of transformation: Clement of Alexandria. On the face of it, Clement is an out-and-out castigator of such myths. The depiction, on a signet ring, of an amorous bird hovering over Leda is for Clement nothing less than a representation of Zeus' immoral licentiousness (*Protr.* 4.60.2). But Clement does not single out metamorphosis myths for special opprobrium: he expends much more effort in mocking cults to non-anthropomorphic gods, and in deriding the reverence lavished on statues and other images of pagan divinities. When he does highlight the notion of metamorphosis, it is, paradoxically, in the course of a resounding paean to the New Song—the Song of Christianity. This Song possesses a wonderful power *to transform*. It has, claims Clement, made men out of stones and men out of wild beasts—because men without

---

[19] Cf. Babut (1974) 174.   [20] See Rist (1972) 140–63.

understanding are no better than stones, no better than beasts (*Protr.* 1.4.1–4). Clement, who was either a formidably learned man or one who convincingly gave the impression of being one, effected his own transformation of the Greek myths which he deployed in such profusion.

REFLECTIONS ON TRANSFORMATIONS OF HUMANS

Truth and nonsense

One possible reaction to the idea of a human being changing into something non-human is: it is preposterous. That is the line taken, time after time, by Palaiphatos in his *On Unbelievable Tales*.[21] Virtually everything about this author is uncertain, even the authenticity of his perhaps artificially constructed name ('Spoken long ago'). As to his date, Jacob Stern's investigation concludes that a floruit in the late fourth century BC is not implausible.[22] What is not in doubt is the ridicule which Palaiphatos heaps upon anything in the mythological tradition which strikes him as contravening the notion of plausibility (*to eikos*).

Tales of astonishing transformation come high on his list of offenders. The authentic Palaiphatean tone is given by his version of the tale of Niobe (8):

They say that Niobe, a living woman, became a stone (*lithos egeneto*) upon the tomb of her children. But whoever believes that a human being can become a stone, or a stone become a human being, is simple-minded. The truth is as follows. When Niobe's children died, someone made a stone image of her and placed it on the tomb. People passing by would say: 'A stone Niobe is standing on the tomb. We ourselves saw her.' So people today say, 'I was sitting next to the bronze Herakles' or 'next to the marble Hermes'. That's how it was in this case: Niobe *herself* did not *become stone*.

Throughout his work Palaiphatos displays total certainty about the truth/falsity distinction. People said that Atalanta and Melanion changed into a lioness and a lion; but the truth was different. In

[21] See Stern (1996); Brodersen (2005).   [22] Stern (1996) 1–4.

fact the two had gone into a cave to make love, but had been killed by the cave's residents, a lioness and a lion. Seeing the animals emerge, the fellow hunters of Atalanta and Melanion had drawn the wrong inference (13). The same misunderstanding happened in the case of Kallisto, allegedly transformed into a bear; her companions got the wrong end of the stick after she had wandered into a grove and had been eaten by a bear (14). Palaiphatos does not dismiss stories of metamorphosis out of hand: he simply finds a prosaic truth behind them. A woman *obviously* cannot turn into a cow, so when people said this of Io there must be a reasonable explanation. The truth is that she got pregnant, ran away in fear of her father, and (so people put it): 'she is fleeing like a mad cow' (42). For good measure, the idea that human beings could originate from *Meliai* (Ash Trees) is absurd. It's just that there was once a man called Melios... (35).

The only genuinely interesting part of Palaiphatos' otherwise intellectually monotonous treatise is a series of observations which he makes in his introduction. Everything which existed in the past, he asserts, still exists in the present, and will continue to exist in the future. The anti-evolutionary corollary is that the many *eidē kai morphai* ('shapes and forms') which are alleged once to have existed, but which no longer exist, cannot *ever* have existed. The mythical tradition about metamorphoses of human beings is predicated upon a contrast in form between before and after; Palaiphatos denies the reality of such a contrast. But why should myth-tellers have taken a different view? Tales about fantastic events and persons are to be laid at the door of poets and 'writers of tales' (*logographoi*), who invented them in order to astonish (*thaumazein*). In so many of the stories which we have considered in this book, astonishment is an internal theme within a narrative, describing the impact of the sacred upon characters who register its presence. For Palaiphatos, the arousing of astonishment becomes a calculated narrative strategy adopted by myth-tellers towards their gullible public.

Death, bodies, and 'souls'

Greek views about life after death usually assume that human beings lead just one life, after which the deceased will experience some kind of post mortem existence, varying in its degree of grimness or beatitude: the gloomy Homeric afterlife differs from the brighter prospect on offer to Eleusinian initiates. However, according to other, more 'marginal' beliefs, the soul of an individual could pass into a succession of different containers (i.e. corporeal forms) after, on each occasion, the punctuation mark which is death. I shall consider two examples of these beliefs: those attributed to Pythagoras, and those set out in some of Plato's dialogues.

In the climactic, fifteenth book of his great poem about transformations, Ovid depicts Pythagoras as the leading spokesman for his universal theme. But what exactly *is* the relationship of Pythagoras to the metamorphic tradition? His teachings were identified with the belief in the continuity of the soul through many incarnations. When an individual died, his or her soul was said to transmigrate into a new body; what kind of body depended on the moral life which the individual had previously led. Clearly, there is an affinity between this belief and the metamorphic tradition, since the belief, like the tradition, called into question the definiteness of the boundary between the human and the non-human. Moreover, Pythagorean teachings and the metamorphic tradition alike explore the persistence of identity through flux, and the tension between continuity and change in the life of a person.

Yet at the same time there are major differences between the tenets of Pythagoreanism and traditional myths of metamorphosis. First, most traditional metamorphoses are *alternatives* to death, alternatives which come into play because the events which precipitate the changes of form are so extreme that death would be too conventional a conclusion for the lives of the individuals concerned. By contrast, transmigration comes into play only after a person's body has died (even if their soul continues for ever). Secondly, myths about transformation involve one-off irruptions of the divine, irruptions which are by definition uncharacteristic of everyday life and which therefore generate astonishment: the metamorphic route followed by, say, Niobe or Daphne is emphatically not an exit strategy for everyone. By contrast, transmigration does seem to be—or so it can be argued— the end for everyone. In that case, transmigration would be the reverse of astonishing: it would be the standard outcome for all those living amid the flux of existence.[23] Thirdly, mythical humans whose form is changed do not normally undergo the process repeatedly: at most there is a double change, as when Kallisto becomes first a bear and then a constellation. Transmigration knows no such limitation.

A final, more modest difference may be mentioned, because it touches on a point which I have emphasized earlier. Pythagorean teaching has implications for how one should live. If any of us might in theory return to life in the form of an animal or a vegetable, then all of us should be wary about how we treat animals and about what we eat. This is the gist of a famous anecdote recorded by Xenophanes, where Pythagoras cites the example of a man who recognized the voice of a dead friend in the sound made by a squealing puppy.[24] Now this anecdote assumes a continuity of voice between two embodiments of the same soul. The contrast with many metamorphosis narratives is worth noting. As we have seen, *dis*continuity in vocal production can be a classic marker of the difference between pre- and post-metamorphosis existence (as in Ovid and Kafka).[25]

Plato too engaged with the possibility that the human *psuchē* ('soul') might be re-embodied, perhaps many times, after death, in forms which might or might not be human.[26] Classic accounts are to be found in the *Republic* and in *Phaidon*.

Just before the end of the *Republic* Plato includes an episode—the Myth of Er—which reports the alleged experiences of a man who, having died in battle, came to life on his funeral pyre, and related what he had experienced in the other world. In this account the *psuchai* of the dead are shown making choices between possible future lives, some of which belong to animals. The *psuchē* which had once belonged to Orpheus selects the life of a swan; that of another bard, Thamyris, the life of a nightingale; that of Thersites—the butt of mockery in the *Iliad*—the life of an ape (620). However,

---

[23] But very little in relation to Pythagoras can be taken as cast-iron certainty; for some of the many imponderables about transmigration, see Burkert (1972) 120–65.

[24] Fr. 260 KRS = D.L. 8.36; cf. Burkert (1972) 120–1.

[25] See above, 6 and 138.

[26] For the general contrast between the holistic, Hebraic tradition of the unified concept of the person, as opposed to the Platonic notion of a strong mind/body contrast, see Ware (1997) 91–2.

human-into-animal is not the only possible direction of travel. There are also animals (for example 'a swan and other musical creatures') which choose to return as human beings, and human beings who opt to retain their humanity, even a particular *type* of humanity: Odysseus, poignantly, selects the life of an ordinary, private man. None of these changes entails, it seems, an instantaneous shift in corporeal shape, since each alteration is preceded by an intervening spell in the other world—a major difference from the immediate transformations familiar from traditional mythology. Most crucially of all, individuals are allowed to make a formalized choice about which shape they will inhabit, whereas in most myths about the metamorphosis of humans the victim has no option but to take what comes. It is true that such myths sometimes evoke an expression of will, as when Daphne implores Zeus to be removed from humanity in order to elude Apollo. But to describe these moments as opportunities for *choice* would be to misconstrue the degree of empowerment which they entail. In the *Republic*, by contrast, choice is the very focus of the transformation, since it illuminates the ethical state of the subject.

Phaidon tells a similar story. Once more the argument turns on the possible nature of existence after death, coupled with the question of the immortality of the soul; once more the discussion is dominated by the ethical implications of choice. One respect in which the *Phaidon* account differs from that of the *Republic*, however, is in its degree of circumstantial urgency: in *Phaidon*, what will happen after death is only too personally relevant to Plato's beloved and condemned master Socrates. By definition, the tale told can be no more than 'likely' (81d), since getting a reliable first-hand report about life after death is far from easy. What is 'likely' is that the souls of the dead pass into the bodies of creatures corresponding to the practices of each soul's former life (81e–82b):

'Well, those who have cultivated gluttony or aggressiveness or drunkenness, instead of taking pains to avoid them, are likely to put on the forms (*genē*, literally 'kinds') of donkeys and other similar animals; don't you think so?'

'Yes, that is very likely.'

'And those who have deliberately preferred a life of irresponsible lawlessness and violence go into the forms (*genē*) of wolves and hawks and kites; unless we can suggest any other more likely animals.'

'No, the ones which you mention are exactly right.'

'So it is easy to imagine into what sort of animals all the other kinds of soul will go, in accordance with their conduct during life.'

'Yes, certainly.'

'I suppose that the happiest people, and those who reach the best destination, are the ones who have cultivated the goodness of an ordinary citizen—what is called self-control and integrity—which is acquired by habit and practice, without the help of philosophy and reason.'

'How are these the happiest?'

'Because they will probably pass into some other kind (*genos*) of social and disciplined creature like bees, wasps, and ants; or even back into the human race again, to become (*gignesthai*) decent citizens.'[27]

There is a family resemblance between such likelihoods and those metamorphosis myths which express an ethical parallel between conduct and destination: the cannibalistically cruel Lykaon turns into a wolf.[28] But in *Phaidon* as in the *Republic* psychological and moral attention is focused upon the fate of the *psuchē*. While traditional metamorphosis myths assume some kind of general psychological continuity between the states of the subject before and after transformation, such myths never investigate the nature of that continuity with the degree of analytical rigour aimed at by Plato.

In later antiquity belief in the transmigration of souls would arouse opposition among Christian and pagan thinkers alike. Particularly controversial was the idea of transmigration between human beings and animals or even plants.[29] Tertullian, the brilliant north African rhetorician and advocate of Christianity (second to third centuries AD), argued for the absurdity of the idea of a human soul's passing into an animal body, on several grounds, which boil down to the incompatibility between the two (*De anima* 32). A century later Gregory of Nazianzus dismissed the notion of transmigration—'a *muthos* of the foolish, a vain trifling found in books'— both because a rational soul could not inhabit the body of an animal or plant, and because the Last Judgement would be pronounced upon a soul inhabiting 'its' body—which was incompatible with the idea of one soul passing into several bodies.[30] There was, however, no

---

[27] Trans. Tredennick (1954), with amendments.

[28] For the proverbial characteristics of the wolf, see Buxton (1987).

[29] See Gilhus (2006) 87–90, to which I am much indebted in what follows.

[30] Gregory in Moreschini and Sykes (1997) 7.22–52; cf. Gilhus (2006) 88–9. On the whole question of the importance of the resurrection of the body in Christian thought, see Bynum (1995).

blanket dismissal by Christian writers of the whole idea of transmigration: the great theologian Origen (second to third centuries AD) did (at least as interpreted by Jerome) entertain the possibility of the transmigration of the souls of angels, human beings, and demons into the bodies of animals if they wished to avoid the torments in store for them as a result of transgressions committed.[31]

Rejection of belief in transmigration found expression in pagan as well as Christian writings, though here too there is complexity. In the case of the Neoplatonist scholar and commentator Porphyry (third century AD), for instance, there is evidence both for and against the proposition that he believed in transmigration across the species barrier.[32] The commonest sticking point, for Christian and non-Christian writers alike, was the difficulty of assuming a compatibility between the soul of a (rational) human being and the body of an (irrational) animal. Various strategies were devised to circumvent this. Among the most ingenious was that of another Neoplatonist, Sallustius (fourth century AD), who argued that the soul of a human being could not actually enter the body of an animal, but must remain outside it as a kind of protecting *daimōn*.[33] What is certain is that the divide between humans and animals, which was so good to think with in the metamorphic tradition, led to an extraordinary diversity of interpretative strategies among the countless commentators on, and advocates or opponents of, the views previously developed by Pythagoras and Plato.

Natural kinds

Myths about transformed humans may be located, then, within a wider speculative project directed at understanding the fate of the individual soul after death. But that is not the only debate in which these stories may be seen to have played a part. The belief that one form of life can turn into another had evident implications for thinkers who reflected upon the distinctiveness of natural kinds.

[31] Jerome, *Letter to Avitus* 4; see Gilhus (2006) 89.

[32] Sorabji (2004) 213; Gilhus (2006) 89–90.

[33] Sallustius, *On the Gods* 20; cf. Gilhus (2006) 90. See also Sorabji (2004) 216, and in general 213–16.

One question repeatedly posed by such thinkers was: have such kinds always existed as they do today? Empedokles answered this with an emphatic negative. In his view, the development of living things in our world had taken place in stages, each characterized by a different 'formal' arrangement:

Empedokles [reports Aitios] held that the first generation of animals and plants were not complete but consisted of separate limbs not joined together; the second, arising from the joining of these limbs, were like creatures in dreams; the third was the generation of whole-natured forms.[34]

The nature of the second generation in this process is elaborated in another fragment:

Many creatures were born with faces and breasts on both sides, man-faced ox-progeny, while others again sprang forth as ox-headed offspring of man.[35]

The images conjured up by Empedokles anticipate the weird mixtures described in Apollonios' version of the Circe episode, and also recall some of the hybrids (especially Acheloos) which we discussed earlier.[36] Empedokles did not narrate—any more than Hesiod did in his account of the Five Races of Man in *Works and Days*—a seamless, evolutionary progression, by infinitesimal gradations, through which one stage of humanity grew out of another. But he clearly believed that the natural kinds which he saw around him had not existed for ever.

Such a view not only contrasts with the position later adopted by Palaiphatos, according to whom that which existed in the past still exists in the present; it also runs counter to the opinion expressed by an altogether more substantial mind: that of Aristotle. According to the majority of interpreters, Aristotle held that natural kinds were fixed.[37] It is true that he acknowledged the minuscule differences between types of living things, along the scale which runs from the inanimate to plants to animals; it is also true that at one point he speculates about how—if, 'as some allege', human beings and

---

[34] Fr. 375 KRS.
[35] Fr. 379 KRS.
[36] See above, 119–20; 84–5.
[37] See e.g. Lennox (2001) 131–59.

quadrupeds had been 'earthborn'—they might have grown up (answer: from larvae or eggs).[38] However, these qualifications need to be seen against the background of the broader Aristotelian project of *discriminating* between types of living thing. His underlying assumption that 'like breeds like' rules out any notion of evolutionary change in the development of species, and a fortiori any notion that monstrous, hybrid forms might play a role in such evolution.[39] Exhaustive observer of the natural world that he was, Aristotle was well aware of the potentially astonishing changes of form undergone by certain insects and other creatures.[40] But he was concerned, through his explanations, to normalize and regularize such changes, rather than regarding them as evidence that one natural kind could turn into another.[41]

In fact in one amusing passage Aristotle insists on a discrimination between natural kinds precisely in a case of metamorphosis. The context, from the treatise *On Rhetoric*, is a discussion not of biology but of metaphor (1406[b]):

As for what Gorgias said to the swallow which, flying over his head, let fall her droppings upon him, it was in the best tragic style. He exclaimed, 'For shame, Philomela!' There would have been nothing shameful in the act if it had been a bird that had done it; but for a girl, it was shameful. The reproach therefore was appropriate, insofar as he was addressing her in her past state, not in her present state.

Even in this little vignette—mildly scatological, if Philomela is thought of as a bird; grossly scatological, if she is thought of as human—we are presented with a typically Aristotelian discrimination. The philosopher stresses not the continuity between the individual's states before and after metamorphosis, but rather the distinction between them, and, specifically, the moral and linguistic implications of that distinction.

After Aristotle, the debate about natural kinds continued. To take just a single example: in his poem *On the Nature of Things* Lucretius seems at one point to affirm Aristotle's emphasis on the enduring

---

[38] *HA* 588[b]4 ff.; *GA* 762[b]28–31; cf. G. E. R. Lloyd (1968) 89.
[39] See G. E. R. Lloyd (1996) 113.
[40] E.g. *HA* 550[b]–552[b]; *GA* 758[a]–759[a].
[41] Cf. G. E. R. Lloyd (1997) 553–5.

stability of natural kinds (1.172–3): 'That is why everything cannot be generated from everything, because a certain power (of generation) inheres in certain things.' Yet elsewhere, in his account of humanity's prehistory, he finds room for the presence of a host of misshapen monsters, androgynes, creatures bereft of limbs or with limbs mis-attached to the body, and which died out because they could not reproduce—in other words, some natural kinds had become extinct (5.837–57). But Lucretius makes clear that the 'monsters' which failed to survive were *not* mixtures on the pattern of centaurs, or the half-human, half-bitch Scylla, or the lion-goat-snake Chimaira: such creatures of fantasy, Lucretius maintains, could never even have been begotten (5.878–924).

Critical attitudes toward the world of mythological narrative were anything but uniform, and certainly not uniformly adversarial. They were a product of dense, complex, and serious engagement. Throughout antiquity those who argued about the nature of the gods, or about the boundary between human and animal nature, or about the fixity of natural kinds, kept turning to mythology as a shared reference point, a common cultural language. Within that language, tales about metamorphosis continued to provoke, to enrage, and of course to astonish.

10

Final Thoughts on Contexts

In Part I of this study I analysed Greek metamorphosis narratives in a range of historical, literary, and artistic contexts. So far in Part II I have looked for cross-contextual patterns, a 'logic', underlying the beliefs investigated, and I have juxtaposed the metamorphic tradition with the views of thinkers who engaged with it from a variety of critical standpoints. There remains one question to ask. How far can a contextual *approach to interpretation claim to throw light on a* strange, indeed an astonishing, *belief such as that in metamorphosis?*

The frequency with which *thambos* recurs in Greek metamorphosis narratives demonstrates that, already for the Greeks themselves, metamorphoses were liable to unsettle and shock in virtue of their strangeness. A fortiori, these narratives may be felt by outside interpreters to embody such strangeness to an even greater degree. How, then, are we, as observers of ancient Greece from the viewpoint of another culture, to come to terms with the strangeness of metamorphosis beliefs?

One approach would be to characterize such beliefs as naive or childlike.[1] This view is deeply suspect, not only on general grounds of ethnocentric bias, but also for the particular reason that some of these beliefs are embedded in powerful, mature, and sophisticated works of the imagination—for example, the *Odyssey*, Greek tragedy, and Aristophanic comedy—which have rarely been equalled and never surpassed in the history of humanity. The charge of naïveté collapses as soon as it is entertained.

A second gambit would be to regard as misplaced *any* attempt to engage with these beliefs, for the reason that ancient Greek and 'our'

---

[1] In what follows I draw on G. E. R. Lloyd (2007) 112–14.

world views are incommensurable. This gambit too must be rejected. There are many contexts *within our own culture* where we come across phenomena of astonishing change—let us cite, at random, the Eucharist, Kafka's *Metamorphosis*, and *Terminator 2*. Such phenomena give us a certain amount of purchase (*mutatis*, as always, *mutandis*) on analogous phenomena in Greek antiquity, even though the identification of apparent parallels between 'their culture' and 'our culture' represents merely a modest first stage in the process of understanding.

A third strategy would be to propose that such apparently strange beliefs as that in metamorphosis are to be understood *merely as metaphors*. This, it will be recalled, is the view taken by Forbes Irving:

> We can assume, I think, that most ancient Greeks were not seriously worried that they would suddenly become animals; we should perhaps assume, therefore, that metamorphosis stories will normally depend for their appeal on involving the audience, probably not fully consciously, in some metaphorical or symbolic perception of the story.[2]

On this view—notwithstanding the repeated caveats implicit in 'I think', 'most', 'seriously', 'perhaps', 'normally', etc.—metamorphosis belongs *essentially* to the world of metaphor and symbol. However, the danger with such an approach is that the outside observer may overlook the possibility that the Greeks may actually, *in certain contexts*, have meant what they said. After all, are we to imagine that rhapsodes' performances of the Circe episode from the *Odyssey*, or a staging of *Prometheus Bound*, were interrupted by constant cries of 'You cannot be serious?' I cannot prove that the answer to this question was not, or was not occasionally: 'Yes'. Nevertheless, my strong inclination is to say that to locate metamorphosis beliefs always and only at the level of metaphor is to misrepresent the Greeks' experience.

A fourth strategy, directly opposed to the third, would posit that such beliefs as those we have been considering were *always* taken equally seriously, regardless of the context. This strategy too is unconvincing. The poet and critic Ruth Padel once described the Greek gods as 'like electricity—at work *all the time*, in their bodies,

---

[2] FI 60; see Ch. 2 above.

minds, homes, and cities'.[3] But Hellenists are professionally prone to romanticization. If we do accept the metaphor of electricity, we should remember that voltages vary from circuit to circuit. In order to measure religious voltage, there is no substitute for the close reading of texts and images, paying due attention to *variations between contexts.*

The notion of context is, in short, crucial for a viable approach to 'the astonishing'. Now in stressing the importance of a context-ualizing interpretation, I am dipping my toe into a famous anthro-pologico-philosophical debate. Sir Edward Evans-Pritchard once famously highlighted two assertions by the Nuer of southern Sudan, that 'a twin is a bird' and that 'a cucumber is an ox'. He contended that, for the Nuer, these assertions are perfectly rea-sonable, given the actors' assumptions that, in the first case, they are speaking of the *personality* or *soul* of a twin, which is felt to belong to 'the above', and, in the second case, that a cucumber is indeed *in certain contexts* an 'ox', that is, when it is an object of sacrifice (which is what oxen are for the Nuer).[4] The ensuing debate obliged scholars to reflect on the process of 'making sense' of supposedly strange beliefs from another culture, and on the role that invocation of context should be allowed to play in that process.

One of the most trenchant disputants was Ernest Gellner, who bridled at what he saw as Evans-Pritchard's efforts to make sense of 'alien' beliefs at all costs.[5] Gellner argued that, when trying to grapple with an assertion such as 'a twin is a bird', one must be prepared to entertain the possibility that—when all allowances have been made for context, symbolic meaning, etc.—such an assertion might have been absurd or meaningless, or at least contradictory.[6] This is surely right. Any account we might want to give of, say, a religious assumption or practice, must allow for the possibility that it *might* have been perceived by the original actors—or some of them, or sometimes, or in some contexts—as absurd, nonsensical, irrational, or whatever the analogous terms might have been in the language spoken by those actors.

---

[3] Padel (1992) 3; my emphasis.   [4] Evans-Pritchard (1956) 128–33.
[5] Gellner (1970).   [6] Gellner (1970) 41.

Gellner put another spoke in the excessively charitable contextualist's wheel when he observed that 'the manner in which the context is invoked, the amount and kind of context and the way the context itself is interpreted, depends on prior tacit determination concerning the kind of interpretation one wishes to find . . . After all, there is nothing in the nature of things or societies to dictate visibly just how much context is relevant to any given utterance, or how that context should be described.'[7] Here again, Gellner was right: the choice of which context to invoke is undeniably one of the interpreter's most powerful weapons.

However, it would certainly be a mistake to adopt a *wholly* negative view of (in Gellner's words) 'tolerance-engendering contextual interpretation'.[8] *Some* degree of 'tolerance' *must* be allowed to qualify what may otherwise seem to an outside observer to be an incomprehensible 'alien belief'; the trick is to do the analysis—be it anthropological or historical—in such a way as to be alert *both* to symbolic meaningfulness *and* to the possibility of absurdity, illogicality, nonsense. Thus—to come back to cases studied in the present book— I argued that an understanding of Greek views about the symbolism of tears and blood was a prerequisite for a more persuasive (indeed, tolerance-engendering) account of tales about the role of these fluids in the astonishing transformations of human beings into plants. By contrast, in other cases it is clear that an alertness to absurdity and nonsense is indispensable for a sound interpretation: I tried to make this point in my discussions of Aristophanes, Palaiphatos, and Plutarch (in *Gryllos*). In yet other instances, the best policy is caution: I argued that I, for one, *simply do not know* how far a tolerantly contextual interpretation should be permitted to reduce the strangeness of the prediction about Kadmos, Harmonia, the snakes, and the ox-cart at the end of *Bacchants*.[9] My aim throughout this book has been always to take notice of the context, but to do so *appropriately*. It is for the reader to judge whether this objective has been reached.

What, finally, was the place of metamorphosis within the Greeks' perception of the world? The sacred was, we can agree with Ruth

---

[7] Gellner (1970) 33.   [8] Gellner (1970) 32; cf. 30.
[9] See 61–2 above.

Padel, a pervasive element of the cultural environment. As Martin Nilsson wrote: '[The antique landscape] is saturated with religion in a manner quite foreign to us. One could hardly have taken a step out of doors without meeting a little temple, a sacred enclosure, an image, a cult-pillar, a sacred tree.'[10] You could put yourself in touch with the sacred at any time: for instance, by cursing or praying or sacrificing, or exposing yourself to a healing dream. With a little more physical and psychological effort, you could travel to consult an oracle. But what kind of religious experience was implied by this 'pervasiveness' of the sacred? Robert Parker wrote of the religious procedures of assembly, courts, and army that '[i]n large measure they can be seen as soothing background music of religious reassurance ... Embedded religion is comfortable, familiar, and easy to live with: it is in the background of awareness.'[11] But there is *in some contexts* an unsettling edginess to Greek religion, an edginess which such a formulation does not capture.

The notion of metamorphosis lay at a greater distance from everyday life than the ubiquitous ritual practices which we have just mentioned. Even Theophrastos' Superstitious Man did not fear being changed into a dog or a bat, in spite of all the religious danger which he spied around him.[12] (If he *had* feared it, he would certainly have told us.) But metamorphosis *could* be highlighted, fore-grounded: by a poem, a play, a carved or painted image, a ritual, a rumour, an anxiety. For a god—any god, at any time, in any circumstance—it was always an option. For a human being, it might suddenly come to seem—in certain contexts—to be a possibility, even a not-so-remote possibility. The metamorphic tradition expressed in narrative form the astounding, destabilizing irruption of divinity, and the existence of remarkable continuities between human life and the natural environment. Stories told in this tradition were a way of articulating, and perhaps even partially coping with, the astonishing strangeness of life's outcomes.

---

[10] Nilsson (1952) 118–19.   [11] Parker (2005) 104.
[12] Thphr. *Char.* 16.

Bibliography

Alcalde Martín, C. (2001), *El mito de Leda en la Antigüedad*. Madrid.

Amigues, S. (1992), 'Hyakinthos. Fleur mythique et plantes réelles', *REG* 105: 19–36.

Anderson, W. S. (1963), 'Multiple Change in the *Metamorphoses*', *TAPA* 94: 1–27.

Armstrong, R. (2006), *Cretan Women: Pasiphae, Ariadne, and Phaedra in Latin Poetry*. Oxford.

Arnott, W. G. (2007), *Birds in the Ancient World from A to Z*. London.

Auger, D. (1979), 'Le Théâtre d'Aristophane: le mythe, l'utopie et les femmes', in *Aristophane: les femmes et la cité*. Les Cahiers de Fontenay, 17: 71–101.

Babut, D. (1974), *La Religion des philosophes grecs de Thalès aux Stoïciens*. Paris.

Ballario, P. (1995), *Fiabe e leggende delle Dolomiti*. 6th edn. Florence.

Bannert, H. (1978), 'Zur Vogelgestalt der Götter bei Homer', *WSt* 91: 29–42.

Barkan, L. (1986), *The Gods Made Flesh: Metamorphosis and the Pursuit of Paganism*. New Haven.

Barrett, D. (1964), *Aristophanes: The Wasps, The Poet and the Women, The Frogs*. Translation. Harmondsworth.

Barrett, W. S. (1964), *Euripides: Hippolytos*. Edition and commentary. Oxford.

Barta, P. I. (ed.) (2000), *Metamorphoses in Russian Modernism*. Budapest.

Baumann, H. (2007), *Flora mythologica: griechische Pflanzenwelt in der Antike*. Rev. edn. Kilchberg.

Besançon, A. (2000), *The Forbidden Image: An Intellectual History of Iconoclasm*. Chicago (trans. of *L'Image interdite: une histoire intellectuelle de l'iconoclasme*, Paris, 1994).

Bettelheim, B. (1976), *The Uses of Enchantment: The Meaning and Importance of Fairy Tales*. London.

Blakely, S. (2006), *Myth, Ritual, and Metallurgy in Ancient Greece and Recent Africa*. Cambridge.

Blech, M. (1982), *Studien zum Kranz bei den Griechen*. Berlin.

Bodson, L. (1978), *'IEPA ZΩIA: contribution à l'étude de la place de l'animal dans la religion grecque ancienne*. Brussels.

Bond, G. W. (1963), *Euripides: Hypsipyle*. Edition and commentary. Oxford.

Bordt, M. (2006), *Platons Theologie*. Freiburg im Breisgau.

Borthwick, E. K. (1968), 'Seeing Weasels: The Superstitious Background of the Empusa Scene in the *Frogs*', *CQ* NS 18: 200–6.

Bottéro, J. (2001), *Religion in Ancient Mesopotamia*. Chicago (trans. of *La Plus Vieille Religion en Mésopotamie*, Paris, 1998).

Bouché-Leclercq, A. (1879–82), *Histoire de la divination dans l'Antiquité*. 4 vols. Paris.

Bowersock, G. W. (1990), *Hellenism in Late Antiquity*. Ann Arbor.

Bowie, A. M. (1993), *Aristophanes: Myth, Ritual and Comedy*. Cambridge.

Bowker, J. (2002), *God: A Brief History*. London.

Bowra, C. M. (1969), *The Odes of Pindar*. Translation. Harmondsworth.

Bremer, J. M. (1975), 'The Meadow of Love and Two Passages in Euripides' *Hippolytus*', *Mnemosyne* 28: 268–80.

Bremmer, J. N. (2000), 'Scapegoat Rituals in Ancient Greece', in Buxton (2000b) 271–93 (originally publ. in *HSCP* 87 (1983) 299–320; now revised in Bremmer (2008) 169–214).

—— (2008), *Greek Religion and Culture, the Bible and the Ancient Near East*. Leiden.

Brewster, H. (1997), *The River Gods of Greece: Myths and Mountain Waters in the Hellenic World*. London.

Brodersen, K. (2005), '"Das aber ist eine Lüge!"–zur rationalistischen Mythenkritik des Palaiphatos', in R. von Haehling (ed.), *Griechische Mythologie und frühes Christentum*, Darmstadt, 44–57.

Brown, C. G. (1991), 'Empousa, Dionysus and the Mysteries: Aristophanes, *Frogs* 285 ff.', *CQ* NS 41: 41–50.

Brown, P. (1978), *The Making of Late Antiquity*. Cambridge, Mass.

Brunel, P. (1974), *Le Mythe de la métamorphose*. Paris.

Bubbe, W. (1913), *De metamorphosibus Graecorum capita selecta*. Diss. Halle.

Bühler, W. (1960), *Die Europa des Moschos*. Hermes Einzelschriften Heft 13. Wiesbaden.

—— (1968), *Europa: Ein Überblick über die Zeugnisse des Mythos in der antiken Literatur und Kunst*. Munich.

Bull, M. (2005), *The Mirror of the Gods: Classical Mythology in Renaissance Art*. London.

Burckhardt, J. (1898–1902), *Griechische Kulturgeschichte*. Berlin.

Burke, P. (1978), *Popular Culture in Early Modern Europe*. London.

—— (1997), *Varieties of Cultural History*. Cambridge.

Burkert, W. (1972), *Lore and Science in Ancient Pythagoreanism*. Cambridge, Mass. (trans. of *Weisheit und Wissenschaft: Studien zu Pythagoras, Philolaos und Platon*, Nuremberg, 1962).

Bushnell, R. W. (1982), 'Reading "Winged Words": Homeric Bird Signs, Similes, and Epiphanies', *Helios* 9: 1–13.

Buxton, R. G. A. (1980), 'Blindness and Limits: Sophokles and the Logic of Myth', *JHS* 100: 22–37.

——(1982), *Persuasion in Greek Tragedy: A Study of Peitho.* Cambridge.

——(1987), 'Wolves and Werewolves in Greek Thought', in J. N. Bremmer (ed.), *Interpretations of Greek Mythology*, Beckenham, 60–79.

——(1989), 'The Messenger and the Maenads: A Speech from Euripides' *Bacchae* (1043–1152)', *Acta Antiqua* 32: 225–34.

——(1991), 'News from Cithaeron: Narrators and Narratives in the *Bacchae*', *Pallas* 37: 39–48.

——(1992), 'Psychologie et paysage dans l'*Europe* de Moschos', *Actes du XXVème Congrès International de l'A.P.L.A.E.S.*, Strasbourg, 33–41.

——(1994), *Imaginary Greece: The Contexts of Mythology.* Cambridge.

——(2000a), 'Les Yeux de Médée: le regard et la magie dans les *Argonautiques* d'Apollonios de Rhodes', in Moreau and Turpin (2000) 265–75.

——(ed.) (2000b), *Oxford Readings in Greek Religion.* Oxford.

——(2002a), 'Time, Space and Ideology: Tragic Myths and the Athenian *polis*', in J. A. López Férez (ed.), *Mitos en la literatura griega arcaica y clásica*, Madrid, 175–89.

——(2002b), 'The Myth of Talos', in C. Atherton (ed.), *Monsters and Monstrosity in Greek and Roman Culture*, Bari, 83–112.

——(2004a), 'Similes and Other Likenesses', in R. L. Fowler (ed.), *The Cambridge Companion to Homer*, Cambridge, 139–55.

——(2004b), *The Complete World of Greek Mythology.* London.

——(2009), 'Feminized Males in *Bacchae*: The Importance of Discrimination', in S. Goldhill and E. Hall (eds.), *Sophocles and the Greek Tragic Tradition*, Cambridge, 232–50.

Bynum, C. W. (1995), *The Resurrection of the Body in Western Christianity, 200–1336.* New York.

——(1998), 'Metamorphosis, or Gerald and the Werewolf', *Speculum* 73: 987–1013.

——(2001), *Metamorphosis and Identity.* New York.

Calame, C. (2003), *Myth and History in Ancient Greece: The Symbolic Creation of a Colony.* Princeton (trans. of *Mythe et histoire dans l'Antiquité grecque: la création symbolique d'une colonie*, Lausanne, 1996).

Calder, W. M., III (1974), 'Sophocles, *Tereus*: A Thracian Tragedy', *Thracia* 2: 87–91.

Cameron, A. (2004), *Greek Mythography in the Roman World.* New York.

Campbell, M. (1991), *Moschus: Europa.* Edition and commentary. Hildesheim.

Canney, M. A. (1926), 'The Magic of Tears', *Journal of the Manchester Egyptian and Oriental Society* 12: 47–54.

Carden, R. (1974), *The Papyrus Fragments of Sophocles*. Berlin.

Caruana, W. (1993), *Aboriginal Art*. London.

Carver, R. H. F. (2007), *The Protean Ass: The Metamorphoses of Apuleius from Antiquity to the Renaissance*. Oxford.

Cassin, B., and Labarrière, J.-L. (eds.) (1997), *L'Animal dans l'Antiquité*. Paris.

Castiglioni, L. (1906), *Studi intorno alle fonti e alla composizione delle Metamorfosi di Ovidio*. Pisa (reprinted Rome 1964).

Cazzaniga, I. (1950–1), *La saga di Itis*. Milan.

Chantraine, P. (1954), 'Le Divin et les dieux chez Homère', in *La Notion du divin depuis Homère jusqu'à Platon*, Entretiens Fondation Hardt, i, Geneva, 45–94.

Clark, E. G. (1998), 'Bodies and Blood: Late Antique Debate on Martyrdom, Virginity and Resurrection', in D. Montserrat (ed.), *Changing Bodies, Changing Meanings: Studies on the Human Body in Antiquity*, London, 99–115.

Clark, S. (1997), *Thinking with Demons: The Idea of Witchcraft in Early Modern Europe*. Oxford.

Collins, B. J. (ed.) (2002), *A History of the Animal World in the Ancient Near East*. Leiden.

Conacher, D. J. (1980), *Aeschylus' Prometheus Bound: A Literary Commentary*. Toronto.

Constantakopoulou, C. (2007), *The Dance of the Islands: Insularity, Networks, the Athenian Empire, and the Aegean World*. Oxford.

Cook, A. B. (1894), 'Animal Worship in the Mycenaean Age', *JHS* 14: 81–169.

Csapo, E. (1993), 'Deep Ambivalence: Notes on a Greek Cockfight', Part I, *Phoenix* 47: 1–28; Part II, ibid. 115–24.

Dakaris, S. (1993), *Dodona*. Athens.

Dallapiccola, A. L. (2002), *Dictionary of Hindu Lore and Legend*. London.

Darrieussecq, M. (1996), *Truismes*. Paris.

Darnton, R. (1984), 'Workers Revolt: The Great Cat Massacre of the Rue Saint-Séverin', in id., *The Great Cat Massacre and Other Episodes in French Cultural History*, New York, 75–104.

Davies, M. (1986), 'A Convention of Metamorphosis in Greek Art', *JHS* 106: 182–3.

De Jong, I. J. F. (1987), *Narrators and Focalizers: The Presentation of the Story in the Iliad*. Amsterdam.

Delgado Linacero, C. (1996), *El toro en el Mediterraneo*. Madrid.

—— (2007), *Juegos taurinos en los albores de la historia*. Madrid.

De Sélincourt, A. (2003), *Herodotus: The Histories*. Translation, rev. J. Marincola. London.

Detienne, M. (1973), 'L'Olivier: un mythe politico-religieux', in M. I. Finley (ed.), *Problèmes de la terre en Grèce ancienne*, Paris, 293–306.

De Visser, M. W. (1903), *Die nicht menschengestaltigen Götter der Griechen*. Leiden.

Diels, H. (1879), *Doxographi graeci*. Berlin.

Dierauer, U. (1977), *Tier und Mensch im Denken der Antike*. Amsterdam.

Dimock, J. F. (1867), *Giraldi Cambrensis Opera* (=vol. v of *Rerum Britannicarum Medii Aevi Scriptores*). London.

Dirlmeier, F. (1967), *Die Vogelgestalt homerischer Götter*. Heidelberg.

Dobrov, G. (1993), 'The Tragic and the Comic Tereus', *AJPh* 114: 189–234.

Dodds, E. R. (1960), *Euripides: Bacchae*. Edition and commentary. 2nd edn. Oxford.

Duminil, M.-P. (1983), *Le Sang, les vaisseaux, le cœur dans la collection hippocratique*. Paris.

Dunand, F., and Zivie-Coche, C. (2004), *Gods and Men in Egypt 3000 BCE to 395 CE*. Ithaca, NY (trans. of *Dieux et hommes en Egypte 3000 av. J.-C.—395 apr. J.-C.: anthropologie religieuse*, Paris, 1991).

Dunbar, N. (1995), *Aristophanes: Birds*. Edition and commentary. Oxford.

Easterling, P. E. (1982), *Sophocles: Trachiniae*. Edition and commentary. Cambridge.

Eisenstein, S. M. (1988), *Eisenstein on Disney*, ed. J. Leyda; trans. A. Upchurch. London.

Eliade, M. (1939), 'Ierburile de sub cruce...' [*sic*], *Revista Fundaţiilor Regale* 6. 11: 353–69.

——(1940–2), 'La Mandragore et les mythes de la "naissance miraculeuse"', *Zalmoxis* 3: 3–48.

Erbse, H. (1980), 'Homerische Götter in Vogelgestalt', *Hermes* 108: 259–74.

Evans-Pritchard, E. E. (1956), *Nuer Religion*. Oxford.

Fantuzzi, M. (2000), 'Nikandros [4]', in *Der Neue Pauly*, Stuttgart, viii. 898–900.

Farnell, L. R. (1896–1909), *The Cults of the Greek States*. 5 vols. Oxford.

——(1921), *Outline-History of Greek Religion*. New edn. London.

Fauth, W. (1975), 'Zur Typologie mythischer Metamorphosen in der homerischen Dichtung', *Poetica* 7: 235–68.

——(1981), *Eidos Poikilon: Zur Thematik der Metamorphose und zum Prinzip der Wandlung aus dem Gegensatz in den Dionysiaka des Nonnos von Panopolis*. Göttingen.

Feeley-Harnik, G. (1981), *The Lord's Table: Eucharist and Passover in Early Christianity*. Philadelphia.

Feeney, D. C. (1991), *The Gods in Epic: Poets and Critics of the Classical Tradition*. Oxford.

Feldherr, A. (2002), 'Metamorphosis in the *Metamorphoses*', in P. Hardie (ed.), *The Cambridge Companion to Ovid*, Cambridge, 163–79.

Fitzpatrick, D. (2001), 'Sophocles' *Tereus*', *CQ* ns 51: 90–101.

Flint, V., Gordon, R., Luck, G., and Ogden, D. (1999), *Witchcraft and Magic in Europe*, ii: *Ancient Greece and Rome*. London.

Fontenrose, J. (1959), *Python: A Study of Delphic Myth and its Origins*. Berkeley and Los Angeles.

Forbes Irving, P. M. C. (1990), *Metamorphosis in Greek Myths*. Oxford.

Fränkel, H. (1921), *Die homerischen Gleichnisse*. Göttingen.

Fraser, P. M. (1972), *Ptolemaic Alexandria*. 3 vols. Oxford.

Frazer, J. G. (1921), *Apollodorus: The Library*. Edition and translation. 2 vols. London.

Frischer, B. (1982), *The Sculpted Word: Epicureanism and Philosophical Recruitment in Ancient Greece*. Berkeley.

Frontisi-Ducroux, F. (2003), *L'Homme-cerf et la femme-araignée*. Paris.

Gantz, T. (1993), *Early Greek Myth: A Guide to Literary and Artistic Sources*. Baltimore.

Geertz, C. (1973), 'Deep Play: Notes on the Balinese Cockfight', in id., *The Interpretation of Cultures*, New York, 412–53.

Gellner, E. (1970), 'Concepts and Society', in B. R. Wilson (ed.), *Rationality*, Oxford, 18–49.

Gilhus, I. S. (2006), *Animals, Gods and Humans: Changing Attitudes to Animals in Greek, Roman and Early Christian Ideas*. London.

Ginsberg, W. (1991), 'Dante, Ovid, and the Transformation of Metamorphosis', *Traditio* 46: 205–33.

Gomes, J., et al. (1999), *Warping and Morphing of Graphical Objects*. San Francisco.

Goody, J. (1993), *The Culture of Flowers*. Cambridge.

Gould, J. (2001), *Myth, Ritual, Memory, and Exchange: Essays in Greek Literature and Culture*. Oxford.

Graf, F. (1988), 'Ovide, les *Métamorphoses* et la véracité du mythe', in C. Calame (ed.), *Métamorphoses du mythe en Grèce antique*, Geneva, 57–70.

Graham, A. C. (1991), *The Book of Lieh-tzŭ*. Translation. London.

Granarolo, J. (1979), 'Europe et l'Europe', *Annales de la Faculté des Lettres et Sciences Humaines de Nice* 35: 67–82.

Green, J. R. (1985), 'A Representation of the *Birds* of Aristophanes', *Greek Vases in the J. Paul Getty Museum* 2: 95–118.

—— and Handley, E. (1995), *Images of the Greek Theatre*. London.

Griffin, J. (1977), 'The Epic Cycle and the Uniqueness of Homer', *JHS* 97: 39–53.

Griffith, M. (1983), *Aeschylus: Prometheus Bound*. Edition and commentary. Cambridge.

Griffiths, J. G. (1960), 'The Flight of the Gods before Typhon: An Unrecognized Myth', *Hermes* 88: 374–6.

Hackforth, R. (1952), *Plato's Phaedrus*. Translation and commentary. Cambridge.

Hall, J. M. (1997), *Ethnic Identity in Greek Antiquity*. Cambridge.

——— (2002), *Hellenicity: Between Ethnicity and Culture*. Chicago.

Halliwell, S. (1998), *Aristophanes: Birds, Lysistrata, Assembly-Women, Wealth*. Translation. Oxford.

Hansen, W. (2000), 'Foam-Born Aphrodite and the Mythology of Transformation', *AJPh* 121: 1–19.

Harzer, F. (2000), *Erzählte Verwandlung: Eine Poetik epischer Metamorphosen (Ovid—Kafka—Ransmayr)*. Tübingen.

Hatano, G., et al. (1993), 'The Development of Biological Knowledge: A Multi-national Study', *Cognitive Development* 8: 47–62.

Hawthorne, N. (1846/1974), *Mosses from an Old Manse*. London, 1846, reprinted in *The Centenary Edition of the Works of Nathaniel Hawthorne*, x, Columbus, Oh., 1974.

Henrichs, A. (1984), 'Male Intruders among the Maenads: The So-Called Male Celebrant', in H. D. Evjen (ed.), *Mnemai: Classical Studies in Memory of Karl K. Hulley*, Chico, Calif., 69–91.

Heubeck, A., and Hoekstra, A. (1989), *A Commentary on Homer's Odyssey*, ii. Oxford.

——— West, S., and Hainsworth, J. B. (1988), *A Commentary on Homer's Odyssey*, i. Oxford.

Heyne, C. G. (1802), *Homeri Carmina cum Brevi Annotatione*. Leipzig.

Hollis, A. (1994), 'Nonnus and Hellenistic Poetry', in Hopkinson (1994) 43–62.

Hopkinson, N. (1984), *Callimachus: Hymn to Demeter*. Edition and commentary. Cambridge.

——— (1988), *A Hellenistic Anthology*. Cambridge.

——— (ed.) (1994), *Studies in the Dionysiaca of Nonnus*. Cambridge.

Hordern, P., and Purcell, N. (2000), *The Corrupting Sea: A Study of Mediterranean History*. Oxford.

Hornung, E. (1982), *Conceptions of God in Ancient Egypt: The One and the Many*. Ithaca, NY (trans. of *Der Eine und die Vielen: Ägyptische Gottesvorstellungen*, Darmstadt, 1971).

Houlihan, P. F. (2002), 'Animals in Egyptian Art and Hieroglyphs', in Collins (2002) 97–143.

Hourmouziades, N. C. (1986), 'Sophocles' *Tereus*', in J. H. Betts, J. T. Hooker, and J. R. Green (eds.), *Studies in Honour of T. B. L. Webster*, i, Bristol, 134–42.

Hughes, Ted (1997), *Tales from Ovid*. London.

Hugh-Jones, S. (1979), *The Palm and the Pleiades: Initiation and Cosmology in Northwest Amazonia*. Cambridge.

Hunter, R. L. (1989), *Apollonius of Rhodes: Argonautica Book III*. Edition and commentary. Cambridge.

—— (1993a), *The Argonautica of Apollonius: Literary Studies*. Cambridge.

—— (1993b), *Jason and the Golden Fleece*. Translation of the *Argonautica* of Apollonius of Rhodes. Oxford.

Hutton, R. (1999), *The Triumph of the Moon: A History of Modern Pagan Witchcraft*. Oxford.

Innes, M. M. (1955), *The Metamorphoses of Ovid*. Translation. Harmondsworth.

Izquierdo, I., and Le Meaux, H. (2003), *Seres híbridos: apropiación de motivos míticos mediterráneos*. Madrid.

Jaeger, W. (1947), *The Theology of the Early Greek Philosophers*. Oxford.

Jannaccone, S. (1953), *La letteratura greco-latina delle metamorfosi*. Messina.

Johnston, S. I. (ed.) (2004), *Religions of the Ancient World: A Guide*. Cambridge, Mass.

Jones, C. P. (1986), *Culture and Society in Lucian*. Cambridge, Mass.

Jorissen, H. (1965), *Die Entfaltung der Transsubstantiationslehre bis zum Beginn der Hochscholastik*. Münster.

Kakridis, J. T. (1971), *Homer Revisited*. Lund.

—— (ed.) (1986–7), Ἑλληνική Μυθολογία. 5 vols. Athens.

Kern, O. (1930), 'Die Metamorphose in Religion und Dichtung der Antike', in J. Walther (ed.), *Goethe als Seher und Erforscher der Natur*, Leipzig, 185–204.

Kessler, D. (1986), 'Tierkult', in *Lexicon der Ägyptologie*, Wiesbaden, vi. 571–87.

Kindstrand, J. F. (1998), 'Claudius Aelianus und sein Werk', *ANRW* ii.34.4: 2954–96.

Kirchhoff, A. (1860), 'Homerische Excurse. 4', *RhM* 15: 329–66.

Kiso, A. (1984), *The Lost Sophocles*. New York.

Klein, N. M. (2000), 'Animation and Animorphs: A Brief Disappearing Act', in Sobchack (2000) 21–39.

Knight, V. H. (1995), *The Renewal of Epic: Responses to Homer in the Argonautica of Apollonius*. Leiden.

Knott, K. (1998), *Hinduism: A Very Short Introduction*. Oxford.

Krasniewicz, L. (2000), 'Magical Transformations: Morphing and Metamorphosis in Two Cultures', in Sobchack (2000) 41–58.

Kratz, D. M. (1976), 'Fictus lupus: The Werewolf in Christian Thought', *Classical Folia: Studies in the Christian Perpetuation of the Classics* 30: 57–79.

Kron, U. (1992), 'Heilige Steine', in H. Froning, T. Hölscher, and H. Mielsch (eds.), *Kotinos: Festschrift für Erika Simon*, Mainz, 56–70.

Lada-Richards, I. (1999), *Initiating Dionysus: Ritual and Theatre in Aristophanes' Frogs*. Oxford.

Lafaye, G. (1904), *Les Métamorphoses d'Ovide et leurs modèles grecs*. Paris.

Lamberton, R. (2001), *Plutarch*. New Haven.

Lancellotti, M. G. (2002), *Attis, between Myth and History: King, Priest, and God*. Leiden.

Lane Fox, R. (1986), *Pagans and Christians*. London.

Larson, J. (2001), *Greek Nymphs: Myth, Cult, Lore*. Oxford.

Latacz, J. (1979), 'Ovids *Metamorphosen* als Spiel mit der Tradition', *Würzb. Jbb.* NF 5: 133–55.

Lattimore, R. (1965), *The Odyssey of Homer*. Translation. New York.

Leaf, W. (1900), *The Iliad*, i. 2nd edn. Edition with notes. London.

Lee, H. D. P. (1955), *Plato: The Republic*. Translation. Harmondsworth.

Lennox, J. G. (2001), *Aristotle's Philosophy of Biology: Studies in the Origins of Life Science*. Cambridge.

Lévi-Strauss, C. (1970), *The Raw and the Cooked*. London (trans. of *Le Cru et le cuit*, Paris, 1964).

Lewis-Williams, D., and Pearce, D. (2005), *Inside the Neolithic Mind: Consciousness, Cosmos and the Realm of the Gods*. London.

Lietzmann, H. (1979), *Mass and Lord's Supper: A Study in the History of the Liturgy*, with Introduction and Further Inquiry by R. D. Richardson. Leiden (Part I originally publ. as *Messe und Herrenmahl: Eine Studie zur Geschichte der Liturgie*, Berlin, 1926).

Lightfoot, J. L. (1999), *Parthenius of Nicaea: The Poetical Fragments and the Ἐρωτικὰ Παθήματα*. Edition and commentary. Oxford.

Livingstone, A. (1986), *Mystical and Mythological Explanatory Works of Assyrian and Babylonian Scholars*. Oxford.

Livrea, E. (1987), 'L'episodio libyco nel quarto libro delle *Argonautiche* di Apollonio Rodio', *Quaderni di archeologia della Libya* 12: 175–90.

Lloyd, A. B. (ed.) (1997), *What is a God? Studies in the Nature of Greek Divinity*. London.

Lloyd, G. E. R. (1968), *Aristotle: The Growth and Structure of his Thought*. Cambridge.

Lloyd, G. E. R. (1983), *Science, Folklore and Ideology: Studies in the Life Sciences in Ancient Greece*. Cambridge.

—— (1996), *Aristotelian Explorations*. Cambridge.

—— (1997), 'Les Animaux de l'Antiquité étaient bons à penser: quelques points de comparaison entre Aristote et le *Huainanzi*', in Cassin and Labarrière (1997) 545–62.

—— (2007), *Cognitive Variations: Reflections on the Unity and Diversity of the Human Mind*. Oxford.

Loraux, N. (1995), *The Experiences of Tiresias: The Feminine and the Greek Man*. Princeton (trans. of *Les Expériences de Tirésias: le féminin et l'homme grec*, Paris, 1990).

Ludwig, W. (1961), '*ΓΙΝΕΤΟ* bei Moschos und Kallimachos', *Hermes* 89: 185–90.

Lutz, T. (1999), *Crying: The Natural and Cultural History of Tears*. New York.

Marcattili, F. (2005), 'Argoi lithoi', *ThesCRA* iv. 186–7.

Martin, L. H. (1991), 'Artemidorus: Dream Theory in Late Antiquity', *The Second Century* 8: 97–108.

Martín Rodríguez, A. M. (2002), *De Aedón a Filomela*. Las Palmas de Gran Canaria.

Massey, I. (1976), *The Gaping Pig: Literature and Metamorphosis*. Berkeley.

Mayr, E. (1982), *The Growth of Biological Thought: Diversity, Evolution, and Inheritance*. Cambridge, Mass.

Meiggs, R. (1982), *Trees and Timber in the Ancient Mediterranean World*. Oxford.

Mellink, M. J. (1943), *Hyakinthos*. Utrecht.

Metamorphing: Transformation in Science, Art and Mythology. Booklet issued to accompany exhibition of the same title, at London Science Museum, 4 Oct. 2002–16 Feb. 2003.

Miles, G. (ed.) (1999), *Classical Mythology in English Literature: A Critical Anthology*. London.

Miller, P. C. (1994), *Dreams in Late Antiquity: Studies in the Imagination of a Culture*. Princeton.

Mills, R. (2003), 'Jesus as Monster', in B. Bildhauer and R. Mills (eds.), *The Monstrous Middle Ages*, Cardiff, 28–54.

Momigliano, A. (1933), 'L'Europa come concetto politico presso Isocrate e gli Isocratei', *Rivista di filologia e d'istruzione classica* 61: 477–87.

Moreau, A. (1999), 'Le Discobole meurtrier', in id., *Mythes grecs 1: origines*, Montpellier, 127–46 (originally publ. in *Pallas* 34 (1988) 1–18).

—— (2000), 'Médée la magicienne au *promètheion*, un monde de l'entredeux (Apollonios de Rhodes, *Argonautiques*, III, 828–870)', in Moreau and Turpin (2000) 245–64.

—— and Turpin, J.-C. (eds.) (2000), *La Magie*, ii: *La Magie dans l'Antiquité grecque tardive. Les mythes*. Montpellier.

Moreschini, C., and Sykes, D. A. (1997), *St Gregory of Nazianzus: Poemata arcana*. Edition, translation, and commentary. Oxford.

Mossman, J. (1995), *Wild Justice: A Study of Euripides' Hecuba*. Oxford.

Murr, J. (1890), *Die Pflanzenwelt in der griechischen Mythologie*. Innsbruck (reprinted Groningen, 1969).

Murray, R. D. (1958), *The Motif of Io in Aeschylus' Suppliants*. Princeton.

Myers, K. S. (1994), *Ovid's Causes: Cosmogony and Aetiology in the Metamorphoses*. Ann Arbor.

Needham, J. (1986), *Science and Civilisation in China*, vi: *Biology and Biological Technology*. Pt. 1: *Botany*. Cambridge.

Nilsson, M. P. (1952), *A History of Greek Religion*. 2nd edn. Oxford.

—— (1967), *Geschichte der griechischen Religion*, i, 3rd edn. Munich.

Nisbet, A. (2000), 'Savage Thinking: Metamorphosis in the Cinema of S. M. Eisenstein', in Sobchack (2000) 149–79.

Obeyesekere, G. (1992), *The Apotheosis of Captain Cook: European Mythmaking in the Pacific*. Princeton.

Olck, F. (1899), '*Βολβός*', *RE* iii. 669–73.

O'Meara, J. J. (1949), '*Giraldus Cambrensis in Topographia Hibernie*. Text of the First Recension', *Proceedings of the Royal Irish Academy*, 52, Section C: 113–78.

—— (1982), *Gerald of Wales, The History and Topography of Ireland*. Translation. Harmondsworth.

Onians, R. B. (1951), *The Origins of European Thought about the Body, the Mind, the Soul, the World, Time, and Fate*. Cambridge.

Osborne, R. (1993), 'Competitive Festivals and the *Polis*: A Context for Dramatic Festivals at Athens', in A. H. Sommerstein et al., *Tragedy, Comedy and the Polis: Papers from the Greek Drama Conference, Nottingham, 18–20 July 1990*, Bari, 21–38.

Otto, W. F. (1929), *Die Götter Griechenlands*. Bonn.

Pack, R. (1955), 'Artemidorus and his Waking World', *TAPA* 86: 280–90.

Padel, R. (1992), *In and Out of the Mind: Greek Images of the Tragic Self*. Princeton.

Page, D. L. (1973), *Folktales in Homer's Odyssey*. Cambridge, Mass.

Papathomopoulos, M. (1968), *Antoninus Liberalis: Les Métamorphoses*. Paris.

Parker, R. (1983), *Miasma: Pollution and Purification in Early Greek Religion*. Oxford.

—— (2005), *Polytheism and Society at Athens*. Oxford.

Pasquali, G. (1920), *Orazio lirico: studi*. Florence.

Piccaluga, G. (1966), 'Τὰ Φερεφάττης ἀνθολογία', *Maia* 18: 232–53.

Pines, S. (1963) *Moses Maimonides: The Guide of the Perplexed.* Translation with notes. Chicago.

Pollard, J. (1977), *Birds in Greek Life and Myth.* London.

Polunin, O. (1980), *Flowers of Greece and the Balkans: A Field Guide.* Oxford.

Powell, J. U. (ed.) (1925), *Collectanea Alexandrina.* Oxford.

Price, S. R. F. (1999), *Religions of the Ancient Greeks.* Cambridge.

——(2004), 'The Future of Dreams: From Freud to Artemidorus', in R. Osborne (ed.), *Studies in Ancient Greek and Roman Society,* Cambridge, 226–59 (revised version of *Past and Present* 113 (1986) 3–37).

Privitera, G. A. (1991), *Omero: Odissea.* Italian translation. Milan.

Pülhorn, W. (1984), 'Archemoros', *LIMC* ii. 472–5.

Quirke, S. (1992), *Ancient Egyptian Religion.* London.

Radt, S. (1977), *Tragicorum Graecorum Fragmenta,* iv: *Sophocles.* Göttingen.

——(2002–), *Strabons Geographika.* Edition, German translation, and commentary. Göttingen.

Raeck, W. (1984), 'Zur Erzählweise archaischer und klassischer Mythenbilder', *JDAI* 99: 1–25.

Raquejo, T. (2004), *Dalí: Metamorphoses.* Madrid.

Reckford, K. J. (1987), *Aristophanes' Old-and-New Comedy,* i: *Six Essays in Perspective.* Chapel Hill, NC.

Reed, J. D. (1997), *Bion of Smyrna: The Fragments and the Adonis.* Cambridge.

Reid, J. D. (1993), *The Oxford Guide to Classical Mythology in the Arts, 1300–1990s.* 2 vols. Oxford.

Reinhardt, K. (1961), *Die Ilias und ihr Dichter,* ed. U. Hölscher. Göttingen.

Ribichini, S. (1983), 'Metamorfosi vegetali del sangue nel mondo antico', in F. Vattioni (ed.), *Sangue e antropologia nella letteratura cristiana: Atti della terza Settimana di Studio, Roma 29 novembre–4 dicembre 1982,* i. 233–47.

Riemschneider, W. (1952), 'Polyidos', *RE* xxi.2.1659–61.

Riginos, A. S. (1976), *Platonica: The Anecdotes Concerning the Life and Writings of Plato.* Leiden.

Rist, J. M. (1972), *Epicurus: An Introduction.* Cambridge.

Robert, C. (1878), *Eratosthenis Catasterismorum reliquiae.* Berlin.

Roessel, D. (1989), 'The Stag on Circe's Island: An Exegesis of a Homeric Digression', *TAPA* 119: 31–6.

Rouse, W. H. D. (1940–2), *Nonnos' Dionysiaka.* Edition and translation. 3 vols. London.

Roux, J. (1970–2), *Euripide: Les Bacchantes.* Edition and commentary. 2 vols. Paris.

Russo, J., Fernandez-Galiano, M., and Heubeck, A. (1992), *A Commentary on Homer's Odyssey*, iii. Oxford.

Rutherford, R. B. (1996), *Homer. Greece and Rome*. New Surveys in the Classics No. 26. Oxford.

Ruthven, M. (1997), *A Very Short Introduction to Islam*. Oxford.

Saïd, S. (1987), 'Travestis et travestissements dans les comédies d'Aristophane', in P. Ghiron-Bistagne (ed.), *Anthropologie et théâtre antique*. Actes du colloque international, 6–8 mars 1986, Montpellier, 217–48.

Salisbury, J. E. (1994), *The Beast Within: Animals in the Middle Ages*. New York.

Sallares, R. (1991), *The Ecology of the Ancient Greek World*. London.

Sanz Morales, M. (2002), *Mitógrafos griegos*. Madrid.

Sarton, G. (1959), *Hellenistic Science and Culture in the Last Three Centuries B.C.* New York.

Scarborough, J. (1996), 'Botany', in S. Hornblower and A. Spawforth (eds.), *The Oxford Classical Dictionary*, 3rd edn., Oxford, 255–6.

Scarpi, P. (1996), *Apollodoro: I miti greci*. Edition, with Italian translation by M. G. Ciani. Milan.

Schmidt, E. A. (1991), *Ovids poetische Menschenwelt: Die Metamorphosen als Metapher und Symphonie*. Heidelberg.

Schnapp-Gourbeillon, A. (1998), 'Les Lions d'Héraklès', in C. Bonnet, C. Jourdain-Annequin, and V. Pirenne-Delforge (eds.), *Le Bestiaire d' Héraclès*. 3ᵉ Rencontre héracléenne (*Kernos* Suppl. 7), Liège, 109–26.

Schrier, O. J. (1979), 'Love with Doris', *Mnemosyne* 32: 307–26.

Seaford, R. (1980), 'Black Zeus in Sophocles' *Inachos*', *CQ* ns 30: 23–9.

—— (1996), *Euripides' Bacchae*. Commentary. Warminster.

Seeliger, K. (1924–37), 'Weltschöpfung', in W. H. Roscher (ed.), *Ausführliches Lexikon der griechischen und römischen Mythologie*, Leipzig, vi. 430–505.

Segal, C. (1998), 'Ovid's Metamorphic Bodies: Art, Gender, and Violence in the *Metamorphoses*', *Arion* 3rd series, 5.3: 9–41.

Seidensticker, B. (1982), *Palintonos Harmonia: Studien zu komischen Elementen in der griechischen Tragödie*. Göttingen.

Sergent, B. (1984), *L'Homosexualité dans la mythologie grecque*. Paris (reprinted in Sergent, *Homosexualité et initiation chez les peuples indoeuropéens*, Paris, 1996).

Seznec, J. (1953), *The Survival of the Pagan Gods*. Princeton (trans. of *La Survivance des dieux antiques*, London, 1940).

Sharrock, A. (1996), 'Representing Metamorphosis', in J. Elsner (ed.), *Art and Text in Roman Culture*, Cambridge, 103–30.

Shewring, W. (1980), *Homer: The Odyssey*. Translation. Oxford.

Silk, M. S. (2000), *Aristophanes and the Definition of Comedy*. Oxford.

Simon, E. (1979), 'Archemoros', *Archäologischer Anzeiger* 31–45.

—— (1998), *Die Götter der Griechen*. 4th edn. Munich.

Sinclair, J. D. (1939), *The Divine Comedy of Dante Alighieri*, i: *Inferno*. Translation and commentary. New York.

Skulsky, H. (1981), *Metamorphosis: The Mind in Exile*. Cambridge, Mass.

Smelik, K. A. D., and Hemelrijk, E. A. (1984), ' "Who Knows Not What Monsters Demented Egypt Worships?" Opinions on Egyptian Animal Worship in Antiquity as Part of the Ancient Conception of Egypt', *ANRW* ii.17.4.1852–2000.

Snodgrass, A. M. (1982), 'Narration and Allusion in Archaic Greek Art', 11th J. L. Myres Memorial Lecture. London.

—— (1998), *Homer and the Artists: Text and Picture in Early Greek Art*. Cambridge.

Sobchack, V. (ed.) (2000), *Meta-Morphing: Visual Transformation and the Culture of Quick-Change*. Minneapolis.

Solodow, J. B. (1988), *The World of Ovid's Metamorphoses*. Chapel Hill, NC.

Solomon, M. (2000), ' "Twenty-Five Heads under One Hat": Quick-Change in the 1890s', in Sobchack (2000) 2–20.

Sorabji, R. (1993), *Animal Minds and Human Morals*. London.

—— (2004), *The Philosophy of the Commentators 200–600 AD: A Sourcebook*, i: *Psychology (with Ethics and Religion)*. London.

Stanford, W. B. (1965), *The Odyssey of Homer*, i: *Commentary*. 2nd edn. London.

Sterckx, R. (2002), *The Animal and the Daemon in Early China*. Albany, NY.

Stern, J. (1996), *Palaephatus: ΠΕΡΙ ΑΠΙΣΤΩΝ. On Unbelievable Tales*. Translation and commentary. Wauconda, Ill.

Summers, M. (1933), *The Werewolf*. London.

Sutton, D. F. (1984), *The Lost Sophocles*. Lanham, Md.

Taillardat, J. (1967), *Suétone: ΠΕΡΙ ΒΛΑΣΦΗΜΙΩΝ. ΠΕΡΙ ΠΑΙΔΙΩΝ (Extraits byzantins)*. Paris.

Taplin, O. (1977), *The Stagecraft of Aeschylus: The Dramatic Use of Exits and Entrances in Greek Tragedy*. Oxford.

—— (1993), *Comic Angels and Other Approaches to Greek Drama through Vase-Paintings*. Oxford.

Teeter, E. (2002), 'Animals in Egyptian Religion', in Collins (2002) 335–60.

Te Velde, H. (1980), 'A Few Remarks upon the Religious Significance of Animals in Ancient Egypt', *Numen* 27.1: 76–82.

Thomas, K. (1983), *Man and the Natural World: Changing Attitudes in England 1500–1800*. London.

Tredennick, H. (1954), *Plato: The Last Days of Socrates. Euthyphro, The Apology, Crito, Phaedo.* Translation. Harmondsworth.

Valckenaer, L. C. (1781), *Theocriti, Bionis, et Moschi carmina bucolica.* Leiden.

Veenstra, J. R. (2002), 'The Ever-Changing Nature of the Beast: Cultural Change, Lycanthropy and the Question of Substantial Transformation (from Petronius to Del Rio)', in J. N. Bremmer and J. R. Veenstra (eds.), *The Metamorphosis of Magic from Late Antiquity to the Early Modern Period,* Leuven, 133–66.

Veneri, A. (1996), 'L'Elicona nella cultura tespiese intorno al III sec. a.C.: la stele di Euthy[kl]es', in A. Hurst and A. Schachter (eds.), *La Montagne des Muses,* Geneva, 73–86.

Verdenius, W. J. (1954), 'Platons Gottesbegriff', in *La Notion du divin depuis Homère jusqu'à Platon.* Entretiens Fondation Hardt, i, Geneva, 239–93.

Vian, F. (1963), *Les Origines de Thèbes: Cadmos et les Spartes.* Paris.

——et al. (1976–2006), *Nonnos de Panopolis: Les Dionysiaques.* 19 vols. Editions, French translations, and commentaries.

Von Mücke, D. (2006), 'Goethe's Metamorphosis: Changing Forms in Nature, the Life Sciences, and Authorship', *Representations,* summer: 27–53.

Walsh, P. G. (1994), *Apuleius: The Golden Ass.* Translation. Oxford.

Ware, K. (1997), ' "My Helper and my Enemy": The Body in Greek Christianity', in S. Coakley (ed.), *Religion and the Body,* Cambridge, 90–110.

Warner, M. (1994a), *From the Beast to the Blonde: On Fairytales and their Tellers.* London.

——(1994b), *Managing Monsters: Six Myths of our Time.* London.

——(1998), *No Go the Bogeyman: Scaring, Lulling, and Making Mock.* London.

——(2002), *Fantastic Metamorphoses, Other Worlds: Ways of Telling the Self.* Oxford.

Waser, O. (1905), 'Empusa', *RE* v. 2540–3.

Weicker, G. (1902), *Der Seelenvogel in der alten Litteratur und Kunst. Eine mythologisch-archäologische Untersuchung.* Leipzig.

West, M. L. (1966), *Hesiod: Theogony.* Edition and commentary. Oxford.

——(1978), *Hesiod: Works and Days.* Edition and commentary. Oxford.

——(1997), *The East Face of Helicon: West Asiatic Elements in Greek Poetry and Myth.* Oxford.

——(2007), *Indo-European Poetry and Myth.* Oxford.

Westermann, A. (1843), Μυθογράφοι. *Scriptores poeticae historiae Graeci.* Brunswick.

White, D. G. (1991), *Myths of the Dog-Man.* Chicago.

White, R. J. (1975), *The Interpretation of Dreams. Oneirocritica by Artemidorus*. Translation and commentary. Park Ridge, NJ.

Wilamowitz-Moellendorff, U. von (1906), 'Die Textgeschichte der griechischen Bukoliker', *Philologische Untersuchungen* 18.

—— (1931–2), *Der Glaube der Hellenen*. 2 vols. Berlin.

Wiles, M., and Santer, M. (1975), *Documents in Early Christian Thought*. Cambridge.

Winnington-Ingram, R. P. (1948), *Euripides and Dionysus: An Interpretation of the Bacchae*. London (2nd edn, with introduction by P. E. Easterling, Bristol, 1997).

Wyatt, N. (2007), 'Religion in Ancient Ugarit', in J. R. Hinnells (ed.), *A Handbook of Ancient Religions*, Cambridge, 105–60.

Zgoll, C. (2004), *Phänomenologie der Metamorphose: Verwandlungen und Verwandtes in der augusteischen Dichtung*. Tübingen.

Ziolkowski, T. (2005), *Ovid and the Moderns*. Ithaca, NY.

Index

Page references to Figures are given in bold type. Names of modern scholars are usually omitted, except in the case of extensive discussions of the views of the scholars concerned.